THE BOOK OF
ELABORATIONS

ALSO BY OSCAR MANDEL

DRAMA

The Fatal French Dentist (1967)
The Collected Plays (two volumes, 1970–71)
*The Patriots of Nantucket: A Romantic Comedy of the American
Revolution* (1976)
Amphitryon, after Molière (1977)

POETRY

Simplicities (1974)
Collected Lyrics and Epigrams (1981)

FICTION

Chi Po and the Sorcerer (1964)
The Gobble-Up Stories (1967)

CRITICAL TRANSLATIONS AND ANTHOLOGIES

The Theater of Don Juan (1963)
Seven Comedies by Marivaux (1968)
Five Comedies of Medieval France (1970)
Three Classic Don Juan Plays (1971)
The Land of Upside Down by Ludwig Tieck (1978)
The Ariadne of Thomas Corneille (1981)
Philoctetes and the Fall of Troy (1981)

NONFICTION

A Definition of Tragedy (1961)
Annotations to Vanity Fair (1981)

THE BOOK OF
ELABORATIONS

ESSAYS BY
OSCAR MANDEL

A NEW DIRECTIONS BOOK

Some of the essays in this book were first published in *The American Scholar, The Cresset, The Dalhousie Review, The Georgia Review, New Directions in Prose and Poetry 49, The New England Review and Bread Loaf Quarterly*, and *The Virginia Quarterly Review*, as well as reprinted in *The Key Reporter* and *The Pushcart Prize VIII*.

Oscar Mandel's poems are reprinted from the author's *Collected Lyrics and Epigrams*, Illuminati, 1981.

Grateful thanks are given for permission to quote from the following copyrighted works: Charles Altieri, *Enlarging the Temple: New Directions in American Poetry During the Sixties*, by permission of Bucknell University Press; John Ashbery, "The Other Tradition," *Houseboat Days* (Copyright © 1976 by John Ashbery), by permission of Viking Penguin, Inc.; John Berryman, "Down and Back," *Love and Fame* (Copyright © 1970 by John Berryman), Farrar, Straus & Giroux; Don DeLillo, *Ratner's Star* (Copyright © 1976 by Don DeLillo), by permission of Alfred A. Knopf, Inc.; Nikolai Erdman, *The Suicide*, translated by Peter Tegel (Copyright © 1979, 1981 by Peter Tegel), Pluto Press; Wallace Fowlie, *Rimbaud* (Copyright © 1966 by The University of Chicago), by permission of The University of Chicago Presss; Robinson Jeffers, "A Little Scraping," *The Selected Poetry of Robinson Jeffers* (Copyright 1933 and renewed 1961 by Robinson Jeffers); Thomas LeClair, "Avant-Garde Mastery," by permission of *TriQuarterly*, a publication of Northwestern University; Frank O'Hara, "The Day Lady Died," *The Collected Works of Frank O'Hara*, edited by Donald Allen (Copyright © 1960 by Maureen Granville-Smith, Administratrix of the Estate of Frank O'Hara), by permission of Alfred A. Knopf, Inc.; Marjorie Perloff, *The Poetics of Indeterminancy: Rimbaud to Cage* (Copyright © 1981 by Princeton University Press), excerpt pages 257–58; Theodore Roethke, "I Knew a Woman," *The Collected Poems of Theodore Roethke* (Copyright 1954 by Theodore Roethke), by permission of Doubleday & Company, Inc.; Gary Snyder, "The Market," *Six Sections from Mountains and Rivers without End* (Copyright © 1965 by Four Seasons Foundation); Williams Carlos Williams, "Tract," *The Collected Early Poems* (Copyright 1938 by New Directions Publishing Corporation), by permission of New Directions.

The quotations and essential facts in "Robbers and Killers," pages 235–39, are taken from accounts in the *Los Angeles Times*, May 16 and September 7, 1982.

Manufactured in the United States of America
First published clothbound by New Directions in 1985
Published simultaneously in Canada by Penguin Books Canada Limited

Library of Congress Cataloging in Publication Data

Mandel, Oscar.
    The book of elaborations.
    (A New Directions Book)
    1. Title.
PS3563.A44B6   1985   814'.54   85-11432
ISBN 0-8112-0962-8

New Directions Books are published for James Laughlin
by New Directions Publishing Corporation,
80 Eighth Avenue, New York, N. Y. 10011

Contents

THE BOOK OF
ELABORATIONS

FOREWORD

One day it occurred to me to inquire whether something would come of *staring* at a few of my own poems—whether some additional life worth preserving might be coaxed from them by a seductive attention; either the life (as far as I would recollect and sift it) which had engendered the poems, or a life—still mine, of course—which that staring might father upon the poem; and why not both? The attention was paid, now from a beach chair in Marbella, now from a sofa in Los Angeles. Some poems remained rock-mute. Others, unnerved, gave way. Corridors opened. Befores and afters, antecedents and repercussions manifested themselves. To collect them, I brought in the usual tools, from pencils to word-processors. Of these musings, then, spontaneous yet also reconsidered, of this inward-reach into the unsure self and outward-stretch into the difficult world, the present volume is the result.

"Unsure self" and "difficult world" are not words thrown at the wind. For it is with a high consciousness that I have ventured, with all my hesitations bravely confessed, to set in print notions about the world (and the universe by the way too!) to which it might be objected that only experts have any right. But this so difficult world, every fraction of which it takes a lifetime and more to master, does bombard us day and night, all of us, experts and clodhoppers alike. We are all subjected to dizzying amounts of "input." Have we ordinary people no right to have our say concerning these myriad events and situations? May only experts and celebrities open their mouths? May not a layman whose name you have never heard speak up? Your answer is, "Yes he may; but at the dinner table, or over a drink in a bar." Here, however, is where the "professional writer" begs a special exemption. His métier is precisely to accept the risks that come with opening one's mouth in public. He claims a special power (or weakness) of vibrating to that torrential "input," and the duty or privilege of "putting out."

Self-comforted by such thoughts and making the most of my unprofessionality with regard to almost anything you care to name, I remained pretty faithful to an amiable rule I had set myself from the beginning, which was to avoid anything smacking of research. Now and then, I admit, the trend of my thoughts obliged me to play, indolently enough, at scholar in the library. But mostly you will be strolling over the mews and avenues, the squares and alleys of a man's unmended brain such as years of quiet living and thinking have made it. Should you stay with me, you will discover that I sometimes repeat myself (so do some features of a town), that I can be dreadfully wrong (in your opinion), and downright offensive (to your feelings). As La Fontaine has it in one of his fables, "On ne peut contenter tout le monde et son père"—a fellow can't please the whole world and his dad into the bargain. Bear with me, if you will, until at the turn of a street some figure carved on a doorway or the fashion of a gable strikes your fancy again.

A word about the sequence of these sixteen chapters. They were written in I forget which order, as one poem or another led me on. I had no architectonic forethought. Years passed; some of the chapters were printed in periodicals; I performed cosmetic work on almost all of them, printed or not; and now finally I have tried to arrange them a little, beginning with those whose matter seemed more autobiographical than the others, and concluding with chastened remarks about the making of books. But so perfunctory is the "orchestration" that I can recommend a leisurely picking here and picking there. Read *in* the book, I say; you need not march through it as though, novel-like, some climax were to be reached.

My warm thanks are due to the journals in which some of the essays originally appeared: *The American Scholar, The Cresset, The Georgia Review, New Directions in Prose and Poetry, The New England Review, The Virginia Quarterly Review*, and *The Dalhousie Review*; and to the editors of *The Key Reporter* and *The Pushcart Prize* VIII, where two of the Elaborations were reprinted. Details will be found in footnotes to the appropriate chapter titles.

O.M.

WHEN IT RAINS

When it rains I am wet
And when the sun shines I am dry.
I am no hero,
When the world hits I cry.

I am my harmony,
Choir of wishes,
But I do and die
As the bullet preaches.

Passive, uninsistent, quick to despond, easy to intimidate, though smart with my tongue—there you have me posing in my frame. Place a hare fugitive at the center of my escutcheon. I made a coward's history in my family at the age of six, when I was led away to school. In my otherwise beclouded memory, the day stands out in a sharp if intermittent light. I fled from room to room, roaring away—so far as a child of six can roar. In between gusts, I argued with my mother from behind pieces of furniture with (I am told) superb but futile intelligence. I should not be surprised if, inspired by terror, I conjured up some pedantic line of reasoning against the very foundations of universal education. I was that sort of child. At about the same age I held my own one day, in a café on the Keyserlei in my native Antwerp, against an uncle of mine who objected to a toy steamship on whose rudder a "Made in Germany" had been stamped in ink. I wet my finger, promptly erased the inconvenient words, and argued my uncle into a stupor, maintaining, I don't know how, that the object had become innocent. I liked to babble. On that first day of school, I certainly called my mother evil, unfeeling, unnatural. I cried and blubbered my heart out. My last stand occurred in a corner of our small parlor, behind a leather armchair, under the telephone hanging on the wall. Two hands finally caught me in a grip, and I was carried off to school. This corner reappears once more, and

3

only once more, out of the fogs of memory, for I see my mother at the telephone receiving the news of the death of her own mother: a frozen noiseless image, bereft of before and after—an emergence from that singularly disturbing kind of death, all of our life that we have forgotten.

After this last stand of mine under the telephone, I see myself sitting in a well-worn, wooden-floored classroom of the Ecole Communale No. 3, a mere five hundred steps or so distant from our dwelling on the same Avenue de Belgique. My mother is standing half-reassuringly in the back of the room. Our teacher, Mijnheer Vos, is doing the initiating honors. He has all my attention. Suddenly I turn around: my mother is gone. "Real life" has begun. Into my memory goes the human odor of brown planks and desks aged by generations of warm bodies.

Mr. Vos was a kind but fierce-looking little man all but eclipsed by his own rich mustache. An expiring cigarette was glued to his nether lip, but it never kept him from talking. In these early days he picked me up every morning at the house to take me to school, his large callused hand securely wrapped around my frail one. I don't know what children were taught in their first year. Was it then or later that I dwelled so lovingly on a certain page in a geography book where a good-humored educator had drawn, in several colors, a vast peaceful landscape of hills and meadows, pretty red-roofed villages, sheep and cows, a train chuffing down a valley, a stream and a brook, and an airplane, a balloon, and a dirigible in the sky? Around such images are born our deepest and vaguest inclinations. I have always been in love with these restful landscapes into which humanity blends itself without shoving, clawing, destroying. Some three or four years later, I would gaze for long minutes at an illustration in a Rabelais for children showing very simply an arched stone bridge over a brook, and a man fishing from it. All such scenes, whether they come to me "in the flesh" in a Dutch village, or in a tale, a picture, or music, enchant me to this day.

To be escorted to school by good Mr. Vos was not enough to pacify me. Every morning I vomited, unseen, into the kitchen sink before leaving the house. But my first genuine vision of little Oscar in a classroom after that first day in school belongs to my second year. A summons comes from Authority. Someone leads me trembling from my second-year back to my first-year classroom. The hinged lid of my old desk is opened. A wretched heap of decaying bananas and rolls appears—the food given me by my mother every morning, which I had been too nervous to eat. Day after day I had stowed the victuals into the desk, hoping (I suppose) that it would all go away—somewhat on the same principle by which, like all children, I closed *my* eyes when playing hide-and-seek—and wiped off a "Made in Germany" stamp from a toy in order to purge it of guilt.

Ah the humiliation!

My teacher that second year was an easy-going, ruddy-faced, solid, and handsome fellow, who "allowed" the top boys in the class to kiss him on the cheek after a dictation or an examination. None of us innocents were aware that we were brushing our lips against greasy, odious sin. We came off none the worse for the little kisses, and I hope our teacher got something of a gratuity to make tolerable the pittance set aside by the State for his noble profession.

It was a sheltered life beyond the imagination of today's children. At the age of fourteen, however, in a village near Pau (in southern France), I had a playmate more experienced than myself. We were both from Antwerp, and belonged to a group of refugees rounded up by the French gendarmerie at the railway station of Pau less than a week after the French surrender to Germany. They had packed us into several buses and sent us to the remote village of Bernadets. It was less than a village—a scattering of farmhouses over fields and hills, with a few lined up along a gray gravel road beside the schoolhouse and *mairie*. We were unloaded and lodged above the stables belonging to the local manor house. For a few weeks we enjoyed a most refreshing life. We drew water from a pump a good kilometer away, fetched our magnificent black bread from the baker once a week, ate good meat around a wooden table set up among the horses and the cows, and strolled about the countryside, greeting every stranger and being welcomed in return. Someone there must have lured, toyed with, and rewarded my playfellow (I forget his name), for the boy kept inviting me to join him—to pay a certain visit— to be caressed—to receive this or that in recompense. Not for another ten years was I to understand what was being asked and offered that day—and heavens, the garish novel that might be made of this scene! What came to my rescue was my entrenched cowardice and timidity, coupled (as they have always been) with intellectual bite. I refused, and nothing more was heard of that.

Images come floating in. I see the two boys walking along a path. The other boy deliberately steps on a large insect and mangles it to death. I cry out in horror and indignation. But peace. That other child died long ago. His father rashly took the family back to Belgium after the French capitulation, for the Nazis were playing mellow for a month or two and the man had left all his property behind. My own father pleaded with him to fly still further. We too had left all our property behind, but for my father nothing far could be far enough from the Nazis. Hopeful greed overcame—and destroyed—this and many another family.

In these early years, I stood fearfully against a wall during recess time, praying to be overlooked by all the brawlers and the thugs around me. Lined up to enter or leave the classroom (yes, we were marched in and out, and organized according to size, and no harm done), I was always *nearly* the smallest, and quite sure that I must be the weakest. In fact, the smaller boys were more pugnacious than the tall ones, who were sure of themselves. But then, absolutely everybody looked to me confident, obstreperous, and dangerous. There must have been other toddlers like myself at the Ecole Communale, but the frightened child does not think of looking for other frightened children; and besides, it never occurs to him that he might not be the only one.

I have no recollection of any process of learning to read. All I can see, through a crack of my thick oblivions, is a large class-room, great windows to my left shedding their brown light, and before me, on the blackboard, a row of monosyllabic words: an immobile and calm image inscribed with no apparent reason to survive in the memory any more than any other. Instead, the first *reading* I recollect bears an emotional charge that does explain its survival—and the charge, significantly I think, is one of broken-hearted pity. I see the book, I see the glossy page, and I see the story, a page long at the most, of a poor family—"of honest workers," no doubt—sitting round the dining table. There is nothing on this table except one potato on each plate. An engraving in the margin illustrates the point. The children eat their potato with fork and knife. But they are still hungry. They are crying. The mother, who has waited without eating hers, divides *her* potato among them. She will go hungry. She has nothing at all to eat.

The little schoolboy is drawn again and again to this story, as if hoping that on one of his returns to it everyone will be dining to his heart's content. Poor, poor people!

I must comment that I am glad that this, rather than some tale of climbing mountains or building airplanes or winning a battle, is where my conscious reading life begins. I recognize myself. As for the other stories in my schooltext, they are all heaped in the dark of my brain. But not the mysterious italicized word which concluded them all. The word was *inédit*, that is to say, "previously unpublished." Clearly the good author of our text had obtained them from his own genius. But that word nagged me as aggressively as any intellectual problem tormenting a philosopher or scientist. What could it mean? Had a lady called Edith had a hand in the matter? Like a true philosopher or scientist, I tried for a year to bend the reality to my one and only hypothesis, but it never contented me, and nothing better ever occurred to me—not even the thought of asking my friends or my elders.

By the third or fourth year in school, my fears had dissolved and given way to the good feeling of being at home among friends, and becoming one of the older boys. I could now discuss with adult gravity the death of our director, the old gentleman having succumbed to a congestion in his bathtub one wintry day. I bicycled with my friends, played at marbles or tussled in the Place Boduognat between my house and the school—in those days a leisurely "round square" with the hero of Brabant on his pedestal at the center, plenty of space around him for games, opulent chestnut trees, and at the edge a little traffic—mostly the Trams No. 12, 15, and 17 clanking along. What pleasant and harmless little fellows we were. What a world away from an American school in a major city today, with its drugs, copulations, knife fights, unkemptness, vulgarity. When we fought "to the death" on the Place Boduognat, the conqueror was careful to keep his victim from touching the gravel, lest he dirty his little suit! For a whole year we played at being animals. I was the panther. Which explains how it came about, when my literary ambitions began to stir, that I undertook a novel concerning two panthers in Sumatra. But our greatest pleasure, I think, was to play detective and stalk our prey—someone's older sister or a

placid uncle—from the Avenue de Belgique to the rue du Péli-
can, thence to the Keyserlei, on, perhaps, through the Meir toward the Cathedral—lurking behind shop doors, leaping across
streets, concealing ourselves behind bulkier pedestrians . . .

A boy named Schippers had gone to America with his parents
and returned after two years. When he spoke cynically of the time
when his "old man" was going to "croak" (or some similar
expressions), we stood open-mouthed—outraged—never had we
heard such vicious talk in our lives. An unconscious piety had
been spat upon. That was very different from the "dirty jokes"
concerning penises which went around during our school excursions to the tulip fields of Holland or to the pyramid at Waterloo.
Even these were bandied about by a minority. For me, at any rate,
"dirty jokes" were as alien then as they have been all my life
since.

I was secretly fascinated by streetcars, always stood beside the
conductor, and raptly imitated him at home or when walking in
the streets, uttering suitable noises to render to myself the wheels
crossing rail junctions or the brake hissing away. The conductor
moved a large handle horizontally across a panel in order to give
the streetcar speed. The panel had seven or eight markers which
showed the gradations of velocity. Between the third and fourth
of these markers there was a wider gap, and when the handle
swept across this gap the car received a "critical" surge of power.
It was a charmingly modest surge—a streetcar in Antwerp in the
early thirties!—but that surge gave me a thrill time after time
which I only found again many years later, sitting in an airplane
and feeling its trembling flanks at the mighty acceleration of
takeoff. And so it is. A dollar can thrill in its own good time as
effectively as a million at another.

I kept, as I have said, this love of streetcars to myself; and this is
a wonderful subject too—the mysterious silences of children; for
every child broods over secrets whose need for secrecy would
make no sense at all to the adult. He has loves and fears which he
could ever so easily confide to his parents or his friends, and the
loves would be satisfied and the fears relieved; but he says nothing; he longs or suffers mutely; and, were he questioned, could
give no reason why. How many years, for example, did I long for
a little toy dirigible hanging from the ceiling lamp of a cousin's

room—a grown cousin who would gladly have given to the child a toy she herself never looked at. But I pined away for it (as I had puzzled over that troublesome *inédit*) and never dreamed of breathing a word to anyone.

Names drift in from these years. Little Bertels with the crooked legs who ran faster than anybody in the world, and whom everybody adored. Such bliss when he chose me, one day, to walk home with arm in arm! Quiet, pleasant Van den Bergen, the blond-headed presence of maturity. The one friend who remains to me from this buried layer in the many strata of my life— Jacques Gutwirth, businesslike, prosaic, but as cheerful and good as an old slipper. Léon—Léon what? Léon, at any rate, the dapper, refined, unbeatable Léon, always first—the entire six years which we spent together in elementary school—no one could ever dislodge him, and the rest of us had to content ourselves with a jostle for the second prizes. And Jacobowsky, the Jew from the poorest part of town: a miserable, unteachable boy whose shabby clothes bring the tears to my eyes forty years after he wore them. He should have blown his nose a great deal more often than he did. He was, or seemed to be, a dumb ox. The wise and kind teacher we had in our fifth and sixth years would sometimes fall out of all patience with Jacobowsky, lay him across the boy's own desk—at the back of the classroom, where else?—and thwack him with his cane. As our teacher had been wounded in the leg during the First World War, he had the weapon near at hand. Man and boy must be dead long since, our limping teacher of natural causes, but Jacobowsky surely in some concentration camp, he with his family, for the poor, I shudder as I write it, could not escape.

A kind of terror comes over me when I reflect that of myself, also, many people possess a fugitive image or two in the remotest places of their minds, not even remembering my name. Furthermore, they have a knowledge of me which I myself have lost. Others, who have known me longer and better, can replay substantial and coherent scenes in which I am the leading actor, but which I have utterly forgotten. Have I not first claim to any and every portrait of myself? Who are they, that they should know me better than I do? I am willing enough to share the remembrance of my experiences, but how mortifying to have numberless fractions of my life stolen from me (I could almost say), and stored in the attics of a hundred alien memories, usually as unwanted clutter.

When the war fell on us one morning in May 1940, we fled, father, mother, sister, and myself, each with a small suitcase in hand. I want to extract a single recollection from those turbulent times. We had gathered with a large crowd of fugitives in Royan, a fine seaside resort at the broad mouth of the Gironde, the body of water reaching southward from that point to Bordeaux. On the shore facing Royan, in a forest, lay a body of Polish troops which a flotilla was attempting to evacuate to England. The Germans were bombarding troops and ships. Now and then, from the window of our hotel, we could see an unlucky Messerschmitt, with the swastika yet visible on its fuselage, diving to the ground in flames. Across the Gironde the clouds of black smoke spurted one after the other. Horrifying reports were heard in Royan. Yet beyond the hell of that forest lay England and salvation. News had come that civilians would be admitted on board the ships. There was a rush among the refugees, and particularly among the Belgians, for our Leopold III had just yielded Belgium to the Germans—an act of wisdom we were too agitated to appreciate at that moment—the French prime minister had made the announcement over the radio—our tears had fallen—rage mingled with gloom—and Belgians got sour looks from their French neighbors. Thus on a sunny and windy afternoon a throng collected on the quays of Royan to be ferried to the other side. Now, however, the bombers flew in, and this time they chose the all too visible crowd for an appetizer. We all fled to the trenches. Great sprays of water rose in the Gironde. Detonations filled our ears. I trembled—and that was nothing new; for while falling bombs never could ruffle my stoical and rather apathetic sister—when the sirens sounded at night it was almost impossible to drive her out of bed into the cellar—mine was a different constitution: always the first to fly from my mattress to the underground shelter. Now, with the peculiar heroism of the true coward, I took my stand again, eight years after my epic struggle against school under the telephone on the wall; declared between hysteria and clarity that I for one would not cross the river and go to those perilous woods; said I would if necessary take my chances alone on the continent; begged for a supply of money from my father; and wished them all a good journey to England if they chose to go. My parents had always treated me with respect. That is to say, my gift of gab and my assertive wit had long since turned me into a spoiled little tyrant to my family. My sister was ice and I was fire. I must have known that my parents would yield. And of course we remained in France.

> I do and die
> as the bullet preaches.

Many years later, in the different inferno of the American army, unwilling and unable to yell slogans and stick bayonets into dummies—when my drillmaster asked me sarcastically what I would do if a North Korean lunged at me with *his* fixed bayonet, I replied, "I would let him kill me," and was thereafter left alone, or rather given up, by the good ruffian.

My first day of school was by no means the single catastrophe from which my later anxieties and terrors descended. The trouble had begun earlier. As an infant, I had been entrusted to a German governess, while my mother went about the business of being a favored member of the leisure class of Antwerp. Inevitably, my governess became more mother to me than my mother. She, my sister, and I took our meals together in the kitchen under an unused chimney vent, memorable to me because that is where the bogeyman dwelled, threatening little boys who refused to eat the crust of their bread. But now I think of it, this bogeyman and his friends had a great number of secondary residences elsewhere in the house. Evil lurked in our long dark corridors, behind heavy Victorian drapes, in broom closets among utensils and siphon bottles, and of course more sinister still in the cellar, where our storage bins were, and where I was occasionally sent to bring up an object. Large houses are made to terrify little children; yet they also infuse into the soul the delightful opulence and perfumes of all things mysterious. Today the child takes a notion of mystery from science fiction, but it is the mystery of complicated gadgets, so very different from the "Celtic twilight," the worlds of Perrault and Grimm, of crooked streets and chiming bells in ancient villages, and now and then a ghost—like the white wraith I once saw distinctly from my bed, on waking up one night, very late, I forget in what year of my childhood—only the terror is unforgettable, my scream, and then a tactful retreat by the apparition. In those years I was lodged alone in a loft reached from our long corridor by a ladder. No one heard me, and I said nothing about my ghost the next day. I was in any case the sort of child who wakes up screaming. Death was always lurking for me by my bedside at midnight. No wonder that, in the end, my parents took me to a village in Luxembourg for a few weeks of spiritual repose.

This governess of ours was a large and buxom creature who took very proper care of us. In the happiest of hazes I see myself on a Sunday riding in a basket at the back of her Flemish boyfriend's bicycle alongside one of our canals; I see the baby I was, scuttling about the pine needles in the clearing of a wood; I even see the two in an embrace—but, as this is not a novel, I see them standing fully clad in a single instant of light in my memory. Wretched oblivion! Not only do we lose great territories of our mature being, we can only conditionally affirm that we were alive the first five or seven years of our biological existence; for is it to have lived if we were unconscious of being alive? Yes, like so many amoebas.

I know that this life that dies away from us forms and determines us. The child is father to the man. But I mourn because the child did not know the child. I seem to be connected to my beginnings only through an all but indescribable halo or fragrance emanating from vanished experiences, like the light that reaches the earth from stellar bodies long since exploded into nothingness. I would give much, for instance, to remember and relive a brief holiday when my governess took me along to her family's farmhouse in or near Munster-Gladbach. Almost nothing comes of my straining, however. It is like groping for a word—we run after it—we think we have it—we feel its very sound, shape, length—the initial letter—the vowel in the middle—but an evil haze foils us every time we think we have caught it. So that episode in the farmhouse eludes me: the vapors of a shape are always about to compose themselves into a shape, but they never do. All that I grasp is a trace of warmth inside and winter outside, homeliness, well-being, good rustic bread, old solid wood—and nothing more.

A little clearer are the recollections of Christmas under my governess's regime. She celebrated it with traditional German fervor, and I am thankful that our parents left the children in her care under the Christmas tree. It was a time of candles and tinsel, picture books proposing fabulous tales, toys and sweets, songs around the table—or wait, is my imagination inventing fictive banquets out of one or two crumbs of meager reality? I shall never know, but whatever happened, long ago, begot in me an indelible fondness for Christian symbols (or pagan symbols Christianized) of the tender and merry sort—not that insufferable Christ spread bleeding on the cross; and here I recall, through the cold drizzle of an Antwerp December, floating over the city from the harbor side of town, the sweetness of the cathedral bells. Is there a sound in the world more winning than that of certain bells—not all of them, far from it!—but most especially the bells that play a porcelain tune, as they do in Flanders and Holland. I should like to go to my eternal sleep to the sound of such bells— and to be in a frame of mind, in that dreadful hour, to respond with a final decorous joy as they chime me away.

In the end, this attachment to my governess alarmed my mother, and the good lady was dismissed. That was a *dies irae* if ever. My howls and lamentations rose to the ceiling, if not to the heavens. My mother was tearing my mother from me. And I suppose that all my future fears and tremblings, my timidities and my agonies, are derived from the unmerited blow I was dealt on that day. But children live with their own logic. Instead of pursuing my natural mother with immortal resentment, and my governess with relentless fidelity, I behaved like a little monkey, promptly forgot the governess, and transferred my clinging to the victor. But clung with a new tenacity and ferocity, as was to be expected from the once-bitten-twice-shy child, so that my mother paid heavily for her heedless youth. The child was now a nervous, anxious little being, calling for a glass of water or a pillow to be turned over at all hours of the night, demanding to be kept up in his pajamas to watch the grown-ups play bridge, cuddled and coddled, perhaps adorable, but unquestionably a burden.

That was the great weaning. It left me the frightened and vulnerable boy who cowered so on his first day of school. In all likelihood there were other reasons for my fragility. But I am no longer interested in the search for origins and causes of psychological states. It is a search which always leads back to the same banalities. No hair-raising causes will be discovered by anyone asking why I was afraid of other boys, of rough play, of anything brutal. All banalities. Even these details—shall I tell you the truth? they go against my grain; I force them out of my memory. What philosophical novelties shall be derived from a child calling for a glass of water in the night?

Another weaning took place at the age of twenty-three, when I left the paternal nest once and for all and plunged into the American Midwest. I had been engaged by Ohio State University to teach English Literature and Freshman Composition in exchange for my doctoral studies. "Doctoral studies" makes a fine sound, and the young man on the night train to Columbus ought to have been a suitably grave and poised clerical candidate. But the truth is that I remained a child to an unconscionably late age—a virgin too—and my only superiority to some frightened nine-year-old sent off on a journey alone consisted in an ability to keep the mask of maturity over my infantile viscera. I spent a restless night in the train, and on a grisly dawn came to a semblance of life out of my half-slumber, my mouth pasty, an acute anxiety nagging at me, and loose bowels that mischievously redoubled the original anxiety.

What was I doing in Columbus, Ohio?

Should I not have fought tooth and nail to get a place for myself at Yale or Harvard? Was Columbus, Ohio, was Ohio State University the right place for an ambitious poet? I will never know whether Yale or Harvard would have offered me that place. I was still too much the child to know about right and wrong places, and still, after all, a stranger. My time had been so largely confiscated by the primary task of learning English that I had missed a number of important practical facts of professional life. My parents, modest persons who knew nothing about university life, assumed that all I did was for the best. The best, in this instance, was a salary of ninety dollars a month, which, in 1948, proved enough for a lowly room with an erratic gas heater and a frugal diet in the cafeteria. My mother almost wept when she heard that I was spreading margarine instead of butter on my bread.

The word "butter" brings to mind my first benign collision with the Midwest. It may have occurred on my very first evening when, forlorn (oh so forlorn that my hard heart still aches for the wretch of twenty-eight years ago), I wandered into the streets for a meal—though I nibbled rather than ate, I was so forlorn—and reached one of those spotlessly tiled fast-food diners where you sit on stools at a counter, and where to come in is to declare to the world, I am forlorn. Requesting butter for my bread, I was asked in return kindly to repeat. I tried again. Blank. Was I so much the foreigner? I tried again. A light came into the countergirl's face. BUDDER! And I was cheerfully served.

Of course it is unseemly to mention (in a book as serious as these elaborations) a trivial relaxation of the word butter to the pronunciation budder; yet does it not, in its almost imperceptible way, strike the true American note? Could it not stand for the general American relaxation? Feet on the table? First names at first encounters? Free verse and that casual "omnism" which characterizes authentic American poetry? "Take it easy" and "relax" are almost the first idioms a foreigner learns. Why make the effort to pronounce the double t when an easygoing double d will do the trick? The double t almost smacks of antiquated aristocratic systems. It goes with stiff collars and neckcloths. Homo, says Ohio, need not be as erectus as all that.

My subject is anxiety, but I am making a mental note to consider some day how it is that this take-it-easy amiability manages to coexist with efficient work habits. For it has clearly nothing to do with South American mañanism, long tea breaks in English factories, extended vacations in France, or the old idleness of the aristocracy. Americans are relaxed but productive. Unable to explain this paradox, I return to my private business.

Hateful anxiety! This poisonous derivative of our sublime human consciousness comes to me directly from my father. Forethought and apprehension put him to indescribable torments throughout his life. Surely what makes brave soldiers, daredevil explorers, impavid parachutists and the like must be a certain weakness or haziness in this aptitude for living, in the present, a future of imagined horrors. My father's bouts with his imagination—which literally confined him to his bed—concerned above all confrontations with Authority in general, but the Internal Revenue Service in particular, although its longest finger would not have found a decimal to reprove in his accounts. As for me, what absurdities do I not recall? The first time I had dinner with a girl, I could not swallow a morsel and invented an elaborate illness to explain the untouched dishes before me. When the draft board in New York pronounced me fit for military service, instead of asking whether or when I would be inducted, I waited miserably at home for six months—would not make a simple inquiry on the telephone—but opened the mailbox every day like a man going to his hanging. Stories! Who has not his or her share of ridiculous anecdotes to tell?

So far I have escaped a special torment of anxiety: the invasion of disquieting pains; the physician's troubled look stabbing through your gut; the room full of white machinery to which you are strapped and by which you are devoured; the verdict delayed for all manner of mortal bureaucratic reasons; the onset of the morning when it is delivered; the hours that crawl, the minutes that hasten, the seconds that run; suddenly the physician enters, your heart thunders in your chest . . . O hateful consciousness!

Now I catch a glimpse of myself in Columbus at dawn queued up with a group of fellow-students before certain Quonset huts where all of us had rented space in advance, each from his own home. I recall with extreme vividness that I was the clown of the group—a very Mephisto of sarcastic jest—and, like a good clown, dying within. The huts were odious—I was plummeting from the cosseted life with my parents to a paramilitary slum at the fringes of Ohio State University on a bleak morning among strangers in a Midwest I knew only from a map. I left my suitcase in the hut and fled into the streets of Columbus surrounding the university. I knocked at every door of every clapboard house (each with its porch and front lawn) where rooms were to be had until I found something more like a home than a military barrack. But my loneliness was extreme. I rocked silently on the porch (the semester had not begun) and went gratefully to bed at eight or nine in the evening. Grossly despondent letters went to my parents and my friends. The Midwestern townscape filled me with grief. Odious frame houses! Shabby High Street! I have never ceased to be astonished that the richest country in the world has such an unerring genius for ugliness. Are democratic economies forever incompatible with beauty? Does beauty become comatose when labor is expensive?

Never again have I felt so "repudiated" by America as during my first weeks in Columbus, Ohio. Yet presently I discovered that one of the tenants in my new home was Professor Kevin

Guinagh (I remember the name because his elegant volume of *Latin Literature in Translation* is on my shelves to this day), a charming specialist in Antiquity who was going to lecture for a year at the university.

For this is an authentic part of the "American experience": in the midst of an improbable setting of farmland, frame houses, football games, high-school proms, hot dogs, utility poles, used-car lots, and Jesus Saves in neon letters, you shall find, seven thousand miles and two thousand years away from Rome, a Professor of Latin Literature who might have given Maecenas a lesson.

Friends were made; I found a nook in the university; and I achieved notoriety as the skinny person in a bowler hat and vest who carried a tightly rolled umbrella in emulation of a bank clerk on Threadneedle Street, the one and only inhabitant of Columbus, Ohio, who on football afternoons walked *against* the joyous hordes on their way to the game, a counterflow of one, cutting himself a passage home between all those large and happy bodies. No, I was not built for Ohio, though Ohio and I managed to live together in uncommunicative peace for three years. Little did I anticipate that I should be spending five in Nebraska!

That revolting tendency to diarrhea in hours of anxiety—and I enter these insalubrious details against three-quarters of my will—almost ruined my debut as a teacher. The system at Ohio State University was to assign the graduate assistant to an experienced instructor, who observed once or twice a week from the back of the classroom while the beginner took over the lecture. My career happened to begin with a class on "The Rime of the Ancient Mariner." Of course I was luxuriantly overprepared. I am sorry to say that I had even taken to heart some absurdities of a high intellectual coloring foisted upon the poem by Professor Robert Penn Warren. But I could scarcely stand up. My bowels were in full mutiny. The Mariner's sufferings had been nothing compared to mine, though I had never shot a bird in my life—or angled a fish—or waylaid a rabbit. Yet stand up I did (as always), with some ultimate residue of strength; even answered some questions—to my own amazement—the students asked before class; and "taught" Coleridge's poem to my mentor's satisfaction. She did not detect my agony at all. I had passed the test after all; yet during the three years I stayed in Columbus, I never once entered a classroom without nervous palpitations. This is a common enough ailment among teachers. But mine vanished under peculiar circumstances. When I was stationed in Georgia as a soldier, I found a little relief from my misery by teaching an evening class for the University of Georgia on the army base itself. Instead of trepidation, I felt elation—the elation of an abused slave allowed the dignity of a man for three hours a week. My nervousness never returned.

As for the frightful timidities which impaired my relations with girls when I was a youngster, I could tell all too many ludicrous tales on that ever attractive subject. As a teen-ager, I recall literally hiding in a clothes closet on West End Avenue, in New York, when some visitors who had a daughter came to call on my parents. I could not cross a young female in the street without blushes and tremors. To ask for a "date" (and by the way, why have we no creditable word in English for this socio-sexual operation?)—with the prospect of a humiliating No—this took a torrent of courage—many a time I would gladly have turned Tibetan monk rather than place a fatal coin in a public telephone to call a damsel. I say a public telephone because public was private—at home there was no making or receiving a call out of hearing of my parents. And what was I concealing from my parents? Did they object to my seeing a girl? On the contrary. But for heaven knows what reason, I was convulsed with embarrassment before them, and, embarrassed by my embarrassment, unable to place my diffidence on the table for a family discussion.

I was short and scrawny, hated to be seen on a beach, and once, standing on the subway platform of the Rockefeller Center station, I saw a shiny-lipped girl whom I ardently desired and to whom I had actually spoken once in our high school give a start on catching sight of me from the top of the stairway, and turn up the steps in order to avoid me. And for good reasons. I stare in retrospect at the hapless boy, so skinny and so timid, and wonder how he ever got to the open ground where I see him, many years later, head reasonably high and handsomely balanced. Early in my infancy, and in spite of loving parents, my path led me into a cave of terrors from which it took me thirty years to emerge.

The secret of that emergence is suggested, I think, by these two lines:

I am my harmony,
Choir of wishes . . .

for they too are authentic ingredients in the mix. They signify that the enemy was always without. I myself was then, as I am now, as much of one piece as a human being can be. You will find me singularly untroubled by "inner conflicts." Surprisingly happy outcome of a childhood filled with anxieties, terror of death, downright hallucinations, screams in the night, desperate clingings to mother's skirts, and certified nervous breakdowns. Anxiety is not remorse. Fear is not self-contempt. It is the world that hits, not I myself. If I am ashamed of an action, why then I am ashamed, but the shame does not spread over my life like a cloud of poisonous gas, killing good and ill alike. As I am tolerant of others, mild minded, and expect little of mankind, so I am no terrible taskmaster to myself. My Gothic period gave way to a Classic one, *tout doucement*, without plan or help. I practice an Aristotelian moderation in my virtues without requiring the philosopher to plant the idea in me. Any virtue (if I may use the ancient word) pushed to its extreme will necessarily injure the virtuous man's own comfort and convenience—so much for the hedonic claim—and at the same time thwart the flowering of other sound virtues in himself—thus the ethical part of the argument. As: the man who is extravagantly sincere must *therefore* be wanting in compassion. For a great many virtues to live together in the soul, they must make little compromises, they must not each one try to take up too much room. So it is in crowded households. Each dweller had better shrink a little—giants go lodge elsewhere, with Polyphemus in the wilderness. I am, to speak simply, moderately good in many ways, and live at peace with my shortcomings, which are, in truth, as moderate as my virtues. The violent problems I read or hear about—divided homes, staggering demands by fanatical parents, incests and rapes, darksome self-loathings, shattering sexual encounters, guilt-ridden infractions of social taboos, forbidden lusts and desires, unspoken frustrated ambitions, lifelong revenges, flights to the mercies of drugs, lacerations of loved ones—God in heaven, what a plague of mental diseases, unknown to the animal world, fell on mankind when mankind acquired its mind!—all this is alien to me—I am like Lucretius on the shore watching the shipwreck in the tempest far off.

I see now, as I write, why my adolescent passion for psychology quickly passed, and gave way to a mixture of aestheticism and philosophy which looked outward to the objects in the world— and to the great ethical or ontological issues—rather than inward into myself. Soon after entering New York University in 1943, the gospel of psychology was revealed to me. "Oh my divining heart!"—a great welter of unformulated sensations and apprehensions about the human mind suddenly took shape, and, shaped, provided all the explanations I needed—it seemed to me then—to possess the essential secrets of existence. For two or three years, I sifted every word, deed, and thought of mine with the determination of a greedy gold digger in ancient California. I ran all my friends, acquaintances, and relatives through the sieve too. There were, of course, endless conversations—a good place for them was the Peacock expresso coffee shop off Washington Square—another a bench on the Square, anchored in a coming and going of students, children at play, bums, shoeshine men— I must not forget to mention a stylish fellow who adorned his shoebox with brass-topped nails and offered to recite all the state capitals of America as a bonus to his customers—I made use of him years later in a play called *Honest Urubamba* . . . and so I psychologized away, wormed through motives, badgered myself, and could make no headway in a novel, because every third sentence seemed to demand a volume of motivational commentary. But if sinners make the best saints, neurotics, as everyone knows, make the best psychologists; and as I grew healthier, my interest in psychology declined. In my third year I tried a course in philosophy; read Spinoza with astonishment; and upbraided twentieth-century psychology for not recognizing that mostly it had but rediscovered, and tagged with a new jargon, what Spinoza had taught three centuries earlier. My interest in myself waned as well. My introspections diminished. I was no problem to myself—my enemy, I repeat, was not within, it was always the menacing world. I concluded, besides, that the psychological repertory is quickly exhausted. In health or in illness, our motives are few, repetitive, predictable, and finally tiresome. To speak the whole truth, I am more interested in the history of galaxies than in the question why our friend Mrs. P. is obsessed by her mother though she has grandchildren of her own. Is this misprizing by any chance a weakness in my work as an artist? However that may be, when I moved from the self-regard of lyric poetry to the objective world of drama, it was not to belabor the intimate anxieties of the kitchen, the living room, or the bedroom in the manner of Tennessee Williams or Edward Albee (let alone Eugene O'Neill); I did not love people enough to be so minute with my characters; I became restive after ten minutes of psychological analysis. I discovered that only massive ethical problems, or legends and fairy tales, or jests, and then all metaphysical ultimates gave me the will to write. I yawned at subjects like the growing-up pains of "the local kid" or the naggings of husband and wife.

Contrary to general opinion, I say that the human repertory of motives is stable and narrow. "Of whom may it not be said, I know that man?" writes Samuel Beckett. Rousseau's "je suis autre" is but a chip in this monument of truth. Our belief in the Individual—his dignity, his value, his right to seek his own happiness—is one of the glories of Western civilization; but it causes us to overestimate the diversity of the human species and to exaggerate the possibilities open to individual life. We persuade ourselves that, given his freedom, man can and will do— heaven knows what—perform a hundred delightfully inventive actions—pick extravagant motives for himself—will, in short, be so very interesting, and so very productive, as to shame the tyrants who had held him down—made a *conformist* of him (thunderword!)—in the evil centuries before John Locke—or Francis Bacon—unlatched the gate. Man must be given his freedom, so runs the argument, in order to permit his full development. We always expect the most wonderful consequences to flow from complete self-expression. But when all the entries are recorded, this fullest development and this self-expression result, yes, in a flood of splendid ideas and artifacts, but not in a thrilling expansion of personality. The freest man is apt to be the greatest dullard, for he must rely on himself alone instead of using the accumulated intelligence of the generations. But who is in fact free? Man remains, like the baboon, a tribal imitative

beast. We are forever astonished to discover that the most astonishing thinkers and artists are not in the least astonishing as
persons.

Not (by the way) that "astonishing thinkers and artists" can
make miraculous leaps either, I mean in their inventions. Debussy could not have been born in 1770. Beethoven yes; Debussy
no. The concept of even the sublimest genius can be represented
(until neurophysiology superannuates figures of speech) as a rod
with a hook at one end and an eyelet at the other. That hook
must find a previous eyelet to fit into. In 1770, or in 1800, there
was no eyelet for a Debussy rod anywhere in the cosmos, and no
power of genius—of neural complexity—could create it. The
very definition of a precondition is that a condition cannot
include it. Debussy's inventions might never have occurred at all;
but if they occurred, they did so by hooking into the condition
that permitted them.

I find another poem that bears on the question of human
personality. It is an odd, even a mysterious poem for me. Its spirit
is not mine. It violently demands that which I have been belittling just now. Did I, for an hour or a month in my life, believe in
the entrancing possibility of *creating oneself?* Had Sartre besot-
ted me? Coriolanus speaks defiantly of standing "as if a man were
author of himself," but these are the words of his downfall;
besides, his stern mother soon shows us how mistaken he is. Stern
mother nature did me the same favor, and my poem remains
behind as a sort of mental game played once and then dropped:

Fresh Start

Hand to essence:
    the hair and pimple of fact
    and finger-cushion of feel
(snatching a girl from her mate,
    or hanging my dog with a rope,
    or undrowning an ant:)
the do of do:

Mouth to essence:
    for instance death,
    the undo and the doneout of it:
    no paragraph to hint me how
it sucks me out of me:

Lung to essence:
  like a bare first man
  in undecoded jungle:
I hack through sugared grammars:
  back to thing: place my breathing
  where I pick:

Pushing my birth:
  I womb of I,
  white is my color in the world,
no dad no history:
  hungry trying sand
  and thirsty lapping gravel:
  if I so will I will.

And by the way, I have this very moment—ten minutes ago—minted its best line:

I womb of I

and have sat quietly admiring it (laugh at me, what do I care, I don't know you)—and felt rather happy in that, although I am too old and too dead to beget a new poem, I can still scrub an old one. But I am drifting. My point—in the poem's teeth—is that I am no believer in unlimited personality. Historians who explain the agitations of pharaohs or Chinese emperors need never run farther than to the nearest and homeliest shop of used motives, to pick ambition, greed, fear of humiliation, and other staples off the shelf. Biographers turn in the same merry-go-round. The poor dear resented his father, was a secret pederast, compensated for a limp, etc. I love a good biography; but I love it because of the gossip. Gossip, in my opinion, takes care of the human personality.

Psychologists, psychiatrists, and psychoanalysts come face to face with many a tidbit for gossip to rejoice in. Here are a husband and wife who can make love only after he has dressed in women's clothes and she in a man's. Here is a man with five personalities. Here is someone who is terrified of cats. A thousand and one scenic views of this sort are collected. But a thousand and one is considerably less than an infinity. The behavioral landscape is varied, picturesque, and awful, but it does not take the explorer *very* long to master it. As for the motivational stuff that lies under the interesting surface, I think it is as dull and limited as is the subjacent mud and gravel compared to the colorful grove of trees above it.

We overestimate the range of human motives and behaviors not only because of our worship of the Individual, but also because their extremes are abominable and even unintelligible to each other. Inasmuch as factions of all kinds loathe their nearest neighboring factions, and few factions understand anything outside their four walls, these psychic distances must not be taken as proofs of limitless human versatility.

For example, raised by decorous, affectionate and prosperous parents, retiring and timid by temperament, and unusually prompt in compassion, I occupy a place near one end of the human spectrum, so far from the equally normal and perennial brutalities of mankind that I can scarcely grasp them. That men should be found to pull fingernails out, stomp on faces, apply shocks to genitals, fill bellies with barrels of water, gouge eyes out, flay, burn or bury alive, machine-gun into a ditch, or throw prisoners out of helicopters into the ocean—all this gives me momentarily a sense of belonging to a different species. Presently, though, such actions return to their places in the known, finite range of human behavior. Many of our brethren are and always have been capable of torturing their enemies and taking care of their ailing uncles on the same day, moving from delicacy to bloodiness as easily as an actor changes his costume. And gossip has always known this.

Which brings me back once more to my timidities. I wish I could report that my hatred for these brutalities has roused me sometime in my life to a passionate action against them—an action in which I have staked my very life. Not I! You have seen my portrait. I am no Sir Gawain. I do not volunteer in good causes. Put it kindly and call me a contemplative.

My consolation is that since we all die, we are all punished for our sins. How many of us do not deserve sooner or later to expiate in the dust? As for the Stalins and the Hitlers, imagine the horror if immortality were available to mankind and such vermin could live forever . . .

THE PROOFREADER'S LAMENT

The Proofreader's Lament

Typewriters are amazing enemies
To lions and the crickets in a chirping head—
These were the words young Jason said
When he hankered for a golden fleece

And dropped a dungeon overboard.
And Byron was a gaudy heart, a lout; in fine,
A baron with a nose for the sublime;
His day a color, and his night a sport.

Moreover, loonies there have been
Who climbed five flights into a leaking room
And therefore wove upon a loom
A sun, a zinnia, and a tangerine.

(A pencil on my thumb, I earn my keep,
Don't catch the moon, and look before I weep.)

Looking through my papers in order to condemn some of my poems to the dustbin and others to print, I took to marveling again at the quantity of poems I have devoted to the theme of boredom—*my* boredom, to be plain. As many, I do believe, as Petrarch composed for his Laura, altogether a healthier subject. I offer "The Proofreader's Lament" as a sample. I committed it to paper, if I am not mistaken, in my twenties, when, contrary to what youth is supposed to be and feel, I was already a veteran of that ennui which has laid me low since childhood. I have forgotten why the poem bears its particular title, but I have never changed it, since the relationship and distance between Byron and his proofreader—similar to a contrast between some Rockefeller or Carnegie and his bookkeeper—carries the required sense.

First published in *The Cresset*, May 1982.

Anyway: I could recite scores of these poems. I am even willing to boast that I have no rival in this domain. These lyrics constitute, perhaps, my only tenable claim to originality—though I may as well make a declaration that originality has never interested me, and any velleity of mine in that direction will ever be imprinted with a cheerful, grateful reverence for my predecessors, patterned after the Chinese painters. Do we not have it on the highest authority that no two snowflakes are alike? Why then, such originality as is in any event inevitable satisfies me. I have yet to find a correlation between mere innovation and excellence.

These poems of mine are as "literary" as you please, but why do they discourse about boredom rather than drinking gin, if not because they are born of a singular reality which is made of boredom and not gin? With this in mind, I can invite you, after showing you a second sample, to leave literature behind and walk with me into the singular and insalubrious reality that fathered the poems.

Easter Sunday

> In the tedium of my room all bulbs are lit
> and stunned I attend to the walls
> and sit.
> I am mild as a sofa,
> exact as a vase, rooted in carpets.
> Christ blew the shofar
> and I saw tonight the first green
> pimples in a shivering tree
> and I came home shocked to be seen
> in company with life.
> I am bored. I have had three experiences.
> I want want. I am the antonym of knife.
> Shall I learn gardening? Humus
> under my fingernails might be amusing; I have heard
> of snapdragons. Juvenes dum sumus.
> At the outburst of the resurrection
> a man must cross naked against the light
> and pray softly in a vertical direction.
> I am not morally fit to die.
> I must as yet enact
> what muscles imply.

Lugubrious affliction. Crime against life. The mortal sin of accidia. I have suffered from this disease, or committed this sin, for some thirty or almost forty years—ever since I became a reasonable being—envying the Byrons of this world, the adventurers, the roisterers, the marchers. Everybody else seems to make a decent use of his time. For that matter, most living creatures are too hard at work to suffer from the notorious lethargy of the idle rich. I am idle though not rich. My job is a sinecure. I am not kept busy enough. Lucky enough to have time on my hands, I have spent it largely on nursing my stagnations.

Most people fling themselves on hobbies. Hobbies bore me. In my teens I played cards with my elders, until I awoke one day to the fact that cards bored me sick, even when we played for money. Games are not for me. Nor sports. Most people fling themselves on sports. Sports bore me. In my childhood they intimidated me. I was too obviously smaller and weaker than the others. I was a mollycoddle. And now, after ten minutes of swimming (for instance) I turn sick with the uselessness of it all. I gaze in a rapture of astonishment at the busywork of sportspeople—the hours they spend polishing and blandishing their equipment—diving gear, mountain-climbing gear, sailboat gear, golfing gear—catalogs to read, new models to try out, improvements to worry over, repairs to oversee, the inexhaustible gossip with fellow-enthusiasts—eh, Pascal? you never saw such a flood of *divertissements* in your day—while me, a deep gloom, a metaphysical gloom saps me—unless it be defective glands. "What's the use?" and "It's not worth the effort," and "Leave me in peace." Even though this peace bores me.

Is traveling a remedy? Well, I travel, led in harness by my wife, occasionally diverted, sometimes happy, often bored. Why does she put up with me? Most people love small talk. My small talk runs dry in ten minutes. My wife upbraids me for the dumb look of apathy which, she says, everyone sees on my face when, try as I try, I fail to lift myself to the mild plateaus of chitchat.

Others simply lie in the sun, and like it.

And yet I often think that I am bored by pure mischance. The right opportunities, the lucky encounters, have missed me. I should like to "drain swamps" in the Faustian manner, and only need (I often say) the right companion to give me the vital nudge.

I could run a business, create an Alpine resort, manage a theater; I am aswarm with ideas; endued with good will; desire to be busy; dearly love to plan, organize, solve problems, consult, command, serve—in honorable subordination—but "nothing has ever happened to me," not even the entertaining apprehension of a beast in the jungle that must one day leap at my throat; no, nothing like it; I am quite convinced that no beast in any jungle is destined to waste its teeth on me.

As for literature, I am deathly tired of literature. Enough is enough. I have long since become a prime victim of diminishing returns. I have enjoyed the best there is, and have given of me the best I have, and now what? I try to push on. I read a few books in physics, astronomy, chemistry, biology (as best I can); I dream of learning the theory of music; and why not reteach myself a little piano playing? But nothing comes of these glimmers and this smatter. I am too old and too tired. I re-enact that nightmare Virgil describes of wanting to run when the feet are loaded down with heavy weights. I think of such or such a man who took up Greek in his eighties. Admirable vigor! Where is that Shelleyan wind? Listless, heavy-spirited, and shackled, I have stared hour after hour into nothingness, urging myself at the very least to go out for a walk—call a friend—see a film—but too discouraged to give myself a doglike shake. Every project disgusts me. I desire nothing. "I want want."

A few years ago the *Los Angeles Times* printed an article about one of my colleagues. It came as I was writing a first draft of these almost true notations. I cut it out and reproduce part of it here, substituting an X for the man's name.

"Whenever the world is too much with him, X escapes into the sky. He makes his escape in a sailplane, sweeping through space like a majestic bird carried by the wind.

"Soaring in circles, his steady gaze scanning the patch of blue above, X reflects on the similarities to his continuing quest down on earth, where the search for truth seldom follows short, straight lines but rather loops around in circles of an unpredictable odyssey, until at last the answers are known. Only in glancing back does the voyage seem to have been brief.

"X is collected and comfortable floating in space. Small wonder. He is an authentic pioneer of rocketry, satellites, and far-ranging probes of the universe. Trained as a mathematician, physicist, and astronaut, he is a high-ranking scientist and long-time guiding light of the Jet Propulsion Laboratory. Endowed with a rare talent for bringing clarity to subjects of mind-boggling complexity, X has been tapped over the years for diverse roles. He serves as the 'Voice of Mariner,' a land-based narrator who describes (to a worldwide audience) the voyage of Mariner to the planets. He teaches sophomore physics at the California Institute of Technology 'because I love kids and, if I'm lucky, I might be able to help them.' He is drawing up plans for a new biomedical research laboratory at Caltech; its objective will be, in X's words, 'to use genetic medicine and immunology to strike out at disease.'

"Intense, high-strung, and mercurial, X at 49 keeps exploring new worlds to conquer. He grew up in Akron, Ohio, where his mother, a chemist, introduced him at an early age to the marvels of science. Other students struggled through Caltech; for X it was a cakewalk to earn a degree in physics. Then, turning to the University of Chicago, he took a master's in mathematics.

"With a friend, X devised a formula to beat roulette in Las Vegas. They won $18,000, bought a yacht, and spent a year sailing the Caribbean. Happy but broke, X returned to Pasadena. There he divided his time between Caltech, where he earned a Ph.D. in physics, and JPL, where he helped to direct mathematics and research for the nation's space programs." And so forth. The reporter also reveals that Dr. X repairs clocks, experiments with underwater photography, and sculpts metal assemblies.

This blissful man parks his car next to mine every day; we have a nodding acquaintance; he is tall, hale, and handsome. What a downturn, what a crash from his parking slot over to mine! Here, however, is where your Significant Writer makes his entrance to imagine how, behind the "steady gaze scanning the patch of blue above," when the man X has landed on the mud again, grim rodent doubts and vulture terrors tear at his innards. "Authentic pioneer of rocketry"? Some other pioneer flew off with the honors. "Guiding light of the Jet Propulsion Laboratory"? He was by-passed by a younger buccaneer. "Drawing up plans for a new biomedical research laboratory"? He is the laughingstock of those who know. "Devised a formula to beat roulette in Las Vegas"? To forget that his wife was cuckolding him. Do your work, you Significant Writer with the Uncompromising Insights—insights, that is to say, into the literary fashions of the day, to which you are as much a slave as your John Doe is to his Rotary Club. But literary fashions aside, and stepping trimly over that tiresome cloaca into which our thousands of Significant Writers mechanically toss everything they see—these men, covered with human pimples as they are, are still enthusiastic, alert, brilliant, many-sided, and stupendously alive—I know them where I work, and when they have been duly deflated for their doubts, their jealousies, their machinations, their fears, and their sexual secrets, still they turn the corner of midnight in the laboratories; next dawn they are playing tennis; on the weekend they scale a mountain or two; they amuse themselves with a side interest in Atlantis or Chinese ideograms; it's all true; and in that light I blink, I slink away—not to plant carrots in my garden, not to learn mathematics, not to do volunteer work for the blind, not to play the flute, not to invent a fuel-saving device—but to shuffle up and down the house, fidget over a newspaper, write a letter, read a page of zoology (which I promptly forget), and eat a piece of chocolate.

True, I am a man of letters. But I do not lead the life of a man of letters. For one thing, what is a man of letters whose letters no one has ever read?

> I did not even get
> the compliment of blame,

says one of my poems, very aptly. I might as well claim that I am a cook. If I am a man of letters, furthermore, why am I not sitting in some "intellectual circle"—some wonderful *salon*, or at dinner with the wits of the age? Why was I not, like Robert Lowell, instructed and pampered from my youngest manhood by Richard Eberhart, Ford Madox Ford, Allen Tate, John Crowe Ransom, Robert Penn Warren, Cleanth Brooks, William Carlos Williams, Elizabeth Bishop, and so forth—a star born from a galaxy? All I could boast of was a cousin who had gone to college. Lowell's cousin was, of course, president of Harvard. This very morning I have been reading about Charles Lamb's Wednesdays, with Coleridge, Wordsworth, Hazlitt, Haydon, Hunt, and Godwin in attendance, and "the flight of high and earnest talk that took one half way to the stars"; while at the other side of town, in Holland House, "the constant flow of conversation, so natural, so animated, so various, so rich with observation and anecdote" (in young Macaulay's words) was fed by Byron, Tom Moore, Samuel Rogers, Sydney Smith, Walter Scott, and Macaulay himself. Nothing like this has ever been vouchsafed me, and never will be.

How delicious, this famous life of crisp aphorisms over a cocktail, salty backbiting, venomous egos, venal reviewers, enraged changes of publishers, doting agents, and rumors of impending novels. I, for my part, the son of a merchant who had never seen a writer in his life, have sat since the age of seventeen, "mild as a sofa" and "rooted in carpets," composing hour after tedious hour poems of frozen tedium. I have not even some flaming vice to ruin me in a picturesque manner. If I take a drink, I become pleasantly sleepy. My friends and acquaintances are "nice people." A decidedly sociable and clusterable poet, I am alone in my workshop, and address poems, plays, translations, articles into a void. I read with a sour smile accounts of "exiles" and "outsiders"—these sensationally desperate talents who "entrust their latest work" to excited publishers, these unknown and undiscovered creators about whom three or four articles are written every month, these rejected and persecuted writers whose agonies their intimate friends print in the best critical journals in New York. They are giving lectures before thousands about their loneliness.

Like everything else in the United States, alienation has been industrialized, just as the subconscious is on everybody's lips, and "underground" newspapers and films are mass-marketed, quite as aboveground as Coca-Cola.

If I am an alien to the fashionable or at any rate upholstered tertulias of midtown New York, imagine if you please my remoteness from that "underground" of jolly exile and cozy alienation—the world of the Lower East Side, of the avant-garde in its cockroach splendor, of the bearded bohemians, hippies, freaks— the industry of sandaled outsiders. What outsiders? Once upon a time I spent a year translating some rococo comedies by Marivaux. *That*, I submit, was to be an outsider: not mounting guerrilla theater in the Bowery.

Your standard outsider is in fact a brother-under-the-skin of the Establishment, an unwitting ally of the military-industrial complex. He may throw bombs or merely paint and glue pictures; under either identity—political or aesthetic—if terrorists ruled the world today, it would look as *ugly* as before, and probably much more so. Of course I exaggerate. There are poets, painters, even a few architects, and perhaps here and there some composer I have not heard of, who love *beauty* as heartily as such people used to. No one supposes that mankind rose from its sleep one fine morning and announced that the Middle Ages were over and the Renaissance had dawned. By the same token, our Technocratic Age did not supplant the Renaissance on the first of January 1900. Nevertheless, there can be no doubt that we do live in an Age (duly capitalized) which is distinct enough from a period that lasted some four hundred years to be eligible for a name of its own; and one of its clearest differences from the preceding Age is its aversion to *beauty*.

Here let me deny at once that the *idea* of beauty has advanced, and that our Age has discovered new avatars of this god to which I happen to be blind, dumb, and deaf. To a very small extent some such discoveries have indeed been made, as they are in every age and by every culture; and I hope that I am not as dead as a fossil to them. But after this "small extent" is accounted for, it remains true that both the military-industrial and the artistic complexes have relegated beauty to a remote margin of their concerns. The Technocratic Age deserves a hundred medals, but that which it sports for beauty is one of its humblest decorations.

In such an age, it is Fragonard, not the "beat" poet of San Francisco, who walks about dazed and homeless.

I am no Fragonard; yet something of a semi-Fragonard. Does my boredom arise, I wonder, because the military-industrial-artistic complex does not beckon to even the semi-Fragonard: "Come, produce a work for us"?

I call myself a root looking for an earth.

These "Elaborations" allow me to stroll from one lane to another as the mood takes me, and to return to the first only if a convenient slope eases me back that way. I make this my excuse to speak a little of roots. As it happens, I am "not at home" in a more direct and tangible sense than vaguely missing beauty in the twentieth century. "History" has made me one of the millions of displaced persons of our time. And yet, having been a sort of tumbleweed swept along without any choice of mine causes me no anguish whatsoever. I would perhaps be disoriented in Ceylon, but whether circumstances place me in Antwerp or Los Angeles makes no great difference to me.

This fact struck me many years ago—in 1956—when I found myself alone in a coffee shop in Chelsea called the Number Six. London had recently discovered Italian espresso coffee, and it may be that the slightly funny distance between London and espresso coffee, and again between myself and both of these, produced the following poem:

> Disinherited but dignified,
> alone to the right, the same to the left,
> I sip my profound espresso
> this tolerable night.
>
> Thirty rolls of the sun, with each
> another east and west and in between,
> sipping any nation, forced to be
> the gentleman you cannot reach.
>
> This sterling English I bagged like a thief,
> dropping, so greedy was I, of Vienna,
> Cracow, Flanders and Gaul good coin
> as I ran: sure I must come to grief.
>
> Yet most were kind. Some offered me
> a chair. Few blamed the absence of a face.
> What saved my happiness, in sum,
> was middling courtesy.
>
> Content, I leave a middling tip and rise.
> My home is any fragrant history.
> When stones have failed, and beams are scarce,
> a tent, Vitruvius, must suffice.

In 1956, too, I experienced for once in my life—and for a person of any imagination once is enough—the shock of ecstasy human beings receive on "going home" or "returning to their roots" after a time-span of years, sometimes of only months, sometimes of generations. A substantial sixteen years had passed between my childhood in Belgium and my return to Europe. The spiritual time, however, was much longer than the chronometric, for the child had become a man, a new language had eclipsed the first, and a great war had intervened. When I came ashore in Ostend, it was indeed as if to meet myself again over a chasm of time. Home again! The feeling was false: I was not home; but it was overwhelming. A huge silent sob of joy dilated my whole being. I was not bored at that moment! Three or four such supreme moments justify life. The moment, the hour passed. A calmer bliss succeeded.

As for London, it was new to me, but shimmered with the special charm of a place much studied in books and now revealed to be no fiction. Many a European has enjoyed the same sensation on seeing a genuine cowboy in our sagebrush and yucca West. Fortunately, England at that time was still more or less England, "trailing clouds of glory." Since then I have preferred to travel elsewhere. What is more depressing than a third-rate imitation of America? An imitation, too, in its welcome, so praiseworthy on one level but so dispiriting on the other, of immigrants from anywhere the British flag had ever cowed the natives.

This is hardly a "nice" observation, but I have taken an oath that I will not censor odious opinions in these meditations if I happen to entertain any, and if my stroll has taken me to where they so clearly make up the landscape that I must either shut my eyes to them like a coward or take bold frank notice of them. Let me say then that I subscribe to an old and much-detested illiberal doctrine—subscribe to it at the risk of striking up a brotherhood with certain most unsavory brothers. I am tempted to say that I, too, feel that England ought to have remained nearly pure English, whether pure English is the next thing to Paradise or not. I feel, in the gross, that all countries ought to cling to their "tribal characteristics" and discourage massive immigrations, even when, or especially when, these promise an all too likable access to cheap labor, or better still (how very enticing!) mute slaves. I am not suggesting that England declined because it opened its doors to all comers from its crumbled empire. But after drooping for the reasons everyone knows (social injustice damns a country one way, social justice another), England decayed into something almost alien to itself as a result of its liberal welcome to the disinherited. When Flanders, instead, declined after the Thirty Years' War, it became a sleepy Flanders, and when it recovered, two centuries later, it was itself, integral Flanders, putting on new fineries. This is immensely precious—this peculiar character of a people, unconsciously formed by the steady

abiding generations; and to those who call this Burkean attachment sentimental, I reply that such a sentimentality is far wiser
than satisfaction with good-looking statistics.

What has produced our notorious twentieth-century "alienation"? Is it not, above all, the shocking redistribution of vast
populations in every sector of our globe? Precisely because
human beings are aggressive, they are also timorous: their own
ferocity alerts them to the ferocity which surrounds them. Hence
they dread exile; to uproot them is to leave them perplexed,
panic-stricken; they are always wanting to crawl back to the
hearth; they need to feel the old walls and the reliable kindred
around them. To be blunt, they require a "home base" from
which to exercise their predatory explorations. No; it is not
mindless sentimentality that makes me favor self-contained and
uniform populations. As for the aesthetic side of the question, it
is evident that massive migrations damage the beauty of a land,
as they corrupt its language. Beauty is extremely fragile. The
pressing economic needs of any new population play havoc with
it—and rightfully so, for feeding hungry mouths must take precedence over frescoes on the walls.

Again, I am exaggerating, and simplifying besides. How can
one be perfectly true to these sprawling issues in less than a ten-
volume treatise? I give you my impressions. America, for example, is too complex for single generalizations; whatever one says
about it ought to be contradicted with one's next breath. But
imprudently though humbly I dare suggest that America would
have been a better, happier, and more beautiful land not only
without slaves, but also without promiscuous waves of immigration—without the likes of me! If I assemble half playfully in my
mind the immense benefits brought about by the hybridization or
compounding of the United States, I discover that my imagination subtracts as fast as it adds. I take, say, New England or New
York in 1820, and, instead of expanding my vision of it homo-
geneously to the year 1900, I throw in masses of immigrants
called in from much of the globe to enrich even further the
already sufficiently rich natives. Each wave is a wave of positive
energy balanced by a wave of destructive energy: a violence that
explored, mined, seeded, and manufactured, and a violence of
riots, crime, neurosis, and bigotry. If I place myself Rhadaman-
thus-like in a seat of judgment, I waver for an hour, hesitate

which way is the better, but finally do come down on the peaceful and conservative side. Let America remain English, I hear myself saying in 1820, my eyes fixed on the face and steeple of some little church on a Massachusetts common, yet conscious of all that I am thrusting away.

Including compassion and humanity. When, in London, I buy my bus ticket from a charming Pakistani, my heart goes out to him. Would I not have fled to England too? Yes I would. And could I ever bring myself to do him a cruelty? No I could not. Keeping him out would be difficult enough. Throwing him out, insufferable. But I sigh all the same, and wish in a theoretical cloud that each country would make order in its own house. In Switzerland, too, I join silently with the conservatives when they lock the gates; I do not feel that the Swiss owe it to the world to share in the plenty they were disciplined or lucky enough to create; and I condemn them when they unlock again for the sake of cheap foreign labor.

I once underlined a passage in *The Heart of Midlothian* which is worth transcribing. Scott is speaking of "rude and wild" countries in contradistinction to "well-cultivated and fertile" ones, but the words apply to homogeneous against heterogeneous countries as well: "Their ancestors have more seldom changed their place of residence; their mutual recollection of remarkable objects is more accurate; the high and the low are more interested in each other's welfare; the feelings of kindred and relationship are more widely extended, and, in a word, the bonds of patriotic affection, always honorable even when a little too exclusively strained, have more influence on men's feelings and actions." Rootless though I am myself, and though I might be its first victim, I feel the power of this Tory morality, and regret that so few contemporary intellectuals espouse it.

Regret and do not regret; for the liberal doctrine that resists this nostalgia does so because it sniffs an odor of "fascism" about it—detects at least an unkindness toward all those not elected by divine grace to belong to one or another Switzerland. Our enlightened thinkers may and do entertain views that can be catastrophic; shall we recall their rush of pro-Soviet zeal in the twenties and thirties? But they err commendably out of softheartedness, while the right-winger keeps his finger too readily on the trigger. They are imprudent from a love of man that generously transcends national and other stiff boundaries. As usual, I hang uncomfortably in the middle. I believe I am just sturdy enough of mind to resist having it warped by commiseration, disgust, and other feelings. But feelings have their rights; and, keeping mind and emotion in balance, I can assert that the principle of national homogeneity, excellent though it is, should sometimes be adulterated a little.

Indeed, every principle in the world ought to include a mechanism for putting it to sleep at the right moment. Say, for instance, that an alien group is being exterminated in its own country: how long shall a Switzerland dawdle and look for intermediate solutions before throwing open its borders come what may? On the other side, however, I maintain that in peacetime a nation has a moral right to give precedence to would-be immigrants who will assimilate more easily than others. But it is not my business here (or anywhere) to write a comprehensive tract on social homogeneity. I am advancing a few thoughts, pleading for their admittance into other systems of thought after due tempering, and, above all, begging that they not be damned out of hand because they are *also* the property of bigots. For we have a liberal censorship operating in our country—a quiet exclusion of Tory thought from prestigious journals and other media—an efficient reprobation and prohibition-of-access emanating with disarming innocence from the intellectual elite—and of this we hear much less, inevitably, than what we get in print or over the air when right-wing clowns try to purge a local library of pornographic novels.

Still on liberals: they are unfailingly enthusiastic when it comes to preserving the peculiar nature of remote tribes threatened by the white man, but bare their fangs when the same principle is applied—by bigots, too often—to the white man's own cultures. Compassion is at work again: a white intrusion into the wilds of Brazil or the Philippines means oppression by the whites, and a white exclusion of Blacks or Yellows or Reds or Browns *also* means oppression by the whites. This, for liberals, overrides all other considerations. I am more even-handed, and all but ready to affirm that each culture is the poison of each other. And it is better, sometimes, to be heartless than to poison all sides.

Poisons can be wholesome in small doses, however; and likewise any group can benefit from a modest infusion of alien persons bringing their "outlandish" ideas, styles, and institutions. Furthermore, both parties benefit, for when aliens are few in number they do not suffer from the customary hatreds. But above a certain threshold the benefit turns sour, and the violence begins. Who expected race riots in England in our time? We thought the English were particularly virtuous, and forgot that virtue is mostly an absence of evil opportunity. I am in favor of denying cultures evil opportunities. Let political scientists and sociologists address themselves to this problem of critical thresholds.

For the biologist man is a single species, since a species is defined, more or less, as a group whose members can make babies when they have sex. But remember that mankind has characteristically removed its actions from the instinctive and physiological to the cultural and psychological plane. It is not fanciful, therefore, to suggest that speciation, in mankind, has become a learned and cultivated phenomenon. The physiological barrier has been replaced by distrust and dislike of *others,* and the biological impossibility of begetting babies supplanted by a moral or immoral interdiction of mixed marriages. In this light we may recognize that humanity is less a single species than biologists would have us think. Mankind is divided, if you will, into cultural species.

Again, cultural rather than biological laws determine the boundaries of a human species. What is unthinkable among animals is perfectly normal in mankind and follows from what I have said before: a species of man is simply what man decides it is. At one time and place, two religious groups constitute separate species; in another time and place, they live together, work together, intermarry, hardly notice a difference—and so become two subgroups of a single species. Economic and class differences, language differences—anything at all can divide human groups into separate cultural species.

An ethnological curiosity in the Gulf of St. Lawrence even imitates the sea barriers causing speciation which biologists describe. The Magdalen Islands are nine little remote places where fishermen live. Twelve thousand of them speak French, one thousand English. Long ago they "decided" to separate into two species. They do not socialize together and they do not intermarry, in spite of their remote situation, all but lost in the middle of the ocean, and unvisited and idle during the many months of their wild winters. At the beginning of our century an inspiration confirmed the old division. The English community requested a wholesale swap of homes. The other species agreed. A mutual migration took place, enabling the English to huddle together on the only one of the nine islands not connected to the others by a sandbar or bridge. They *enacted* a biological sea barrier. A purely symbolic one, of course, since any time the inclination comes, a dinghy could take an Anglo-Canadian over to marry a French-Canadian. But the inclination does not come. And perhaps they all enjoy an unconscious atavistic satisfaction in that barrier, as if Nature had whispered to them one of its oldest strategies.

Since man creates his own species, he can also decide, "if the inclination comes," to level the barriers; and nothing in nature prevents him from truly turning the race into a single species. The liberals and optimists make the most of this idea; I instead see the misery and bloodshed which they cause by compressing two species together prematurely, against their will. As happens with charged atoms, they only increase the mutual repulsion by forcing the two factions closer together. My own proclivity is to keep the species at a respectable distance from one another, derive pleasure from their differences, rely on distance to keep the peace, and allow, without hurry, their own imperious needs, should such needs ever arise, to make of two species a single one.

Memories of London propelled me on this longish excursion. Did I quit the track completely? Perhaps not. I had come *pian piano* to the theme of beauty and ugliness, and I may have done no more than pursue it in the political sphere. For the rest, in spite of my Anglophilia, I can allow that London is not the worst place in the world to muse on ugliness. Even before Queen Victoria, England had fallen decidedly behind France, for instance. Consider soporific St. Paul's. Consider the agreeable but basically ordinary domestic architecture of the eighteenth century. Consider the London conceived by Nash. Place all this next to Paris (Paris before 1940)—the results are not flattering for England. And while all Europe was gushing heavenly music in the nineteenth century, England painfully raised itself, at long last, to a Delius, an Elgar! Alas. England remained, perhaps, a nation for concepts, hence a nation for science and literature, rather than a nation in love with the senses.

But, specifically, I had been jotting down remarks about our avant-garde, and was ready to compare it with the bohemia of a century ago when that espresso in Chelsea overstimulated me. A century ago the rebels were all battling for the foam-born goddess. The avant-garde had sprung to life in conscious defiance of industrial blight. Look anywhere: to the Pre-Raphaelites, to the Decadents, to the Symbolists, to the Parnassians—glance at Art Nouveau—read Wilde or Rilke—listen to Debussy—readmire the Impressionists—swell with Mahler—shimmer with Klimt— what, in sum, does that fascinating epoch produce? The final hyperbolical blaze of a dying star—the last feast of Beauty— turned by many, admittedly, into a sick orgy, out of a knowledge, perhaps, that it was indeed the last supper; for after them came ashes; a new generation of "experimental" artists, but this time as snug with ugliness (I repeat) as a sergeant or a manufacturer of petrochemicals.

I could have sunk my roots into that fourth quarter of the nineteenth century, I might have found a home there, though I would not have chosen the garret, and absinthe-drinking, as site and occupation. I would have tried then as I do now to fight the holy fight from the advantageous position of warmly furnished quarters (I do not absolutely require a palace) knowing that beauty was ever a child of luxury. Besides, I was always too timid, cautious, and apprehensive to try rat-infested rooms, drugs, odd sexual practices, orgies, or even staying up late at night. At a recent party, I heard one of the cronies of a well-known playwright relate lurid tales of sexual eccentricities the two enjoyed at the court of some homosexual Burmese or Thai prince (I forget which) who surrounded himself with favorites dressed as girls.

Mine, instead, are Biedermeier ways, transmitted to me by my honest plain parents, and consisting of afternoon teas in Marienbad in the thirties, a solid peaceful merry marriage, a mildly blundering watch over my investments in apartment houses and the stock market, and promptness in obeying the laws. Are such ways compatible with the high calling of Art? Since they were in the days of Franz Joseph Haydn, I have acted as if they were still so today, in America. And when I lack the courage to blame my too infirm abilities for the anchoritic life I lead, I ascribe it to a world of Mailers and Bukowskys in which my well-combed habits and my several reticences would be out of place.

Whatever the cause, this paladin for Beauty is obliged to sit at home by himself, "rooted in carpets," amusing himself with poems or elongated thoughts about Man and Life. Exaggeration? Of course. One is never perfectly honest when writing, yet after you have made allowances for a little facetiousness, all too much of what I have confessed is true. And true it is that the vapors of boredom fill my head as often as do my poetic fancies and these fancy thoughts. Even friendship and love, of which I choose not to speak, have failed to blow the vapors away. Their illuminations have had to contend with my slow clouds, sharp against stubborn . . .

A moderate public recognition of my work and a modest amount of professional activity deriving from it would perhaps have distracted my boredom. But here is a ticklish subject—one of our true remaining taboos. Neither politician nor artist must mention his hunger for applause if he is to survive. Anything one does with one's genitals can be reported in print and at the dinner table. But vanity is still under lock and key. The critics add their silence to the silent chorus. Do not desecrate the eidolon of the artist. Picture him always with that slightly suffering tightness of the lips and the brow wrinkled in dolorous thought. He is a creature driven by an inexorable inner necessity—for we have internalized the possession by a higher power which tribesmen predicated of their shamans and Plato of poets—a creature who may, it is true, wish to regenerate the world, but who is profoundly indifferent to it. I confess to a preference for the frankness of Homer's characters: the heroes fought in order to be remembered by poets, and the poets sang in order to be remembered by heroes. These healthy Greeks were at home with their demanding selves.

The desire for recognition is normal and deeply rooted in our animal nature. "Calling attention to oneself" or "being first in line" are the infant animal's most ancient device for getting fed, and getting fed sooner and better than its less "talented" siblings. This aggression by the self and this assertion of the self persist, of course, in the animal's adult life as the males, at any rate, jostle for dominance, that is to say the eminence, seated upon which one receives more, better, and sooner.

Our desire for praise is but a human refinement of these primordial drives. Why do we perpetuate the Christian affront to nature by either reviling it or concealing it? All the great and noble products of mankind owe their being to this hunger for recognition. Admittedly, intelligence, talent, and good fortune must co-operate, but unaided they cannot give us the push required. We must want to be adored, otherwise we remain bystanders and onlookers—connoisseurs or collectors rather than creators.

> Praise-me-praise-me built the Parthenon
> and peeled electrons shell by shell by shell.
> But who invented praise-me-praise-me?
> Lucifer or Gabriel?

> Grass rhymes selflessly with grass,
> winds, anonymous, mold cumuli.
> Call it fine or call it foul:
> mankind made its bed, and there I lie.

Unliving nature is out of the game. Plants look for success mostly alone yet already begin to push others. Animals roundly badger or compete with their own kind for attention and pre-eminence. Some even do it through "works of art" like gorgeous colors, dances, and "imaginative" forms. Men carry on, then become ashamed, and conclude the game by turning upon the self—in works secretly designed to promote it. What is less secret is that this shame is ultimately a product of the fear which ambition arouses in others. Shaming ambition is mediocrity's revenge upon it.

In my opinion, we can infer a truer modesty from candid ambition than from the usual disclaimers. To require the world's admiration is as much as to say that one's self-esteem does not suffice. How do I decide that my work has merit? By dint of daily self-congratulations? Fatuous assurance! In scornful disregard of anyone else's opinion? *There* is diabolical pride. I hope that those who admire their own works in the face of public indifference or derision are happy. I am not so sturdy. Whatever I manufacture I must sell, if not today, then next year, if not in my lifetime, then after my death, if not to the many, then to the best, or if not to the best, then to the many. Production, whether of a bicycle or a poem, is a social act. A man may produce a model of a bicycle the world does not want. He may keep doing it in the conviction that his is the only right model. He may be incapable of producing another kind. But, if he is not a psychological freak, he will never be happy standing alone in a heap of his unsold bicycles.

Men and women who are truly indifferent to the world's praise remain, I repeat, mute, anonymous, and uncreative. Saints who write and publish tracts on humility are not themselves humble, for the truly humble would not and could not write and publish tracts. And what are we to think of certain world-denying authors—say Mr. Samuel Beckett, who plays his one and only string with such an exasperation of dejection, fiddling the everything of nothing, hidden from the public, refusing the Nobel Prize—but all the same delivering his manuscripts to his publisher, a living refutation of his one and only thesis? The author of Ecclesiastes did not know that in English "All is vanity" would be a delicious and most meaningful pun.

ONE OF THE ASTRONAUTS
ATE A PIECE OF
CONSECRATED BREAD
ON THE MOON

One of the Astronauts Ate a Piece of Consecrated Bread on the Moon

The Reverend blessed a slice of bread,
Aldrin took it to the moon,
To prove man is and shall remain
Half sage, two-thirds buffoon.

I think of my work (any Peter Quince will think of "his work") as austere, spare, and melancholy, but I know that much of it is comical, and therefore comically austere, spare, and melancholy. My friends and acquaintances report me to my face as a witty and sarcastic talker. My wife accuses me of saying anything at all in company (or for that matter at home) provided I can sharpen it into a barb. It all comes, you will say, of the desire to dominate, for a barb is a weapon; adeptly used it "annihilates"; and many a conversation is in actuality a contention between salon adversaries for the title of champion. Yet on the other hand this Hobbesian account is too grim, because good nature and exuberance—a generous delight in the thing-in-itself—these play their part too; one is aware that the game is a mock tournament; and the proof is that one is willing to lose, and one laughs at oneself for losing. I have seen, to be sure, wit used humorlessly, in dead earnest, to injure and not to play; just as all too many athletic folk play with a racket, say, as if they did so only because the law kept them from using guns. If all play is a kind of diminished warfare, we still must make an important distinction between the person who underlines, in his inner being, *diminished,* and the person who underlines *warfare.* However, there is no wit without a pinch of aggression; and that is why, even today, we find it used more by men than by women.

Duels of wit remind me irresistibly of my college friend Sol Marks, a man—or rather boy, as we were only eighteen years old—who could have held more than his own in the company of Beardsley and Wilde. He belonged, however, to that especial race of geniuses who, for lack of the more workbench qualities of steadiness and prudent calculation, wander the world as failures, lost causes, wrecks. Their "mission" is to galvanize the lucky ones in whom there is not only the flame, but also a humdrum fueling of the flame.

We were both freshmen in Mr. Gamzue's English Composition class at New York University on Washington Square. The Comic Spirit had evidently prearranged our meeting, seeing to it that Mr. Gamzue should seat his students in alphabetical order so he might learn their names more easily, and that Mandel and Marks should be consecutive, with never a Maple in between. Marks and Mandel shone as the jewels of Mr. Gamzue's class. The others were the usual amiable dullards. They played the string section, we blasted the trumpets. Naturally we carried off Mr. Gamzue's A's with any and all of our compositions. Mine tended to be serious, however. I recall a passionate "research paper" on the question, IS AUSTRIA GUILTY?—for this was the year 1943—I believe I came out in Austria's favor—while Marks dazzled us with lighter confections.

He was not much taller than I, wore thick spectacles which even so kept him drastically myopic, and had a pock-marked complexion. There was something spicily Mephistophelian about him: thin-lipped, haughtily elegant, demanding, formidably intelligent, a scourge to simpletons, and unbelievably worldly for the offspring of a "nice, decent Jewish family" in the Bronx. It goes without saying that he cultivated an aristocratic shudder with respect to corner delicatessens. We were both in revolt against Judaism; no, not revolt, for revolt would have meant thinking, arguing, writing against it, or attempting to draw others away, or wishing to transform it; we, instead, had simply quit that cozy but battered vessel, even though it carried parents, relations, and ancestors.

Unlike myself, Marks acted out his tastes and convictions. For example, he spent his parents' money on fastidious lunches alone at one of the expensive Longchamps restaurants, while I swallowed cheap food at the Horn and Hardart automat in the garment district hard by the college. I was a baby; he was a tested blade. Tested and already worn, for sad to say, by eighteen he had done most of his cutting and carving. While the rest of us had it all to do, and were mounting assaults on philosophy, political science, or poetry which later in our maturities we would know for the childish flummeries they were, Marks had behind him a respectable career as a Gilbert and Sullivan tenor in provincial companies, he owned a vast collection of rare operatic records (his parents' money again), he was erudite in music and literature, he frequented as a young but distinguished guest the mansion of the then retired operatic star Geraldine Farrar, and he was both enduring and savoring a tragic romantic attachment, begun years before, to a beautiful girl afflicted with fits of insanity. Furthermore, he slipped away about once a month to a hamlet in New Jersey where an older woman (probably in her twenties)—prostitute or mistress, I don't recollect which—amply satisfied his physical desires. Did he ever invite me to share the lady with him? Cursed forgetfulness! Faintly I believe he did—though I know he kept the unbalanced girl away from me—but what of it? Such enormities were far beyond my daring.

We remained close companions for several years, but I am sure he received little nourishment from me. I had so far to go! I was discovering Scheherazade while he probed Isolde. He accepted me, I imagine, because I could at any rate parry his speech with gab, and that was something. He was the master, I ambitious to become one. So we exchanged fine and merry thrusts, or lunged invisibly at the world, each watching the other for a miss. Youth is the time for talking, is it not? Talk is not only expression, it is discovery, it is audible thought, it is thought in action, it moves us forward, we babble our way out of tangles into open country. And oh we babbled—in college lounges or on Washington Square when we derisively cut classes not up to our standards (and was not Washington Square more instructive than many a professor, with its traffic of children, students, loiterers, shoeshine men, freaks, and everybody under the sun?)—we rattled and witticized along the streets of Manhattan on idle Saturday afternoons, in his parents' apartment in the Bronx, with its stuffy furniture absurdly wrapped in cellophane and slip covers, or in my parents' in Forest Hills; and we did not stop talking for the two comical weeks when a third member of our clique, André Ambron, lured us to a canoeing trip in the Adirondacks. Imagine us, if you please, carrying a canoe on our shoulders from one lake to the other. As this requires both hands, it yields us to the trillions of mosquitoes that pasture in the Adirondacks. We lost our way and our cooking was wretched. We were not suited for the outdoors. On a lakeshore, however, I began to learn Italian out of a grammar I had taken along. And one night, we paddled out to the middle of the lake for my first unforgettable look at a clean sky unimproved by the lights of civilization. It was sheer terror. And as we slowly drifted toward shore, the mountains, now a huge uniform black mass ingesting the stars, seemed to me a monstrous tidal wave about to break over my head. Here at last was a half-hour of silence.

Marks was too patrician to succeed in the world of classroom attendance, registration for courses, forms, assignments, and all the regularities of an institution which tries to educate ten thousand souls at a time. He had deserved a Nabokovian boyhood, pert bonneted maids and *thés dansants*. The crowded elevators and the rancid cafeteria of our Main Building revolted him. After a couple of years at college, he simply fled. But to what? I argued and implored, but he would never turn his beloved music into a career. It was too sacred for him, he gave me to understand in a circuitous way. Perhaps he did not dare venture his pride where failure would have broken it. To be a clerk in a post office was safer. Marks became a post office employee who lunched at Longchamps and dined with Geraldine Farrar. When he lost the job or gave it up, I forget which, he merely idled at home, supported by his bewildered parents. And here I lose sight of him. Myself, stubbornly ambitious and as amenable to discipline as a bookkeeper, I perspired for one degree, then another, then a third, never feeling that I was less essentially free for any rules and conditions imposed on me by institutions. The truth is, I lost Marks because I was too weak to sustain our flights of wit when I arrived in Columbus, Ohio, to begin my studies for the doctorate. I was extravagantly forlorn, and my letters to New York became maudlin. Marks lost patience. Or rather, he had none to lose. He wisely rid himself of the sniveler.

More than a quarter of a century later, I sometimes half expect to see his name on a book, something perhaps with a touch of Firbank. But no: Marks could not take the bruises to which ambition must submit. If he is still alive, I hope he has a luxurious nook, shall we say in Scarsdale, and a great deal of music. May he not be sorting mail or be taking his lunches at the automat.

Destined to be a comedian, I inaugurated my literary career at the age of eight or nine with a piece of humorous prose on the dolors of waking up early in the morning. It had all the success with my parents which I deserved as an only son. At the age of twelve, however, I turned serious with a thrilling romance concerning two filmmakers (*cinéastes*) pursuing certain panthers in Sumatra. I loved documentary films. My mother wanted me at all costs to be a Zionist boy scout. I wanted nothing to do with Zionism or boy-scouting. While she thought I was attending wholesome meetings and tying knots with my playmates, I was standing in the corridor of the Cinéac, a Belgian temple of newsreels, documentaries ("The March of Time," for example), and cartoons—also a predilection of mine. The Cinéac's managers even took care of their queued up patrons by distributing magazines in the corridor. Adults never know, never can know, what will strike a child's fancy. They will arrange for festivities and provide entrancing games and presents and never dream that the child really longs for a broken old dish because it has the picture of a steamboat on it. At the Cinéac I never wearied of a cartoon which closed the hour-long program. It was meant to guide the audience out through a given door into the street, and to prevent the good people from surging head-on into the incoming crowd from the corridor with the magazines. A disobedient damsel was shown choosing the wrong direction. The new audience, supposedly famished for newsreels to the point of desperation, trampled her so thoroughly that only a flattened shadow on the floor remained of her. If the Cinéac had shown nothing else but this one-minute black-and-white cartoon, I would have thought my money well spent each time I attended.

As for my interest in panthers, it stemmed from the fact that about ten of us in the same class had been spending a whole year carousing and cavorting in our several houses, each as a different beast, and I had been designated, or had designated myself, a panther. And that is how my novel was born. I suppose that there are indeed panthers in Sumatra—I hope that I did not choose Sumatra without a trifle of research. My parents owned a fine German encyclopedia—but I wonder now, did I ever get beyond the colored plate concerning childbirth, wombs, and fetuses? My information about panthers must have come from one of the large picture-books given to me on a birthday.

Strange sweetness and sadness of memories; but for me more strange, more sad, more mysteriously sad and strange than for most men and women, because of the rent which the war made in my life at the vulnerable age of thirteen. The adult body sits five thousand miles away from the body of the child. I see the child, I feel the child, I grope for it with the feeble tentacles of my sluggish memory, but is this child me? Because he is me, but because he is not me enough, because he is also a stranger in a now foreign country, my heart aches to possess him more fully, and a terrible yearning comes over me to continue the child and bring him to ripeness in Belgium where he was, and was after all so snug, not far from ancient cathedral bells and the tintinabulations of Tram No. 2. This very language—this English—does it not taunt me and call me stranger?

The war naturally deepened my seriousness. My first literary enterprise in America—and my last in French—was a tale I never finished concerning some wartime adventure—an escape from Dunkirk or the like—with plentiful bombings and strafings for which, this time, no encyclopedia was required. The fragment may still be slumbering for all I know at the bottom of a drawer in my mother's apartment. My earlier pieces, alas, are lost to the admiration of posterity.

My first poems are solemn too. Some were imitations of Milton, whom I was just discovering, others, though in English, of Verlaine. My tastes were catholic. Much later, I come to my first play, a bloated work on the subject of Asclepius who resurrects the dead Hippolytus and is killed by Zeus for his pains. My theme was properly tragic: man deserves to die; Asclepius commits a sin by quarreling with death; he is guilty of criminal optimism. I showed this by making my reborn Hippolytus look out at once for his father Theseus with a dagger in his hand. Not an unworthy subject, but I was making orchestral noises before having learned to play the piccolo. I have the play among my papers to this day, and like many an author I am torn between my desire to keep a record of my first imbecile steps and my terror that anyone else should take a peek at them.

My other juvenile plays, and most of my apprentice poems, are equally lugubrious. But the older I became, the more did grins and laughter encroach on tragic pathos. I take this to be a normal pattern. Tragedy is for the young. As heroism is for the young. It is a time for exaltation: we all know that. It is also a time when, as yet unprepared, we must wage awful battles—for love, for money, for consideration. But it is also an age when, our own dissolution lying far in the distance, we are better able to toy with reminders of it. Explain it as you will, artists often evade or transcend tragedy in their old age. *Hamlet* gives way to *A Winter's Tale*, as *King Oedipus* had evolved into *Oedipus at Colonus*. Our *Werthers* lie left behind, curiosities to our own eyes. For myself, at any rate—and I repeat that smallness does smally what greatness does grandly—this evolution toward a sort of Chinese hilarity has been very marked. From preferring the last, agonized works of Rembrandt or those of Beethoven, I came to love the hale accomplishments of their middle periods. I care deeply for Persian miniatures, for Oriental porcelains, and for the idylls of the younger "velvet" Breughel. I worship the madrigals of Monteverdi. And, aging poltroon, I duck the "searing," the "excruciating" plays, novels and films which our young artists are proposing to us every day. I am sure such spectacles would be "good for me," but it was never my way to solicit improvement from the arts.

I did not inherit my comic manner from my father, who laughed easily, his eyes all but vanishing in little pillows as his face wrinkled with merriment, but who was far too gentle for wit; I believe he never made a witty remark in his life. My mother and sister were and are to this day good-natured, bland, and innocent. The three of them sat, so to speak, in a semicircle about the young prankster; I did not get my weapons from them. Was this wit therefore a distraction from my fears at school, or even a weapon for defense, and sometimes for attack? It is an obvious, a trite idea, but a true one, trite and true. The child amused his nerves with his sallies, and then, instead of muscle, used them to win his first scraps of respect.

As for the epigram concerning Aldrin the astronaut, which is certainly comically austere, kindly believe that the event itself is authentic. I had it from a casual newspaper story, and was struck then, as I have always been struck, by the comically outrageous discrepancy between Man the Doer and Man the Thinker. From the beginning, man has been prodigiously clever when he placed his head at the service of his hands, but weird when he allowed his head to float free. We may picture our rather nasty Mother Nature endowing him with an extraordinary brain so that he might build houses, discover fire, wheat, wool, wine, cooking, the wheel, arrows and guns, irrigation, cattle breeding, pulleys, metals, and so on up to nuclear power and beyond, and then shrugging her shoulders when that same brain, abusing the few hours of the day or preferably night when thoughts concerning feeding and fighting were not in demand, went about dreaming of spirits, prayers, incantations, rituals, theories of Creation, Resurrection, witches' spells, angels, the influence of the stars, chosen peoples and superior races, the Trinity and transubstantiation and infant baptism, palm-reading, levitation, predestination, transcendental meditation, metempsychosis, the Immaculate Conception, Mormonism, Nirvana, prohibitions against pictures or wine or switching on lights once in seven days, fasts, goddesses with eight arms and a dozen breasts, the soullessness of women and the glories of chastity, fear of Friday the Thirteenth, the divine right of kings, Manifest Destiny, my arm tires of writing.

To this day, millions of astrology pamphlets are sold in the United States. Astrological predictions appear in almost all our newspapers, and they are not meant for children. It is in Los Angeles and Paris that worldly wise, chic men and women ask you earnestly whether you are a Crab or a Capricorn. We need not refer to the picturesque superstitions of the Amazon. I say that Nature shrugged her shoulders at this unexpected by-product of her gift, our agile brain. So I might give a man a pair of paddles for his skiff to help him go after the fish or escape from his foes, and if in an idle hour he used them as stilts on dry ground to divert himself, it would not matter to me, and it would not imperil his life. These extravagant speculations did not worry our Mother. She wanted the scientific method applied to tangible problems of eating, housing, and fighting, and so they were, obviously from the very beginning. Exceptions apart, philosophizing (the head floating free) did not ruin the harvest or prevent man's subjugation of the other species. True: great slaughters might result from certain speculations—a Thirty Years' War, a massive carving up of human bodies by the Aztecs, six million Jews exterminated on the basis of a theory—but the species survived them, and the survivors of these speculative massacres rebuilt their towns, recruited their forces, and prepared themselves for massacres of their own with methodical smartness.

That head floating free was and is, of course, a head buzzing with words. Language gave men and women the means of using and manipulating, alone or in company, objects and events absent from them in time or space. But words do not "take off" until grammar organizes them. A grammar of words behaves like a set of power tools, each tool equipped with a set of interchangeable heads. A rudimentary instance: a singular and plural applied to one object or situation can instantly be fitted onto ten thousand others. However—to change the metaphor again—language also behaves like a laborer who refuses to disappear after he has done his work. Though paid his wages, he dawdles about the house. And then he begins to blunder and to break things.

Take a clause like "The chief is coming to see you tonight." This is extremely useful. It can give a man power and control. It is a wonderful help to survival. Now make up another clause. "We found a dead man in the ditch beyond." This too can be very useful, very important. And both statements can be verified by the major sense, namely our vision. But when the true work of these clauses is over and the time has come for them to withdraw, they remain in place to make a little mischief. The *dead man* of one clause has no trouble whatever attaching himself to the *is coming to see you tonight* of the other. It is only that splendidly adaptable tool kit performing. Another simile, that of circuitry (perhaps more fact than simile) gives one an even clearer notion of the mischief going on. Almost any bundle or packet or burst of intelligible words will branch into almost any other. Whether the impulse is random dreaming, intoxication, desire, anxiety, or terror is immaterial to my present discourse. What matters is that literally countless human sentences, which are ideas, which are convictions, display mere intelligibility rather than rationality, rather than verifiability.

Furthermore, these merely intelligible notions receive a powerful endorsement from the fundamentally truth-bearing, informative, verifiable, credible nature of language. Now it may seem strange to praise what is so often pilloried for its unreliability. But spreading scandal about language is unworthy of the all too many philosophers who do it. The delinquencies of language—and they are sensational—do not affect its vast homely honesty, upon which mankind has always depended to good effect. Untrustworthy language would have killed the species as rapidly as a noxious mutation in the kidneys. Language had to prove its worth in the field, and it did. Nine times out of ten (the one time out giving ground for scandal) one could indeed believe that the chief would be arriving at sundown and that, on inspection, a dead man would be found in the ditch. But then, why not also believe that a dead man was coming to the house? There is an assurance—a public assurance—in language that is missing from the private, largely visual scenes made up by the imagination.

If one excepts a handful of Greeks in a short-lived and even then precarious season of sense—with perhaps a few ancient Chinamen for company—it took mankind a staggering geologic span of time to correct speculative language, that is to say speculative thought, systematically according to the decrees of logic and sense-verifiability—in short, to make thought rational, distinguish rational discourse from imaginary and imaginative discourse, and oblige language to practice the same humility with respect to speculation that the child, the Bushman, and *Australopithecus* impose and imposed on it with respect to opening a box or cracking a neighbor's skull. Yet I doubt whether the relative number of persons living today who think about metaphysics, ethics, and politics with the same appreciation of cause and effect, the same feeling for logic, and the same discrimination between certitude, probability, and remote possibility that they apply to the repairing of a clock is any greater than it was in the noontide days of Hellenism. Most people still make excellent sense when they talk technology (how to cut up a cow, span a river, or sew on a button) and the most iridescent nonsense as soon as their hands cannot touch or their eyes behold. To put this another way, if Nature withholds her tangible and visible correction, our minds find the truth where we fear it or want it, and we make declarations about labor unions, General Motors, the Albanians, or the Mafia on evidence we would laugh at if we had nothing better when trying to grow radishes in our garden.

True, the world's population is now so vast that in absolute numbers it contains more unsuperstitious persons than in the days of Epicurus. But many more, too, are the drunkards of the imagination, the uncontrolled visionaries, the fuddle-brained reasoners dominated by fear or desire rather than evidence. My quite intelligent and extremely sophisticated friend L. C. spends her days in a laboratory performing exact work for medical researchers, yet she tells me seriously at the dinner table that talking to her plants does, yes it really does, "people are right," does help them grow. Like children who misbehave the worse the farther they stray from their mothers, we grownups get more reckless and cocky with our thoughts when that other Mother is not near us to rap our knuckles for extravagating. I fear, keeping Aldrin in mind, that the rationality which we have won here in the Western world is so flimsy and so rare a growth that it will decay once more (a new "failure of nerve," to use Gilbert Murray's famous phrase) in the normal, alas normal, course of history.

I shudder when I think of the cohabitation of advanced science and appalling social superstitions in the Soviet Union today. The notorious Lysenko episode is as dramatic an exhibition of human weakness as the squashing of Galileo three hundred years before. But the later event occurred in a nation supposedly imbued with "scientific materialism," where God and the priesthood had been banished in favor of rational thinking. Unfortunately, what the Communists achieved in metaphysics they threw away in politics, ethics, psychology, and every other arena of speculation. I will quote a trivial example from today's newspaper—I think it can stand fairly for the whole of what I am thinking about. A Russian circus clown and his wife have taken refuge in the United States. He reports: "All skits had to be submitted to a committee. Nina and I wanted to do one about Mars and Venus, for example, but the committee said, 'You must make it Soviet Russia against the Western imperialists.'" A vast and perfectly stupid mythology of history looms behind this little conversation, the likes of which take place a hundred or a thousand times a day in the Communist world—and this mythology is, in addition, devoid of charm, warmth, beauty, grace, and pity. To read East German newspapers, as I did in Prague in the early seventies, is to plunge into a world of speculative absurdities expressed in modern positivistic jargon but worthy only of remote jungle tribes—or of the astrology columns in our own dailies. A street in a Communist town cannot be paved without war chants, tribal outcries, and a litany of childish legends concerning past and future and good and evil. Worse, the leaders themselves, Soviet, Chinese, Cambodian, are not refined hypocrites (like so many excellent Catholic prelates, bless them, in Renaissance Italy) but all too often fools of their own follies, low intellects, witch doctors with machine guns.

We in the West nurse our own lunacies, of course. May I use the newspaper again? You will wrinkle your nose, but I assure you that the daily paper is a splendid orchard, and I have collected from it enough apples, and enough worms, to keep me active for a lifetime. Here then is a story concerning shoplifting in London's West End and the tricks used by the pilferers. Some of them bring along wrapped parcels with hinged false bottoms. Some install hooks inside their overcoats. Some, playfully technical, use "a spring-loaded hook hidden in the palm of the hand that leaps out to snatch the desired item." Some use hollow books which they place on top of jewelry on the counter. Some use half-open umbrellas "ready to enfold an array of goods." And so on. *Homo faber* in his rational glory. Nothing "mystical" to blur his scientific methods for spearing his fish. However, the last three paragraphs of the article devote themselves to explanation. Since this is our Western culture, psychiatrists and psychoanalysts are consulted. "The Freudian school agreed that rich women steal to obtain the love lift they yearn for from husbands that neglect them. . . . Male offenders suffer from a feeling of sexual inadequacy. Among children it is the lack of parental affection" etc. etc. etc. With a dramatic thump science collapses. Pure voodoo runs loose. In another age, the voodoo might have enlisted the names of Mercury (patron of thieves) or Satan. Ours is all our own, but as predictable and repetitious as incantations always are, and nothing less zany for passing up the supernatural.

But my newspapers are too vulgar for you after all. Here then is doctrine from a reputable scholarly work edited by a certain Professor Ernest Borneman. It is entitled *The Psychoanalysis of Money*, and happily unites the two fabulous systems devised by *Homo cogitans* for the use of twentieth-century man, namely the Marxian and the Freudian:

Judging by all the clinical discoveries made by Freud and his disciples, there is no reason to assume that a desire for the private ownership of the means of production would have to persist in a socialist society with appropriate weaning and toilet training.

Professor Borneman is not, as one might suspect, a master of the humor of anticlimax, but a very sober scientist. Shall we not prefer Colonel Aldrin to him, however? One more note: system for system, the Freudian and meta-Freudian constructions are dafter by far than the Marxian and meta-Marxian, and the reason is, once again, that the farther we travel from Nature's knout, the loonier we become. The grander speculations concerning our political and economic condition are halfway in and halfway out of reach of instant correction by brutal fact; those concerning the inner man play at a safer distance, almost beyond castigation. It also follows that they must perish by being forgotten, not by standing corrected.

Partisans of Marx or Freud will naturally scoff at my "slick" caricature and dismissal of their patron saints. Doctrines so dense in themselves, and surrounded by even denser layers of commentary, are not to be moved, much less exploded, by a flick of the wrist—a citation of some imbecility in a newspaper or another in a scholarly book. But my reply begins with the observation that such citations do not pretend to constitute adequate artillery against these massive targets. They are (to change the metaphor) encapsulations—humorous or dramatic—which a thinking man may permit himself after he has lived some decades in an intellectual atmosphere impregnated with these and of course other doctrines. And he may, I think, permit himself an opinion on massive doctrines even if he is not an expert in them. Surely a Freudian is allowed to express views on Christianity without having mastered the history of the Church in all its permutations, and the monuments of theology with theirs. By the same token we laymen, we commoners, take the freedom to speak our minds about Freud. Indeed, doctrines and movements live and die, in all probability, by the impression they make upon thinking persons in general, and not simply by their status among experts—granted, of course, that the views of a general elite derive in part (but by no means altogether) from those of the inner circles.

This said, I conclude with another capsule—to wit, that where Freud was right he was not new, and where he was new he was not right. This is a verdict I would be the first to qualify and mitigate. But I do not think I could be reasoned into reversing it.

There is, however, a reversal that does tempt me. Though I take the scientific method to be (as a matter of course) the only human way of making contact with the universe the moment we grant its existence, nevertheless I understand that this achievement, like all large-scale human successes, is a tragic one. One cannot subscribe to a complex theory, a great institution, or a comprehensive system of values, without contracting for a series of regrettable renunciations. My appetite for cherries is simple, and provided I eat them in moderation does not entail unpleasant consequences. But to love immense and complicated "objects" like Democracy, the Catholic Church, Equality, the Life of Adventure, or the Scientific Method—here the prudent thinker takes pause before he flings himself, for sooner or later he will be crying over the loss of something he loved, because he loved something else.

I have complained that the Communist myths and rituals are harsh and devoid of charm. Their lack of poetry, their vulgarity, their flatfootedness, all this denotes that they are products made for (if not altogether by) the proletarian imagination. If these myths and rituals sank under the earth this very minute, I would breathe easier for truth *and* for poetry. But who can unconditionally desire that religion, on the other hand, had never fuddled men's brains? Perhaps cathedrals would have been erected to honor the Laws of Gravitation or Bohr's model of the atom— after all, the *sans-culottes* raised up a statue to the Goddess of Reason in Notre-Dame; perhaps Bach would have written an oratorio on thermodynamics; and it may be argued that the secular Mona Lisa is as moving as a Virgin and Child by Van Eyck. Still, here they are, the cathedrals, the paintings, the music, and shall I wish them undone, and can I wish that men and women had never shivered with a sense of God and his angels, and apprehended something far greater than man, a mysterious benevolence or a terrible taskmaster, ruling the universe? Can I regret, more humbly, that I was raised on tales of fairies and goblins? And furthermore, if I am content that these superstitions once existed, must not some part of myself want them to subsist?

More: could I survive—I choose the word carefully, and repeat: could I survive if all the objects created by falsehood on the one hand and tyranny on the other were suddenly gutted, and all that remained was—what the Democratic, or Fascist, or Communist twentieth century has conceived? Our steel, our chrome, our concrete? Ah sweet cathedral bells!

> An diesen Klang von Jugend auf gewöhnt,
> Ruft er auch jetzt zurück mich in das Leben.

Nor can we easily dismiss these superstitions because they are morally disgusting. Some are stupid but beneficent. Some silly but beautiful. In certain moods, moods by no means abnormal, one could wish science to the devil in exchange for a deathbed certainty of life after death, reunion with loved ones, and even, if best must come to worst, eternal damnation. Better the hell of Christianity than the extinction guaranteed by Science.

So there you find me, ecstatic in front of the Cathedral at Laon, and extolling the Scientific Method. I am caught in a logical cross fire from which I do not even want to escape. The cross fire is inconvenient but it is not absurd. How is a double devotion to the children of beauty and those of intellect absurd? One of the tragedies of our time is that *they* are at cross-purposes. The characteristic products of our modern intellect are ugly, or expressed in ugly terms, with such force and frequency that a conscious campaign to eliminate beauty from the world could not have done more efficient work. The work has been so efficiently performed that art itself has all but liquidated beauty. And Aldrin with his chunk of consecrated bread on the moon reminds me that the Catholic Church too has busily kicked itself free of every beauty—short of razing the cathedrals in favor of blank meeting halls—in order to catch up with the universal drab of the twentieth century. Popery without beauty has little left, I fear, but its imbecility.

My own wicked utopia is modeled on a vision of Italy just before Luther spoiled the game. My vision is a fiction, don't (I beg you) misunderstand me; I am not the man to draw authoritative pictures of this or that Age. Well then, I assemble an elite of princes, cardinals, doctors of law, scientists and artists, thoroughly skeptical and disabused in private, epicures, scholars, lovers of beauty and money. Why, they say, disturb the people at their worship? Why maculate our venerable Lady's so edifying impregnation? We do not wish to unmask the saints, disprove Scriptures in public, or turn St. Peter's basilica into the Roman Workers' Recreation Hall. Is religion the opiate of the people? It is as it should be. The intelligent are crawling into the light of truth; let the simpletons keep at their beads. Alberti builds another beautiful church. The Pope passes in gorgeous procession—on his way to a mistress. Raphael paints, long may he live. In one play the suffering of a martyr makes the populace weep. In another, Machiavelli amuses the cardinals with sprightly obscenities. The churchbells send their rhythms over walls and gardens, while a choir sings in the chancel. Leonardo designs airplanes. Columbus has sailed. The astronomers are beginning to stir—let Galileo (my cynical prelate makes free with time) write in Latin and keep his temper so we cardinals can keep ours. Scientific instruments are works of art, science speaks in angelic prose. We build and maintain charitable hospitals. Priests console the dying and the survivors. Intellect and Beauty are indissolubly married . . .

I recollect yet another poem: I called it "Christmas," long ago:

> I hear the churchbells go
> and sow into the night
> their charming seed, the God,
> his courtesy, his might.
>
> I hear them toll again again
> *In dulci iubilo!*
> May only we who murdered him
> his black departure know.

For we deserve it; we intellectuals did the deed, we and only we ought to take the consequences.

Be that as it may, the superstitions I miss are those which the populace picked up from their betters. "Their betters" is not a phrase one uses nowadays, but as I have nothing to gain from hypocrisy I set it down in deference to the facts of the case. Now the rabble manufactures or demands the manufacture of its own myths and debases the great legacies. The Pope sedulously brings his Church "in line with the times"; in China, instead of golden boddhisatvas smiling their faint contempt of the world, second-rate blown-up photographs of Chairman Mao deface the walls;

and we, we have invented a new divine right of kings, the right to make money for us; witness our king-size cigarets, king-size hamburgers, king-size mattresses, and Royal Motels.

In our world poetry and science cannot coexist, not because they are necessarily incompatible, but because our generalized populism is too primitive to reconcile them. If a brace of astronauts, financed by Leo X, had flown to the moon in 1510, the world would have enjoyed high and solemn services, swells of harmonious music, epic words, noble and colorful pageantry, heroic monuments—in short, the great corona of poetry which the deed deserves. We, instead, heard some yippees from outer space, news of baseball scores were sent aloft, a few inarticulate exclamations came over the waves, and someone said, "This is a giant step for mankind," words to be set beside the immortal utterance of another proletarian hero, the nineteenth-century Mormon, upon seeing Utah: "This is the place"; words much celebrated in that decent province.

DITTY ON THE BRAVE MAN'S LOT

Ditty on the Brave Man's Lot

Wilfred Owen died in the World War
the darling of his rifle corps.
He volunteered, the way a great man ought,
and can't complain that he was shot.

I squinted, said I could not see;
the doctors paused; got rid of me.
I hate my land, hate mankind more,
and plan to live to ninety-four.

Some poems are totally authentic "exudations" of the poet's innermost feelings and thoughts; others are exercises of a craftsman "to see whether he can produce a fine work of art on a given subject." Most, I suppose, are like this ditty an ambiguous mixture of authenticity and craftiness.

For one thing, I was never, for I never dared to be, a Felix Krullish malingerer at the military's medical examinations. Instead, after I failed them several times between 1944 and 1953—but failed them honestly—the army caught me unexpectedly in what can almost be called my old age (for a twenty-seven-year-old private is a pathetic ancient) and threw me unresisting into the pit. For another, it is not only untrue that I hate either my land or mankind, it is also clear, if only from the jaunty sound of the couplets—pure doggerel—that the poem expects its select audience to understand the wink.

Yet on the other side, the poem is as sincere a declaration and wish-fantasy as any searcher after poetic sincerity could ask for. When it comes to the military and to patriotism, I have passion to spare—passion that would preoccupy me even if I never set pencil to paper.

True, when the medical board dismissed me for the first time, my heart all but stood still for grief. My excuse is that I was very young. Besides, the Nazis had driven my family into a long, dangerous and hungry flight from Antwerp to Lisbon, and from Lisbon to New York, all our possessions lost, helpless on roads along which thousands of refugees ran, walked, and dragged, hounded by the French police, in danger of capture followed by a forced return north and certain death—but why repeat tales everyone has heard? Remember in short that this was Hitler's Germany—not Wilhelm II's realm—and a war worth fighting in. Such an occasion does not arise more than once every five or ten centuries.

If I could govern myself by principles, the first article of my constitution would read: "I consent to expose my life if the enemy is after my life. If the enemy is after less than my life, less than my life is all I will expose. Like all ethical precepts, this one begs for a volume of commentary. But take it as it stands, crude but firm, and it becomes clear why millions of people have passed profoundly different judgments upon the first and second World Wars. The first Germany, still rooted in the nineteenth century, did not dream of massive enslavements, human guinea pigs, and extermination camps. The war of 1914–18 had been planned by all concerned as quick, clean, customary, professional bloodshed. It ran away from its astonished authors. As for its outcome, who knows? The world might have been better off if Germany had won it. This is at least a ponderable proposition.

As soon as a clear view of the first World War came to the thinking portion of mankind, a fierce revulsion against it took place. Significantly, no such revulsion has occurred in the decades following the end of World War II. The very intellectuals who have clamored against the wars in Algeria and Indochina (to name only these) have not disowned and do not disown World War II. For the war against Hitler is recognized as the truest crusade against the Infidel which man has ever undertaken. I have not gone to my books to verify the wickedness of Attila, but taking that name as one usually understands it, it is fair to say that in Hitler the world found a second Attila, a scourge, a Black Plague in human lineaments—an Attila with technology!—so that the war against his machine must be defined as morally exceptional. Stalin was, if anything, more monstrous yet, but where Hitler exported his plague, Stalin inflicted it chiefly on his own compatriots; there the crusade, there the holy war would have had to be a civil insurrection.

However, at eighteen I was too frail and thin for a crusade. After three years of good feeding in the United States I had not completely recovered from the long flight and deprivation, and stood on a weighing scale which could barely handle a feather like myself. Incredulously the examiner kept thumbing back the weight. The other boys gathered round. I stood in my drawers, my ribcage on scandalous exhibition, smiling in embarrassment as if I had left a few pounds of flesh at home by mistake. Or was something clogging the scale? No; at ninety-five pounds it came alive. The examiner wrote it on my record and circled the number in red. I was not to fight Hitler. Heartbroken, ready for tears, and unwilling to go home just yet, I chose a movie house on 42nd Street to mope in undisturbed. A boy alone in a half-deserted movie house balcony on a weekday afternoon! Let us tiptoe away.

The wars since then have sunk back to routine: nothing, God knows, for which I would risk my one and only life, or oblige you to risk yours. Let them pay for volunteers! And above all, force every man and woman who votes for war in Congress or who runs it in the Administration to serve one year rifle in hand at the front.

And so the fantasy of my ditty, my low regard for the ardent Wilfred Owenses of the first World War—and the wistful admiration I conceived for the Krull who slept in the bunk next to mine at Camp Kilmer, a pesthole in New Jersey to which the inductees from New York were sent.

My wretchedness there was perfect. Past my boy-scouting years, a doctor of letters never expecting to hear any other rat-tat-tat for the rest of his life than that of a typewriter, a conscious gentleman (I had affected a bowler hat in my last years at the university), and perfectly uninterested in Korea, I suddenly became a dirty thing housed in a grimy barrack that stood on a site of purest gravel as far as the eye could see, bullied from my mattress at two in the morning by vociferous corporals or sergeants whose mission it was to diminish the draftees to a mass of trembling and obedient pulp, dragging my feet in boots which kept a certain place above my heel bleeding day after day, and moving the slop about in kitchen, latrine, or barracks as soldiers do to tauten the martial fiber. Ah those pots and pans feeding a thousand at a time! That was a long way from the conceits of John Donne and Herrick's "sweet disorder." I suppose I was feeling, approximately, what must have been Oscar Wilde's sensations on being translated from the Savoy Hotel to Reading Gaol. This is comparing, first a small with a great height, and then a small with a great depth, but a pauper can drown as easily as a prince, and furthermore, while the prince is drowning in ten fathom of brine, the pauper can do the same in ten inches.

The conscript in the adjacent bunk seemed to be even less resilient than I. The stubble on his hollow cheeks intimated a hand too feeble to shave it. It seemed that he would rise from his bed only because he wished to die on the floor. Now and then he groaned or whined. Haled nevertheless before various doctors and captains, interrogated, shouted at, and clapped in the stockade for a week, he showed himself firmly deviated and incorruptibly insane. At last he was returned and confined to our barracks with a broom in his hand until such time as his expulsion papers could be signed. I would find him sprawled out after my day of marching, drilling on the asphalt, loading trucks, scrubbing floors, cutting officers' grass, and worst of all enduring the company of my buddies, fuck here fuck there fuck everywhere—they, it goes without saying, were hugely enjoying themselves, as an army is really the male proletarian's utopia come true—how could armies persist otherwise?—I would find him, staring glassily up from his bunk or twittering about with his broom. He had, however, taken notice of me. I must have had the traitor's sour look which inspires confidence. For he took me aside one Sunday afternoon and asked me in a suddenly normal tone to call up his sweetheart in New York and notify her that he would be out in a week. He even gave me the coins for the call, proof enough of equilibrium. Thereafter we had a number of very pleasant conversations bunk to bunk, though never about the delicate matter in hand. In due time he took leave of the army and went back to his girl, while I, lacking his moral force, sank deeper into the pit. I remember now the particular wretchedness of being unable to sleep, because the boys in the barracks all had their radios switched on, each at his favorite station, and besides kept up a singing and a howling almost till dawn.

Another poem of mine, "Camp Gordon, 1953," evokes the atmosphere. It was written after I left New Jersey, and "celebrates" a bout with pneumonia in Georgia in the first weeks of basic training.

> In recollection of the time of the hot hospital
> down in Georgia in the United States
> with pneumonia caught inhaling murder
> and drilling with the jolly men
> God had blasphemed against the earth:
> > they paid him back the same.
>
> First sick-call
> where they believed my fever
> and authenticated the fainting I had done
> with such dark paradise of soul that day
> marching to the tom-tom of the sun, the cannibal.
> Second the trouble with the human item at the desk
> who asked me "your religion bud?"
> to fill a certain blank in case of death
> and shivering I said None, before God none,
> none by God, Goddamit none,
> until they found a bed for me in a ward
> full of his youngsters, black and pink,
> the ones he jettisoned all over earth:
> > they paid him back the same.
>
> That was a sweet pneumonia
> although my orders were I must survive.
> I did not eat the pills,
> I rubbed thermometers, I groaned,
> but slowly I recovered, I began to hear
> the seven radios of the ward:
> one ad, one Negro southern spiritual howl,
> one hit, one ad, one jazz, one news,
> one quiz of decent ladies,
> all together in my bed,
> whatever God had bellowed to the earth:
> > they paid him back the same.
>
> At night I went in slippers and pajamas
> to a patch of grass
> behind a door I shut.
> I walked criss-cross and in a circle,

> hearing honest insects chirp,
> and while I walked, I sang against my time
> untimed cantatas in remembered scraps.
> I sang like a demented naked man
> the cops haul off the street
> while all the damsels laugh to see his skin.
> Then I returned to bed, the lights went out,
> and no one knew
> I had then overthrown our consecrated State,
> the duly constituted government of man.
> Now I slept, awaiting orders,
> between a private and a corporal
> great God had fumed against the earth:
> > they paid him back the same.

Again the radios appear. How I hated the radios, on top of all the other miscellaneous bellowing! How I hated all that male company, I who had been raised amidst a bevy of girls—my placid sister, her pretty friends, and my chirping cousins. Now and then I would spend an evening hour alone at the chapel trying to wrest Bachlike tunes from the electric organ without knowing how to play. On one of the long marches I carried a smudged paperback book of poems in my back pocket. But I found that "culture" did not work. I was too unhappy for these refinements. I discovered that music and poetry demand a certain comfort of body and soul. Of me, at any rate. I am no Boethius. Were I condemned to death, by a judge or by a physician, all art, all philosophy, in short all "culture," would drop away from me; I would be a simple frightened blubbering child or animal; and all I would clamor for is a sedative.

The lines:

> I had then overthrown our consecrated State,
> the duly constituted government of man,

are not unlike the

> I hate my land, hate mankind more

of the ditty. Once more, such lines can be taken only as approximations of reality. Utterly personal though the Camp Gordon poem is—no one could ever mistake it for a piece coldly crafted in obedience to a tradition—even here we must allow the work of art to impose its own conditions. The poem must run its peculiar course. The propositions it offers cannot be entirely false to the man, for else how would he summon the psychic force to make it in the first place—but they are apt to be "fixations of impermanences," like certain photographs which eternalize some ephemeral look or gesture. What a poem must do is stand in an intelligent relationship to the world as the reader knows it, rather than in a truthful relationship to the poet who writes it. "I hate my land, hate mankind more" is false: perfectly false one day, partly false another, somewhat false on a third, then (I confess) not false at all. But the line's intelligibility to almost anyone who happens to read it does not change, and neither, if I may say so, does its power to interest.

Such power—speaking generally now—comes in part from the univocal hammer effect of a word, phrase, or line. The poet is willing to be partly false to himself—to play an ambiguous game with his inner truth—in order to deliver an unambiguous aesthetic blow to his audience. As you can see, I am a believer in sharp pleasures. The fashion I remember from my university days for ambiguity, ambivalence, and multiple levels of meaning never touched me. I wonder, incidentally, what has become of it, for nowadays one fashion is quickly swallowed by the next: so many careers are clamoring to be made! I hear as if from afar of strange new literary theories, and thundering new prophets for a day, but as my term on earth grows shorter, I become more reluctant to read about reading, or think about thinking. Every hour devoted to a book about a book is an hour taken away from a book that is a book, not to mention the hour subtracted from raw living. All the same, I notice that a certain friend of mine is publishing a work in praise of poetic "indeterminacy" and "hymns to possibility," and infer that the love of multiple and disseminated meanings is still alive. My own preference, I repeat, is for the poem that strikes over the one that splatters. When I come to a fine word or phrase that might yield several meanings, my habit is to shut from my mind—it can be done—all but the hammer meaning until the others positively *ravish* me.

I suppose that a lover of sharp aesthetic pleasures will inevitably distrust downright obscurity even more than "indeterminacy." And I do. At the Delphic oracle I am a suspicious Greek. Difficulty has always had too much prestige. It is a sort of land of Cockaigne half of whose denizens carry forged papers. For the advantage of living there is so great that almost every intellectual is at least tempted to cheat a little to enter. Or what? When I cannot follow Ezra Pound, it is because, like the physicist pursuing a quark, he has beheld things untranslatable to the likes of me? Give me a poem that is above suspicion, like William Carlos Williams's "Tract":

> I will teach you my townspeople
> how to perform a funeral.

It takes, I think, a certain daring to be clear, because to be clear is to be naked to inspection. When I read an enigmatic poet like Mr. Ashbery, a little voice within me asks whether perchance he blurs his thoughts so very anxiously because he has none arresting or rare enough to display in focus.

I cannot leave these hammer words, and poets, without a tribute to a brave, jolly, beery private in my company at Camp Gordon, a folk poet if there ever was one. He was a champion at salting his discourse with fucks in places no one else dreamed of placing them. His masterpiece was a solemn "neverthefuckingless" that he once slowly unfurled before his audience. He surely was the first to have thrust the manly syllable into the open thighs of that virginal word. Here at any rate was a soldier whose profanity I enjoyed. No doubt that, without being able to say so, he felt the desperate poverty of expressions available to the contemporary American foul mouth.

As I was never in battle, my reports of army life are tame. I was nauseated rather than terrified. I found it strange that several boys almost froze with fear between the unpinning of a grenade and their tossing it into the target area. Stories circulated of recruits who had blown themselves to bits—or worse, killed some courageous trainer who had tried to save them. I also witnessed a good deal of fear when we were made to crawl under barbed wire while machine guns dribbled the atmosphere a few inches above our buttocks; or when we were requested to let a few tanks roll their bellies over us. For me these were amusing games, and I preferred lying at peace with the world under a tank to picking up trash on all fours or standing stiff to have my boots inspected. The genuine horrors I never experienced. Could I have survived the adventure of my friend who, squatting in a wet trench, saw the man beside him severed in two by a shell, the head flying one way and the body slumping the other? I also recall several coffee sessions with a sergeant wrecked by his brutal heroism. Parachuted behind enemy lines in Belgium, he had been compelled (so to speak) to shoot a number of farmers and their families who mistook him for a Boche and threatened their would-be savior. He had also, in the course of his mission, strangled a set of sleeping German soldiers one by one with a length of wire. Now he was assigned to quiet duties compatible with shaking hands and uncontrollable jumpiness. Is illness a form of penance?

Mine instead was an epic of pots, pans, and latrines. And even these I finally evaded. A lovely lieutenant colonel who ran the hospital at Camp Gordon befriended the sodden private. He was studying French, I wonder why, in an extension course which I taught several evenings a week. One good turn deserving another, he gave me a certificate informing all concerned that I was subject to a skin disease which made all approaches to soaps and detergents undesirable. Thy name be blessed, lieutenant colonel, though I do not remember it. I carried this precious document to the state of Washington as if it had been Veronica's handkerchief, on board a troopship to Japan, to the slopes of Mount Fuji, to Tokyo, and to another troopship home again. It preserved me from pots and pans and latrines, and left me, instead, with innocent brooms one could take into corners and fall asleep with. This meeting with the lieutenant colonel was one of the luckiest encounters of my life.

I survived Georgia's effusive July and August better than many other draftees because I was a more efficient shirker. On a long march I would collapse, or induce a collapse, without false pride. At obstacle courses I would officiously hold other boys' glasses and contrive to be last in line several times before taking my turn—very slowly, too—over the wicked contraptions. The tallest, largest, and strongest man in the company was a glorious black figure. To my surprise, the heat felled him one day while he was giving his best to this obstacle course. He went berserk, began to flail and rave and knock people down, and had to be subdued by some seven or eight cadres. I instead, besides husbanding my resources, was small and scrawny and thus offered less surface to that assassin of a sun.

The black minority will not hold it against me, I hope, if I set down that my liberal feelings, and my awareness of "socio-historical factors," did not keep me from being thoroughly frightened. While the oppressive American system was mending itself, or not mending itself, I stood in serious danger of being stabbed to death out of mere high-spirited anarchical fantasy. It so happened that my company had no representatives of the black middle or intellectual class. Ours was a small wild population which made me extremely anxious to bring Jane Austen to all the victims of white America, the sooner the better. True, almost all their bloodletting was kept "in the family," but among them was a particularly ferocious imp with bloodshot eyes and an unintelligible local dialect whom even the giant I have mentioned before seemed to fear. This Quilp slept in the bunk next to mine. He hated me from the first minute he saw me—socio-historical factors had determined this—and would gladly have murdered me for two dollars. Why do I say two dollars? Disinterestedly and gratis. In a preliminary way he scraped my heels while marching, jabbed me with his elbows, jostled me at every opportunity, chuckled, sneered, made his knife visible, and finally stole my wallet, to which he was welcome. Luckily his broils and brawls with his own little world stole enough of his attention from me to save my life. He is probably terrorizing a cellblock in a penitentiary at this very moment, unless the gods have deserted him and placed him at the wrong end of a switchblade.

But this was an exception. The other blacks had nothing against me, and frightened me mostly by being a little noisier and a little more anarchical than the white infantry. It was a man as white as this sheet of paper who went about Camp Fuji stealing all our bottles of aftershave lotion after running out of cash for whiskey. As for shirking, there we were all fellows, the black soldiers and I, and my recent boast notwithstanding, they often bettered my efforts. While the rest of us were attending to our daily duties, a knot of blacks could always be found near the barracks, ten or fifteen jovial fellows playing dice as if forgotten by the Table of Organization. This was all predestined so that one of them might be hired to take care of the pots and pans in my place, before the providential lieutenant colonel entered my life. In the morning I would nervously scan the list of names tacked to the bulletin board, and as soon as I saw mine I would suborn the nearest hero who had lost all his money within hours of earning it from the United States, and for whom pots and pans weighed little heavier than the dice that had done him dirt. On such days I myself became a knot of one, an item of army waste dozing discreetly between two bunks, on the wooden floor.

I hate my land. . . .

Not in the least. Only, it was not made to *my* measure, no one consulted me. But I think it had the right to arrange itself for the convenience of its cheerful millions rather than that of a belated immigrant with a taste for Monteverdi's madrigals. I say cheerful because, let novelists and social critics publish what they will, it is a most admirably good-humored society. A frank, outgoing, relaxed, optimistic, plain, and satisfied population. In other societies the plain people had to make do with the scraps of goods and institutions which their betters ordered for their own benefit. Here the plain folk have built for the plain folk. A novelist requiring a birthplace for a fictive president could not have improved on Plains, Georgia. The symbol here is the very thing symbolized. (The neighboring town in called Americus.) And Plains would be perfectly blameless if it told lovers of Monteverdi's madrigals to go elsewhere (where, for God's sake?), and at the very least put a stop to their tiresome disgruntled literature.

Hate my land? Far from it. I ought to love it, to begin with, because it permits poems like this ditty to be printed and sold to the public, instead of hitching its author to a chain gang—in Georgia—in July. Alas, when I return to America after a longish journey abroad, and watch the familiar ground become a carpet to meet the homing plane, I ransack myself in vain for a hint of that incomparable feeling: "Home again!" Nothing stirs. Ungrateful indifference! Here I am free; happy in my work; splendidly paid. Here is a stupendously successful political, economic, social, and legal human venture. That venture reminds me, however, of what is sometimes said about ancient Rome, that it was skillful and inventive in political administration and road-building, but defective in the arts and wanting in charm. This charm is exactly what I miss so much, though I know it to be a thing much less important than a sound minimum wage. I find it moving that so many Americans also miss it, more or less obscurely. They travel abroad to immerse themselves in it; or they build, a little pathetically but on the whole commendably, artificial enclaves of charm: a New Hope in Pennsylvania or a Carmel in California, or on a smaller scale, the many "quaint" shopping towns, malls, and streets designed, it is true, by the commercial interests, but what of that? Still, Americans coming home from a bout with charm in Bavarian villages undoubtedly do feel the elation of a return *ad penates*. Naturally, home is home; I was not born here; I cannot be expected to participate. But neither was I born in a hundred places in the world which do warm my spiritual entrails when I return to them. Apparently then, most Americans get all the charm they require, a little from two weeks in Bavaria, a little at home in a street of ye olde shoppes, and their downtowns do not trouble their digestion. My own aesthetic bump is simply too large for the times. Sometimes I suspect it of being larger than my ethical protuberance. This is entirely my private weakness, and I do not consider mine a sound position from which to fleabite the vast, healthy hide of these United States.

Since contemporary Europe is distinctly uglier than contemporary America, we need not look for a degraded aesthetic gene on this side of the Atlantic. The aesthetic collapse is global and the reasons for it are patently socio-economic. A splendid palace in St. Petersburg or Madrid depends on a vast population compelled to work for next to nothing. When wealth is spread a little more equitably, we see less splendor on one side and at the same time less squalor on the other: Amsterdam. When still more progress is made, the extremes of beauty are priced out of reach and funds are directed to utilities for the greatest number, from better hospitals to new gadgets for the kitchen. In short, when the masses can pay for the goods of this world, these goods will be shoddier in design and in their materials, no matter how well the masses are educated in a myriad schools, than when these goods can be had by some rare prince or cardinal for survival wages. Presently, in an environment dominated by a factory rather than a cathedral, the semicostly arts of music and painting lose their grip on beauty, followed at last by the most private and least expensive art, that of poetry.

No one is to blame. While we grieve over our cities, where the aesthetic slump displays itself on a grander scale than it can in a chamber piece by Alban Berg or a poem by Allen Ginsberg, the hapless taxpayer has his own word to say. Why should he mulct himself to beautify a town he does not possess in any genuine psychic sense? To the extent that he wishes to beautify anything, every man wants to embellish what belongs to himself. The great urban centers of Europe are beautiful only because a lord, or the lucky members of an oligarchy, felt that they were adorning their own property. "Let us have an avenue of trees here—the finest marble for the flooring yonder—and over there another monument." The popes chiseled their names on every drinking trough in Rome. Vanity makes cities beautiful. The contemporary citizen quite naturally concentrates his vanity on his third-floor apartment or his very own house. That is why the major American cities are pleasant enough in their better residential districts but calamitous in the public sector; and paradoxically, an American millionaire must dwell in an ugly metropolis whose heart is a basic "downtown," while the poor in Europe live in the midst of palaces, piazzas, elegant churches, fountains, statues—or what is left of them. Not (by the way) that I would make sentimental conclusions as to what it all means to them. A good job will always be more important to mankind than a set of Berninis upon a bridge.

Hate my land because of an absence of Berninis upon its bridges? Mere literature. Here, for all its twisters of social violence, is a peaceful and stable country; populated by reasonably honest, earnest, jovial, simple people; flexible and adaptive in its institutions, so that its imbecilities do not necessarily take permanent root, as they do elsewhere; abounding in brutal characters, but even more in characters eager to expose, denounce, or reform them; and inclined to look upon the unknown as a problem to be solved rather than as a mystery to gape at in awe. Therefore it is not in any way a "poetic" country, though it is full of practicing poets. The Celtic twilight is absolutely missing. No fairy tale could get itself born in the United States. There is no melancholy, no metaphysical giddiness, no shy hesitation here. The women like the men are straightforward, tough-worded, and aboveboard. But what am I saying that Hawthorne did not tell his countrymen a hundred and twenty-five years ago, when he described America as "a country where there is no shadow, no antiquity, no mystery, no picturesque and gloomy wrong, nor anything but a commonplace prosperity, in broad and simple daylight"? Religion itself sinks or rises (choose which) from the mystical and aesthetic to the ethical and economic. Slang and obscenities in the poetry (with "honesty" as a vicious virtue), hardness in the paintings, pandemonium in the popular music, distances between people which must be conquered by an inhuman delivery of energy, a desolation of drugstores, Woolworths, neon "Christ Saves," parking lots, sagging Midwestern porches, Little League baseball fields, hygienic skyscrapers, outdoor moviehouses, disheveled utility poles, hamburger drive-ins, ah merciful gods! and that perpetual heartiness! I have slipped into scolding again.

An obscure but insistent need to dawdle in an old narrow street, to stop on a humorously arched bridge and lean over to watch the fish among the river grasses, to hang still in the silence of a cathedral square and hear the generations of the dead rustling under the earth—but also a need for the delicate, the fragile, the elegant—a Chinese porcelain, a song by Schumann—these are the hungers, my dear unmelodious America, which you cannot satisfy. Forward, forward to the good life—scuba-diving, martinis at the Waikiki Sheraton, backpacking in the wilderness, a strip show in Las Vegas, poolside suntans, oil millionaires golfing in Texas, a whiff of marijuana by youngsters who really believe they are in rebellion against America, the football game on television, a safari in Tanzania for your holidays—forward, forward, I am not striking a superior pose, believe me, and do not think of myself as an extraordinary being because I remain, in your midst, unaccommodated.

It pleases me to think that our ancestors knew how beautiful their towns were, for they never wearied of making engravings of them. How I love to look at these prints, with their churches, towers, and halls dutifully named, and a buxom maid on the riverbank looking toward the gables with a bundle under her arm. That bundle, alas, reminds me that she was an underpaid, downtrodden drudge, and this at once cuts off my oration. True, I do believe that a degree of well-being accrued to her from that beauty; I believe that our well-being and hers is sapped by ugliness; I believe that the presence and absence of beauty are "factors" which hard-nosed economists should include in their computations; I believe all this; but I do not believe that the Piazza Navona can do *much* good to the wretch who is obliged to sleep on its pavement; and this is the consideration which forbids me to be the impeccable aesthete.

DO NOT PLACE YOUR TRUST
IN BABIES

Do not place your trust in babies:
Himmler was one.
Remember he too took his first steps
on funny pudgy legs,
you should have seen him gurgle
and smile at the smiles he saw.
Ah what a happy family.

Next time you bend over a cradle
tuck a hatchet in your thoughts.

This is an awesome contemplation: our minds cannot close the gap: the discontinuity between a toddler playing with his hoop in the park and running to mamma to have his nose wiped, and the grown man organizing mass murders, barking arrogant commands, lying, pushing, conniving, or himself firing his automatic weapon into the chests and bellies of a thousand wailing, huddled, ragged human beings twenty-five feet away from him. That was the same creature who splashed his rubber duck about the bathtub!

Step by step, almost everything is possible for Nature: from the dumb intertwining of some carbon atoms with others (whose only difference lies in their owning a few subparticles less or more than carbon) to the Pope; from the acorn to the oak; from the toddler to the murderer; all these developments display their normalcy, their inevitability, when we follow them step by step; but when we see only the beginning and the end of the ladder, we are stunned—there seems to be a leap from one reality to another across a vacuum.

Why Himmler? I had better admit that I know *nothing* about Himmler's childhood. I have heard that he raised chickens before enlisting with Hitler; and I have present before me that face of

his: the neat spectacles, the dapper mustache; but I have deliberately kept away from the biography, even the biographical article
in some encyclopedia. For all I know, Himmler was an orphan in
a slum, deprived of love from his earliest infancy. Wouldn't it be
convenient if all our monsters had begun as orphans in a slum,
deprived of love from their earliest infancy? But the world is not
so neat as Himmler's mustache. And since any human monster
suited my poem, I chose him by sound, after discarding the too
obvious figures, Hitler and Stalin. I could have written "Goeb-
bels was one." This would hardly have ruined the poem; but is
there not something sneering and sinister in the name of
Himmler? Something insinuating? provided, to be sure, that we
begin with a trifle of information about the man: I do not believe
in a limitless power of word-sounds, all by themselves, to produce concepts or highly discernible emotions. But they can be a
help once the concept and the emotion are established in the
ordinary way, and this Himmler-leer gave me the goose pimples I
wanted.

The distance between a baby and any greatness at all, in good
as well as evil, is disconcerting, and we fall into another reverie
when we think of Socrates, or St. Francis, or Shakespeare as
infants wetting their diapers. Then, too, the heart misses a beat
when we behold some terrifying mover of men—some police
chief or general or emperor who has fallen from power and
survives to become a next-door neighbor again. There he goes, in
a shabby suit (remember Khruschev?), there he goes to the corner
vendor to buy his daily paper. Why, he is only five feet eight
inches tall! Not long ago he had prisoners tortured in the basement of Police Headquarters. He could have engineered a war
between one set of a hundred million people and another set of a
hundred million people. Now, with all his five feet and eight
inches, he stops for the red light, he fumbles for change in his
pocket.

But to return to our babies—I do not like, in general, to point
out sights in these poems like a guide among the monuments—
still—I hope my "do not *place* your trust" succeeds in being
humorous as applied to a baby (for it is an expression one uses in
connection with dignitaries or bankers)—but at the same time
pregnantly so if we consider who the baby will become. However,

I was going to say, or rather ask: how many poets have written poems against babies? You may reply, A poem like this one is not really a poem against babies, is it? And again: It hardly implies a hatred of babies, does it? Which may be so; but the truth is, after all, that I am no great lover of babies or infants or even children. I find it difficult to sentimentalize over them. The sight of a toddler does not melt me. In fact, the discontinuity I was speaking of is one of power rather than of nature. I mean that the infant's nature is already questionable; his appearance of innocence derives from his endearing helplessness: his helplessness is endearing, you see, not his character. He lacks the brain and brawn to do evil, but not, on his own scale, the will.

I am something of a Christian in this without lapsing from orthodox atheism. For me, a baby is "born in sin" in that he is born as a little ball of irritable greed. Each baby—I should really say each living organism—is born as a sort of would-be "black hole"—that is to say, a locus of all-gulping acquisitiveness—a little mouth that cries, "For me, for me, for me!" even in its sleep (so to speak)—although, unlike the black holes in space, the engulfers that we all are meet with a good deal of resistance—a multitude of objects refuse to be swallowed—and besides, the black holes, the maws, are all competing with one another.

I think it is incorrect to speak of mankind as inherently aggressive. This would imply that the infant takes pleasure in the act of attacking, in the same way as he takes pleasure, for instance, in being tickled or in looking at a bright color. If he did—if the attack gave him as much satisfaction as his bottle of milk—we would have to conclude that man is *sadistic* by nature, for is not sadism precisely a pleasure in the attack rather than in some object which the attack is meant to procure? And mankind is not, by and large, sadistic.

So then, infants are not "instinctively aggressive," they are perfectly willing to ingurgitate the good things of the world without fighting, but they are indeed rapacious consumers and almost as irritable as piranhas. Prod a baby, deprive him of a goody, threaten him a little, and he does not shrink, curl up, vanish into a cowl, or run away—Nature has not provided the baby with the means of doing anything so cowardly—but he bawls, and here Nature has been generous, for an infant's shrieks and wails and howls are surely among the most repellent noises in the world: parrots and hyenas make music in comparison. At this stage, we see man using his earliest weapon, for all that bellowing is really a call for the brain and brawn which he lacks in his cradle, but which the mother and father can supply.

Next, take two healthy infants old enough to sit and crawl, place them in a playpen, and supply them with more toys than any reasonable infant would need. Sooner or later, the two rapacities will collide. Four chubby little hands will reach out for the same toy. God knows, survival is not in question, but war ensues. Faces turn red, arms flail, the children cry like the damned in hell. Again, the vicarious brawn and brain come running into the room, though not necessarily to the infants' full satisfaction. Later, equipped with their own—the brawn for immediate action and the brain for the calculation forward in time—they will drop their bawling the way an army "mothballs" a superseded weapon.

This then is original sin. Original, that is to say inevitable.

In such affairs, one of the two parties is always the loser. But it is not pure chance which selects the loser, a chance so pure that the loser today can hope to be the victor tomorrow. Some children are bigger, faster, and smarter than others. The dice are loaded in their favor. They grow up without feeling the need to invent ideas of compassion, collaboration, meekness. Nietzsche was right, of course. Christian ethics and all moral doctrines in favor of gentleness come from cowards and weaklings like myself. The strong use their intelligence to invent weapons and strategies; the weak, to formulate moral imperatives: a rather clever defensive posture. The weak try to foist on the strong the hopefully effective impediment of a conscience, a substance for which there is, I believe, no gene.

The fairly crass colors of this picture can be subtilized if we consider that few individuals are conquerors all their lives, and few perpetual victims. Therefore, instead of showing the Wagnerian supermen on the one side, whose impulse is only to grab and to conquer, and the meek of the earth on the other, concocting ideas of paradise for the meek, we should perhaps see the conqueror and the victim represented in each person and dividing the psychological field. But paint the picture as we will, mankind still shows its double face: one greedy, the other submissive;

heads, the brute, tails, the pet. Getting hold of the toy will make our wars; losing it will beget pensions for crippled veterans.

Still, the baby is closer to the brute than to the saint. The transition from irritated bawling to striking at the antagonist is a direct one, awaiting only the necessary physiological developments. But the direct path from a baby's cries of weakness and search for refuge in his mother's arms leads merely, as in the lower animals, to the behavior of retreat, concealment, flight, submission. There is no direct and necessary pathway from these instincts to ethical formulations. That angelic feeling-for-others-as-if-they-were-myself is on the path after the path, and even then, the "others" are apt to be old acquaintances like one's immediate kin or one's immediate clan. From *me* to *us* already demands an effort, but as long as that *us* is a small, visible group from which many favors have flowed, almost all human beings are able to make it; and we correctly think of those who cannot, those, that is, who have not even a "me-feeling" for their own family, as monsters. But from there to a love embracing mankind the distance is so vast, and so few human beings are able to make the spiritual voyage, that they too can be regarded, in a laudatory sense this time, as monsters.

There is a passage in Proust's *Le Temps retrouvé* in which Saint-Loup speaks admiringly of the soldiers' courage under fire: "If you could see all these people, above all the ordinary people, workingmen, shopkeepers who never suspected what heroism lay concealed in their own souls and who would have died in their beds without ever having known it, if you could see them run under a hail of bullets to rescue a comrade or carry off a wounded officer; and, struck down themselves, smile as they die because the medical orderly has told them that the trench has been wrested from the Germans again—I assure you, my dear man, that it would give you a fine conception of our Frenchmen and make you understand the historical epochs that seemed to us a bit extraordinary in the classroom." Here we see that limited "identification" (to use the jargon of our day), well beyond the immediate family, but how far short of all mankind, which the vast majority of men (even Germans, M. de Charlus might have retorted) quite easily, I would say quite naturally, bring off; quite naturally, because from the beginning of their history on earth— if our anthropologists are right—men assembled in clans to hunt and to fight under extremely difficult conditions. Their physical helplessness vis-à-vis the predators made it essential that, unlike these predators, they should learn to "love" a large group of nearby human beings.

On the other side of the ledger, I recall a recent experiment by a psychologist which gave Americans a disquieting view of their fellow men and women. The subjects of the experiment, all college students, not riffraff, were instructed, under authoritative and respectable laboratory conditions, to inflict more and more painful electrical jolts on certain "victims" in another room. These "victims" were actually collaborators in the experiment, and their screams of pain were simulated. Under the mildest of proddings and assurances by their white-coated supervisors, the subjects pursued the torture of these victims not only without any pangs, but with a certain glee. These results were confirmed in another study, where college students took on the role of prison guards, and quickly learned to enjoy brutalizing other college students who impersonated convicts.

Let me say at once that I do not gulp these studies like so many consecrated wafers. Just as I would not allow studious-looking psychologists to browbeat me into torturing anyone, so I do not let them bully me with their sensational "scientific experiments." Experiments aside, however, I know that we have traveled far indeed from our origins, that is to say, from our individual and also from mankind's infancy, when we come to the genuine altruistic sensations which in turn lead to our encompassing ethical systems. And they, need one say it, are more often invoked than applied. Unfortunately, it is even an error to interpret a camaraderie of the kind Saint-Loup described as a step on the path to a yet wider circle of fellow-feelings. The bolgias between *us* and *them* that surround us are complex and fluctuating. At one moment Proust's French *poilu* is one with the French army against the German army; but at the first sharp incident, it is his regiment against another, and he is ready to throw the other to the wolves. To speak my whole mind, I take our *humaneness* or *humanity*, as we curiously call it, to be more or less the invention of a prosperous bourgeoisie, and largely confined to it to this day. A well-fed personage in an unwarlike occupation is, naturally, the least irritable member of the species: all honor to the middle class!

After two or three thousand years of exhortations from priests and philosophers, we are still pretty much where we began. Not moral systems learned by rote, but visible signs of helplessness or submission from the *others* make us gentle, even compassionate. This too we inherit from our simian ancestors. Does an epidemic rage in Thailand, or is there mass starvation in Ethiopia? Irritability drops sharply in the rest of the world, and people run to donate money, clothes, food, whatever. Is this not very like the baby in his crib? His helplessness resembles that of an earthquake victim. We are disarmed. We cannot think of the baby as a future Himmler any more than we stint our donations because of the thousand-and-one repulsive acts which, surely, each of the earthquake victims committed in a year's time. Submission by one party naturally satisfies the other party, be he human or simian. Translated to a higher level, this means that we tend to give love when we are submissively asked for it.

It is well known that inmates of our penitentiaries (as rugged a lot as any nation has to show) rate crimes against children—molestation, child-beating, murder—as the lowest species of law-breaking in the book, and often commit assaults within the prison walls against prisoners convicted of such crimes. This indicates how effectively a permanent submissiveness, a helplessness which is the essence of a creature—namely the baby—disarms and, in a word, invites love from mammals like us: even murderers—murderers of offensive adults, that is—rebel against this violation of something like the simian instinct of being appeased in the face (or the rear!) of submissive bodies.

I will not deny that I was rather unsympathetic to children long before I set out to philosophize so garrulously about them. Even as a youngster I preferred the company of adults, and I still do. I am too self-conscious to immerse myself in play with children, and too partial to "rational discourse" to take much pleasure in chatting with them. I delight in the finished product, not the process of making it. It is not only the embryo which roughly recapitulates the history of the vertebrates; even after birth, and for years to come, the toddler is more animal than man. I like him, in short, at the age when, seeing a beggar in the street, he can feel a pang of sorrow. For we are sentimentalizing when we talk about the infant's cuddling, reaching out with his hands and smiling at us as if it were love. True, the word *love* is one of those large receptacles into which we throw anything we have a mind to; it is a generous synonym; but I take love to be something remote from the powers of the infant, who, like the lower species, is capable only of *attachment:* to his source of food, warmth, protection. Much later in life, this attachment does change into love in the noblest sense of the word: and, as the infant's outward signals of attachment are perpetuated in our kissing and our clutching, we are the more easily led into back-reading these signals in the child as something like a glow of love in the adult sense.

This noblest sort of love is, however, as "organic" as any other. I would define it as *the protection of our protection,* and distinguish it from the parents' love for their children, which is (no offense meant) a sort of protection of one's property. The child, then, begins with a helpless attachment to the source of his protection, which is a mere sucking in of love: the black hole again. This evolves into a wish to preserve, a caring for (in both senses of the words), and a meaning well for the sources of love— and this is what I mean by the protection of our protection. Since the child has grown to the point where he is himself a source of protection, we see that the adult is both giver and receiver. Adult love becomes an exchange of protections, an exchange of gratitudes.

Perhaps my impatience with children conceals, or concealed up to now! a pampered man's repugnance to being "sucked in" without reciprocation. The parent, you see, has at least the satisfaction of tending and fructifying his property. Be that as it may, I am no one's favorite uncle, nor a boy-scout master, nor what is called a born teacher. If anything, I am a born learner. I never tire of the company of those who can instruct me, but I am quickly weary of those who seek instruction from me. I have sat raptly listening to an oil millionaire telling me what a wildcatter does; and was annoyed afterward by the silly apologies of a hostess for having exposed me—a certified intellectual—to a rough business adventurer. I love too, of course, the animated argumentative talk among equals—I plunge into it as an athlete dashes onto the tennis court, swinging his racket left and right in the wind out of sheer expectant elation. Making conversation with children— talk which must be condescending, say what you will—bores me. Alas, not a very attractive trait. But I am glad that so many people do delight in playing with children, in teaching them, or simply in being surrounded by them. They find this company restful, I think—not superficially, since children fatigue even those who love them, but deep at the soul's center; a respite, perhaps, from the demands and complications of adult life. I, instead, enjoy children at a distance: sitting, as happened a few months ago, in the Plaza Santa Ana (one of the few charming spots in Madrid), while waiting for my wife to return from certain raids on the shops; and there watching a marvelous animation, from the wooden bench of maturity, of boys and girls in a dozen little groups, squealing, running, digging, skipping rope, following the rules of several games mysterious to me, and resorting at regular intervals to the mothers and matrons knitting quietly on the sidelines, while here and there, a potbellied policeman enjoyed an easy patrol in their midst. But I confess that I love this spectacle much as I enjoy a walk in a zoo. I do not care to be drawn in. To be drawn in means giving up the rational being for a while; watching is making full use of it.

The spectacle in a zoo, or even better, the circus in anyone's home of three or four kittens at play: Beethoven's most delicious (and always brief) outbursts of elfin delight—the finale of the eleventh quartet, the fountain-spray which ends the sixteenth, the rapturous prestos of the thirteenth and fourteenth, give me, I could almost say, no more crystal a happiness than a dance of kittens in a room, bickering among each other or with a ball of yarn—more beauty, more delighted beauty does not exist in nature—and, even though the little beasts are in training for the kill, there are no baby Himmlers among them. I can watch them without unpleasant afterthoughts. One must be blind to prefer a baby to a kitten!

And yet I have known what it is to love children without ifs and buts, and without the sarcasms of my common sense. The children were three little girls, a set of twins and their younger sister, all three belonging to cousins who were as close to my parents' age as to mine. The twins had been born in Belgium just in time for the German invasion of May 1940. The Belgian authorities had promptly whisked their father away as an enemy alien, apparently forgetting that a Jewish Austrian (who had lived all his life in Belgium) was not in altogether the same class as a Hitler's Austrian. The rest of us fled together, uncles, aunts, cousins, old and young, and so I knew the dear twins in their first tribulations, from Belgium across France, across Spain, across Portugal, and eventually to New York; and even there we lived together for a year; and afterward rented lodgings next door to one another. My poor cousin had been delivered to a French concentration camp (yes, the French had concentration camps) in Provence, but the slovenly conditions prevailing during the period of the French disintegration enabled him to literally walk away and to be reunited with wife and children, and the rest of us, in Marseilles. In New York the marriage soured, and the next-door adolescent I was then began to play the role of an older brother, almost a father, to the pretty, lively, and affectionate twins. After a few years, they acquired a sister who became my especial favorite. Details of walks, games, admonitions, hugs, and chatter can be omitted here; they were of the common sort that binds the members of a clan together. Enough if I say that I learned what such affections are; and that my experiences, eked out by a sufficient imagination, have granted me the insight any devoted parent would have, to wit, that my account of these relationships has been as dry as picking out with one finger on a piano the major theme of a tone poem; dry, impoverished, and yet useful and not inaccurate.

A single event, however, stands out in my memory. One evening my cousins went out with my parents. The twins were away too, I forgot why or where, and I was left with instructions to look in every now and then on little Hedy next door. I was almost a child myself, sixteen years old or thereabout, and heedlessly forgot all about my mission. Two hours passed before my duty exploded into my consciousness. Shocked, I ran to my cousins' apartment, and found—no catastrophe, but merely the child standing in her crib, clutching its railing, and piteously crying. I knew at a glance that she must have been crying for a long, long time. I rushed to the crib, all but sobbing myself, quite broken with remorse and pity, and took the baby in my arms, where I kept her, hugging, soothing, and kissing her, until, with the lovable *glissando* of grief toward consolation, interrupted now and then by a sharp spur of recidivist sorrow, she became calm again and blithe. And it is true that the gift of the *imagination*, of which Oscar Wilde speaks so passionately in *De Profundis*, enables us not only to reproduce in ourselves what we feel are the feelings of another human being (and the lack of imagination is precisely what permits cruelty, for the brutal guard of a concentration camp will not or cannot perform this act of representation, which would make it impossible for him to continue being a prison guard)—but further than this, it often paints with stronger colors than those of reality itself, so that I was probably conjuring up a greater despair in Hedy than what was actually there, just as we foist the refined sensations of human beings on animals with which we sympathize. But better too much than too little. I was irradiated, because of my involuntary cruelty, by a love till then unknown to me; and this single hour gave me, as in a precious bowl, the full taste of parental love. As for what the child experiences, need I go farther than the remembrance of my father's infinite love? My arrogant Reason willingly closes its eyes to let me picture him in some paradise this very moment listening joyfully to my thoughts, grieving that he cannot wing his own to me, but patient because I must be arriving there soon enough; and the tears moisten my eyes incongruously as my fingers touch the typewriter's keys. Machinery does not offend my emotions!

Once a child has penetrated our being in some such manner, it is very hard to see it, even in a part of its nature, as a ball of irritated greed. Furthermore, it is painful to analyze our own deepest emotions. I do not like to point out that this "holy" love suffusing me when I held the crying baby in my arms was a compound of emotions A, B, and C which reinforced one another. Not that analysis negates the experience. What really offends us is that the sober mood in which analysis must be conducted forces us away from the solemn or ecstatic mood of the experience under analysis. We want to bask, not ask. The solution, then, is to close our eyes to our own children, and to our own moods, and to philosophize upon other people's.

The adult loves another adult for merits he perceives in the other. He loves the child for its helplessness and submissiveness and because it is his own; merit does not enter the picture. The little girl is now a grown woman, taller than myself, married, divorced, remarried, a stranger I see perhaps once a year at a family reunion. The love she drew from me as a child remains; but this remainder is like the residue, in a corridor, of a light glowing in an inner room. Love's full force is addressed to the pretty little creature of many years ago. And I fancy that she reciprocates in somewhat the same spirit. There is a special strangeness to relationships once close and now distant. When such persons meet again, they rush together with warm expectations of intimacy, but soon find that they have almost nothing to say to each other; so they sit and stare with friendly smiles; they return to the past for subject matter; paradoxically, the present not the past is nebulous; and they part again with the vagueness some animal might have felt on the seventh day of creation, when it realized that God had forgotten to name it.

In his *Doktor Faustus*, Thomas Mann paints the nauseating picture of a little boy who was, as they say, "too good to live," and who dies in fact before reaching school age. From his birth on he smiles at the world; he is preternaturally docile, gentle, considerate, cheerful, obliging to others, humorous, and affectionate. Whatever Mann's intention may have been—I do not like this extravagantly sterile novel enough to have dwelled on it—we are given in effect a vision of the child as the fully ethical adult in embryo; a perfect man in small; *homunculus optimus*. If, in other words, the love we bestow on infants reflected not the lovingness their looks and gestures cause us to imagine, but authentic qualities of the infantile soul, then some of our children would be such creatures as the toddler Mann invented. Unfortunately, the infantile soul, even at its dearest, is depressingly pre-ethical. Therefore when an artist chooses to portray a too-good-to-be-true child, he had better do so in some recognized language of fable, a language which implies at once that we are not being imposed upon with a sugared view of reality, we are being enchanted instead by a vastly desirable fiction.

Mann's stainless child is a child Jesus of and for the twentieth century. As such, its problems are the same as those of all child Jesus representations. No question about it: the Christian religion, with a baby God on its hands, has had to wrestle with a passing strange contraption, worse far than any polybrach Hindu divinity. No wonder apostles and theologians have tiptoed discreetly away from Mannlike details. Did he play at hopscotch with the neighbor's children? Did he get his nose bloodied? Did he hate to eat bananas? An English pre-Raphaelite painting offers us a thirteen-year-old Savior working in the car-

pentry shop of his not entirely presentable dad. A nail has bloodied his palm. Our urge, I am afraid, is not to worship but to run
for the iodine.

Now I do not know whether a person looking at a mosaic of
the child Jesus in the year 800 felt, in a formulated or unformulated way, the fabled, imaginary, sublimated, longed-for quality
of that child, divorcing it imperiously from his own moppet; or
whether, on the contrary, having never seen a Murillo or heard of
realistic novels, to him that Byzantine baby seemed so expertly
copied from Nature that he wanted to ask its mother whether it
had wet her robe. I do not know—but I do know that for us, and
for these last several centuries, that infant in mosaic does have
and has had the fabulous quality that forbids inconvenient questions and therefore solves the problems besetting a baby God.
The Byzantine child Jesus is properly *unearthly*.

He becomes, as we all know, less unearthly—along with the
other personages of his religion—as the generations pass. But he
still convinces us, and still prevents questions that would make
him ridiculous, in his sculptured or painted manifestations in
the year 1100. And he continues beautifully divine in his progress
through the Gothic, child without wem. At last the Flemish
painters take him to the pinnacle. They contrive the perfect but
oh so precarious equilibrium between the human and the divine,
the what-is and the what-should-be. With them, to be a baby and
at the same time to be ethically perfect is no contradiction. They
declare the impossible with a radiant, unproblematic conviction.

The Flemish and all their predecessors were in fact enjoying
the benefits of that immobility of the visual arts (before Calder)
which helps discourage such time-and-motion queries as,
"Didn't the little dear start fidgeting after an hour in his mother's
lap?" After the Flemish, however, a paradoxical ideal sets in.
Painters and sculptors now behave as if the immobility of their
products were a tyrannical dogma that must be defied. They
struggle to endow their figures with a capacity for apparent
motion in time and space. They unfreeze the figure, they round
the body, they ripple the muscles, they pucker the skin. We cry,
Congratulations!—for we are great partisans of liberation. Their
human beings are wonderfully alive, active—and—mortal. For
unwittingly they have created an art superb for ephemeral man,

but no longer suitable for the divine. At that point, religious art survives on energies accumulated over a thousand years, but in reality it is already doomed.

True, Raphael's infant Jesus still asserts himself with full divine authority. The Flemish equilibrium stands for the last time. Perhaps we should place the men of Flanders a notch below the pinnacle after all, and allow Raphael to reign alone at the intersection and interfusion of truth and dream, anatomical precision and pure spirit. We remain untempted to ask of his babies whether they should be diapered. But Leonardo's rolypoly little Jesus and John the Baptist at the Louvre begin to alarm me. Presently the child will be irrevocably a bundle of flesh, and those who narrate the infant sublime—Jesus or any mother's baby—instead of enchanting us with a fiction, will irritate us with a lie.

DR. WATSON TO DULCINEA

Dr. Watson to Dulcinea

I gave my joy long kisses thigh to thigh
   December night, the solstice of our love,
   ascending toward the Christmas of the seed
   and feeding the poor universe with yet
another bone devoted to a bone.

For all we knew that love is fiber, tissue,
   cell leaping with intelligence of cell,
   we ranted "soul" we raved "enchantment":
   two compounds ionized into rebellion.
And yet the rebel's cry, albumin too. . . .

— 1 —

I mean, of course, the Dr. Watson of double helix fame, not Sherlock Holmes's honest companion. Many months after I wrote the first sketch of this chapter of my whimsies—and by the way, I see the date August 1974 scribbled on the last of the long yellow sheets; today is the 18th of February, 1976; ah, but that "today" is long gone as well, for here I am rewriting for the tenth time, and it is "today" again, a year later; and on what date are you reading these words, my dear hypothetical reader?

Flimsy, giddy, unsettled Time, if the philosophers had not thoroughly worn out your one and certain attribute, which is that you pass, what devastating vituperations you would have to bear from me, what deep-dredged musings on Mutability! I envy the writers of past centuries, when all the concepts that are dry with age today were still to be discovered plump and juicy, and Homer, and Dante, and Montaigne, and Schiller could make Pronouncements about Life too trite for us to utter now, so that we latecomers must say queer things, and twist our faces into

First published in *The Virginia Quarterly Review*, Summer 1983 grimaces, in order to be as fresh as they were with their grand and simple truths.

So not a word about Time. I was going to say that long after writing that first sketch, I saw and heard the living Dr. Watson at the institute that employs me. His serious business with colleagues concluded, he came to the students' lounge to chat about his popular and (I have heard) nasty book concerning that same double helix. There he stood with bulging evasive eyes and a wisp of gray hair erect upon his skull as if anxious to go somewhere else. His speaking arrogant words in a very soft voice made me think of a guillotined head falling on a cushion. But what amazed me was to hear him whisper he had long believed that the great molecule consisted of three strands, not two—as if anything in living beings, or in Nature anywhere! went in threes. Only the Christian's God goes in threes, probably in order to prove that he is *un*-natural, *trans*-natural.

Next to Dr. Watson sat his erstwhile teacher and, in a modest way, my friend, the saintly Max Delbrück, also a Nobel laureate. Because Delbrück is a little hard of hearing, what had been intended as a minipanel quickly turned into a vaudeville routine. At every fourth or fifth word Delbrück interrupted his fellow-speaker with a resounding WHAT? (hand cocked to his ear), whereupon Watson would repeat the last fragment of his sentence, looking askance with his Uriah Heep eyes, in precisely the same undertone as before, thus acceding to but at the same time evading his friend's command. Dr. Watson defended himself manfully, however, against the charge of having defrauded a female colleague of credit due to her. And on my side, why, I have seen so few great personages in my half-century of life that I am as thrilled as an ephebe when I look on these real presences. A few nights ago (as of which date?) I was invited to a small party to meet Hortense Calisher. I have never read her work, but what's that to a celebrity hunter? The event in my soul is a surprise that keeps trying to stem itself even as it spreads: surprise, as if a celebrity materializing before me were a fiction mistakenly in company with a fact—while my rational self protests against the childishness of being surprised.

Seriously, I am not a celebrity hunter at all. One needs to be a satisfied cipher, a member of the chorus without heroic aspirations, to "collect" famous people. For myself, when the personage shakes my hand in the limply polite manner he uses for the thousands of cipher-hands he has to press, the message "You Are Nobody" drums to the innermost brain, and I measure my abjectness as I need never do when I am alone in my room. I shake the limp hand, I bring out the expected admiring remark, I snarl *sub rosa* that I, I deserve to be the fatigued congratulated hero, and finally call myself an idiot. Is one not better off at home?

Not for rubies and emeralds should I entrust these degrading thoughts to a leaf of paper. Besides, that is not what the poem is about. The poem concerns itself with the strange coexistence within most of us, and therefore within our civilization, of the "romantic" view and its, shall we say, physiological antithesis. In the first stanza, I have discreetly suggested a contrast between the Nativity as Divine Love (imitated, as it were, on the human level in each romantic embrace) and the bones rubbing together in our unpleasant cosmos. The second stanza implies that we continue to play on both sides of the net. We romanticize even though we know better. We suspend the operations of the critical intellect. We want to enjoy, not know. This is somewhat like admiring a city from a distance. Must we remind ourselves of rotting garbage in alleys while we admire the myriad lights from a mountain or an airplane? Finally, even though our highest romantic visions are a chemical activity, and even though our very protest against the chemical vision is yet another chemical activity, we go on protesting all the same.

Thomas Mann handled this twinning and twining of incompatibles in his best roguish manner when Hans Castorp gazes in fascination at the x-rays of his Dulcinea's lungs. The point is not that the lady suffers from tuberculosis. For the romantic view of woman and of love would be struck the same blow if the x-rays revealed nothing but health. What hits us so hard is the thought of these cells, capillaries, lymph, nervous tissue, these globs of protein, fats, these streams of enzymes and hormones, that crawling, pulsing, oozing, quivering, munching, dribbling internal world of ours, so difficult to conciliate with the pulsations of romantic love—

we ranted "soul" we raved "enchantment"

—the world of "beautiful human beings," "soulful gazes," and "adoration" which, even today, when half the terrorists are women, when tough female soldiers patrol the streets with automatic rifles in their fists, when "foul language" has passed from the garage mechanic to the suburban matron, still, even today, pervades our consciousness and informs our secret dreams. What, we cry, are we talking about the same human being? Can we ever unify these two visions? Or are we doomed to shuttle between Dr. Watson and Dulcinea? Are we obliged to give up our romantic dreams when we become acquainted with our viscera, and do these dreams depend for their existence on gross ignorance?

To be sure, the two streams reach us from different sources. The romantic is the older one, its source is farther from the present time, it grew while flowing across the lands of myth and legend, and the flowers of the marvelous came floating on its surface. The other is more recent. It has its source in the new toughness of seventeenth-century science, it is the river of numerable and verifiable facts: the flowers do not float on its surface, they are quickly decomposed.

Furthermore, this idealizing tendency is a creation of and for the wealthy and leisured classes. Intimations and imitations of it have always reached the proletariat, but romance gets badly bruised in overcrowded rooms. After a brief period of courtship in which a certain mimicry of upper-class romance is practiced, the poor couple quickly declines to a reality of hard work, drink and quarrels, squalling brats, dirty linen, and unsavory sanitary arrangements.

As a result, the poor are always more at home in the "strictly scientific" realm than the scientists themselves. A common working man will belch at dinner to his heart's content. The toughest scientist, instead, will blush, hope no one heard him, and apologize if he realizes that someone did. So much for the scientific attitude!

Notions of "refined love" flourished, I believe, in upperclass Persia, India, China, and Japan. In our own civilization, we are told that the medieval exaltation of the Virgin Mary contributed to this secular exaltation; but if women were idealized in non-Christian societies, we had better reverse cause and effect and surmise that a growing prosperity and stability, and perhaps the example of the Moorish world, gave women a value and loveliness which in turn affected the worship of the Immaculate Virgin. In a society rich enough to take its women away from the labor force, to pamper them, to make them coveted possessions, to sequester them for much of the day, and at the same time not yet oppressed by too much knowledge of pancreases and the like, idealizations of love, dependent upon an idealization of men by women and women by men (though never without a countercurrent of satirical knowledge) would naturally thrive; and here, in the teeth of the Women's Liberation movement, I will claim that nothing of this happened, nor could happen, without the complicity of the women themselves, only too glad to be excused from back- or mind-breaking toil.

— 2 —

The romantic vision is necessarily hierarchical and distinguishes between a high and a low dignity of objects and actions. It begins not so much with a generalized depreciation of the body as with a particular revulsion against excrement, and a covering up of the bodily parts whence they issue. Here I ask the anthropologists: is the disgust with excrement general? universal? do all tribes conceal their urinations and defecations, and bury the products as many animals do?

I have mentioned Mann; but Swift was more daring in this respect, and more penetrating, for he pushed the anguished question beyond the relative decency of lungs—even diseased lungs— to the shocking areas of bladder and anus, in the face of which (if one may put it comically) the Dulcinea world collapses.

His "Strephon and Chloe," for example, is one of the wisest, deepest, and, let me firmly say, one of the sanest English poems of its age. We would be fools to deprecate it on the ground that it makes us laugh. Such topics could not be approached except by way of disarming humor. A work like "Strephon and Chloe" has a philosophical stature altogether more important than anything Pope can devise in his ambitious *Essay on Man* or advance in his monumentally trivial *Dunciad*.

Swift opens with a portrait which rests on the immemorial tradition of antiphysiological idealization, that is to say the tradition of assigning a value of "high" to that which is not physiological.

> So beautiful a nymph appears
> But once in twenty thousand years.
> You'd swear that so divine a creature
> Felt no necessities of nature.
> In summer had she walked the town,
> Her armpits would not stain her gown:
> At country dances, not a nose
> Could in the dog-days smell her toes.

As a result, all the beaux are in pursuit; and now Swift spreads out the romantic wares of flames and darts, bleeding hearts, poetic strains, billets-doux, sighs, ogling, and the rest. Strephon carries Chloe off, and on the wedding day the full romantic personnel of Hymen, rococo Cupids, pigeons and sparrows, the Muses and Apollo are present. Comes the wedding night, and Strephon much perplexed how to invade so much delicacy with his male rudeness:

> Can such a deity endure
> A mortal human touch impure?
> How did the humbled swain detest
> His prickly beard, and hairy breast!

Now, however, the bride has been put to bed; Strephon strips, but shyly keeps his distance at first. Eventually he grows bold. Chloe drives him back.

> How could a nymph as chaste as Chloe,
> With constitution cold and snowy,
> Permit a brutish man to touch her?

The true reason, alas, is not delicacy, but having drunk twelve cups of tea:

> The bride must either void or burst.

She "steals out her hand" to draw the chamber pot into the bed.

> Strephon, who heard the fuming rill
> As from a mossy cliff distil,
> Cried out, Ye Gods! what sound it this?
> Can Chloe, heavenly Chloe,——?

And there is worse to come. As for the mossy cliff (by the way) is this not a masterful and repugnant double shot—at the romantic

pastoral scene and at the female pudenda? Eventually Strephon is
encouraged to follow Chloe's example—

> And, as he filled the reeking vase,
> Let fly a rouser in her face.

As is only right, the little Cupids,

> Abashed at what they saw and heard,
> Flew off, nor ever more appeared.

For they have understood that idealization (in our Cupidinous
tradition) explodes at the touch of the physiological, as a balloon
filled with air does at the poke of a lit cigar.

> Adieu to ravishing delights,
> High raptures, and romantic flights,

cries Swift, and:

> How great a change! how quickly made!
> They learn to call a spade a spade.
> They soon from all constraint are freed;
> Can see each other do their need.

But now comes the surprise; or rather, it has come already, for
Swift has suggested his moral in a passage which precedes the
bedding of the bride. It is by no means a twentieth-century moral,
to wit "that the sooner we drop our romantic flummery the
better," and "let us all learn to accept our natural functions, and
do everything together," etc., etc. On the contrary, Swift is all for
illusion:

> Since husbands get behind the scene,
> The wife should study to be clean;
> Nor give the smallest room to guess
> The time when wants of nature press;
> But after marriage practise more
> Decorum than she did before;
> To keep her spouse deluded still,
> And make him fancy what she will.

In case we should think that he is jesting, he lets this advice
proliferate in the long coda to his poem; and intimates that one
reason why marriages go sour so quickly is precisely that reti-

cence and illusion ("fair decency") are foolishly thrown to the
wind at once.

> They take possession of the crown,
> And then throw all their weapons down.

— 3 —

Most of us manage to survive the passage from the romantic
premarital condition, when even sexual intercourse is surrounded by delicate concealments and silences, and when other
physiological realities are carefully beclouded, to a state of nup-
tial good-fellowship which comes more and more to resemble the
family household we experienced as children. The little noises
and smells are accepted. We tend each other through sicknesses
quite damaging to the chivalric ideal. And if we are lucky, we
discover in our spouses (and they in us) solid qualities to respect
and admire. For Swift himself, this was apparently not feasible.
Together with Esther Johnson, he performed an experiment in
living which is worth studying as an alternative to our usual
physical camaraderie—as an alternative, at any rate, for those
who want no children. Such couples might decide to opt for
marriage without cohabitation, in contrast to our "liberated"
people today, who choose rather to cohabit without marriage.
Swift's way may have its disadvantages, but presumably he was
able to maintain something of the romantic life by keeping his
distance from Stella's "low" physiological activities and concealing his from her.

Actually, the Swiftian solution was less eccentric than one
might think at a first encounter. The rich practiced it daily under
a single roof, for their mansions were large enough to allow for
separate bedrooms and sanitary facilities. A great deal of formality was maintained between man and wife, and they rather visited
each other than lived together in our own humbler manner. Swift
achieved the same purpose in a fashion suitable to the middle
classes. He lived here, and Stella lived there. Each meeting was a
romantic event.

I am not positively advocating this course of life. Yet were I
sure of my lady's faithfulness, I could endure it, I could find
much to relish in it, and I would take full advantage of its

romantic possibilities. We would always meet in our best finery, and we would each wash our dirty dishes alone.

How many "sordid" extramarital affairs are in fact romantic escapes from the sordid? Strephon loves Chloe, and Chloe loves Strephon, but both long for the days when they knew each other less well. This is, in a sense, immature. But then all dissatisfactions with the constraints of reality are immature. It would seem that a modicum of immaturity makes the full man and woman.

For Swift, the romantic life dies never to be reborn at the first foul breath of physiological reality. But one of the most amazing facts about our species is that we are always leaping back and forth between high and low. One moment we indulge in a delicate romantic exaltation, the next we treat love and sex to every piece of invective and every coarse joke known in the language. Listening to us, a visitor from another planet would have to conclude that we all maintain two sexual partners: one whom we respect and one whom we despise; whereas in actuality we are normal schizophrenics conversing about a single person— and about ourselves—on both registers. And why? Because, as Crazy Jane says in Yeats's splendid poem,

> Love has pitched his mansion in
> The place of excrement.

Because of this rather comical and inconvenient accident, this bad joke played by the gods on mankind, we are Januses about sex, we are tangled in the contradiction, we flounder about with the most absurd inconsistencies. The coarsest soldier in the barracks, who never talks about sex except by means of a vocabulary expressing mocking contempt and humorous revulsion—precisely the way he talks about his excremental functions—and indeed, the two vilest four-letter words in the language are, the first, a synonym for sexual intercourse, and the other, a blunt pointer at our bowel movements—this same soldier goes home for a weekend leave and moons over some sweetheart like a swain out of a Victorian album. If the gods had allowed us to make love through our fingertips, this muddle would not have appeared. By the same token, if we had to feed ourselves through the same orifices by which we eliminate our wastes, we would always dine in a private room, we would invent a double vocabulary expressive of our double feelings—a vocabulary of enjoyment and a vocabulary of contempt; and of course we would be telling innumerable "dirty" jokes about eating. As it is, we do have a few "low" words on this subject, for instance "to swill" (and the more expressive German *fressen*), but note the difference: we use the decorous word for normal purposes and the ugly word when the normal act of eating is actually perverted: "You're swilling your food instead of eating it, my friend"—by which we mean that he is eating too fast, and spreading the gravy over his mustache above and his chin below. But the man who says "I f— —d her" (I do not blush, you see, to half-efface the rude word) is not implying in the least that he has botched the job. He is simply in his excremental phase with regard to sex. The next moment he may be all Tancred again.

But now, picture us on the romantic summit, and ask, How can this "unearthly" delight subsist when we know full well, and would have to confess if questioned, that the beloved, man or woman, is subject to the same gross daily physiological blights as an army sergeant? It survives because of a vital distinction between information as idea and information as perception. We live quietly with many a piece of information (for instance, the slaughter of cattle) that would make us retch if absorbed through our own eyes or ears. We know what is behind a holiday, a famous actor, a king at his coronation, but we crave and cherish the idealizations all the same, we carefully keep our distance, we do not constantly punish our dreams of beauty with reminders of kitchen-truths. And here is the reply to fanatics of honesty whom these illusions offend. These illusions are demands, aspirations, desires, which subsist in us whether or not we think they can ever be realized by mankind; hence the romantic life we try to maintain in ourselves, or, far more frequently, ascribe to others (the beloved, the actor, the king), is as authentic a phenomenon of our natures as our grossest visceral facts. We play the romantic role for one another not in the least as a lie, since both partners in the game possess the correct information as idea, but as episodes of idealizing dramatic art, as perpetual holiday, as living enactments of a hope, or rather a hunger, for mankind.

Consider how naively, or rather pseudo-naively, we let ourselves be taken in by cosmetics. It takes a strong hater of mankind—like Swift again—to keep tormenting himself with the realities under the lotions, dyes, colors, and what have you. Like Baudelaire, most of us delight in these ephemeral improvements on Nature. Here, too, we pay homage to the eternal youth and beauty that ought to be and rid ourselves of a primitive and perfectly useless realism, relegating it from the salon to the business quarters where it belongs. A sentimentalist is a person who deludes himself (or others) into thinking that reality can and does operate at the level of romance; but a wise realist cultivates the romantic plot in his garden and culls from it a foretaste of the heaven he has no expectation of ever seeing.

Apropos of heaven, let us recall that our need to idealize by veiling low functions is addressed not only to lovers but also to leaders and to religious figures. Once again, it is one thing to know as an idea and another to see, hear, and smell, or even to be told. God became man, says the Christian. The Incarnation requires full submission to all human physiological activities. Hence there is not the slightest taint of heresy in sending our Savior to the privy. On the contrary, true doctrine demands it. And yet such an image is more destructive of religion than anything the Higher Criticism could ever advance.

The closer the affinity between a given physiological action or condition and our eliminatory functions, the more unromantic it appears to us—even today. A lady will always excuse herself—from anything—on the ground of a headache in preference to pleading a diarrhea or a constipation. A headache—or a broken leg—is a presentable reverse, whereas the stomach in its various manifestations takes us down the ladder toward regions of indecency. Byron exploited this fact to the best comic advantage in a famous episode of the second canto of his *Don Juan*, when the young hero discovers that seasickness and romantic love are incompatible co-lodgers in a man's system. Love, he says, is bold against "all noble maladies," but does not like to meet "vulgar illnesses."

> But worst of all is nausea, or a pain
> About the lower regions of the bowels.

If Don Juan's thoughts had strayed away from Donna Julia because of a bullet in his shoulder, one dignity would have been supplanted by another—love by a wound. Here, instead, dignity is ousted by indignity.

Scientists feel this like other mortals, but Science does not. For Science, a fart is as good as a fanfare. And that is why the "scientific way of life" is reputed (among scientists too) to be unbearably drab. We cling to the romantic vision for our "mental health," if you wish. Romance makes value judgments. Science turns them into a field of inquiry.

— 4 —

I have speculated that the romantic vision begins with a perhaps universal revulsion against excrement. Since mammals are generally fastidious in this respect, it is hard to conceive of man as ever having wallowed happily in his feces, even though babies are known to be less delicate. Since our excrement attracts flies and bacteria (and so forth), it constitutes a source of danger to us. We may suppose therefore that nature's mechanism to separate man from this source of danger is to make the smell "inherently" offensive to adults. Not to infants, because in them it is unnecessary: their parents move them to and fro.

But if this is so, then the romantic vision is not a *mere* illusion. It is an illusion only in the sense that what is bad for our health is not therefore shameful and unmentionable. Shame probably appears because parents, for whom the smell and "mess" are offensive, wean children from their excrement by ridicule and exuberant gestures and noises of disgust. Thus even our civilized shame is remotely grounded in the ultimate physical reality, and if out of this shame the antipodal romantic vision arises, we can go yet farther and connect Spenserian idealism—the complement to Swift's horror—to that shudder against our waste products for which Nature has perhaps provided.

Yet, other states and actions stand low in our estimation without being directly connected with elimination. In the poem from which I quoted, Swift mentions sweat. Now there is such a thing as a "noble perspiration" that bedabbles our brows. Swift, however, mentions places less noble than the brow, and we realize that it is chiefly though not entirely the bad smell which is at issue here. We are extraordinarily sensitive to bad smells, considering that this sense is the least important we have. Why are we repelled by all sorts of body odors? Surely there is no survival value in disliking bad breath. Shall we affirm, then, that these are nonuniversal and late "ornaments" and supplements to the basic human revulsion against excrement?

And what about our snot—the very word is horrid—and what about nose-picking—where there is not even a bad odor to blame? Cleaning our nails in public is "not very nice," but picking our noses is ludicrous and vulgar in the extreme. At this point we are bound over hand and foot to romantic illusion: science discovers no foundation.

Since our romantic valuations remain so unrepentantly alive, our language and our literature are compelled to follow suit. We may be philosophical egalitarians, but we continue psychological hierarchists. In the first place, the "gutter language" which is now permitted in lieu of Swift's mock-bashful aposiopesis ("Can Chloe, heavenly Chloe,——?") has not by any means been elevated to a new dignity simply by being permitted, and encouraged, and repeated *ad nauseam*. Our writers are mistaken if they think that bringing the old foul words into the parlor cleanses the words; no, they befoul the parlor, now as in the past. For language is stubborn.

In the second place, the written language has a peculiar power of magnifying what it names. To name a thing or an action in print is to give it *ipso facto* especial consideration. To write it down for all to read is to frame it and to point the finger at it. That is why so-called realistic writing is in fact hyperbolical. Take again these perfectly innocent physiological emanations of ours, our little noises, our little smells—what do they amount to in our everyday lives? To very little indeed. We scarcely give them a thought. We cordially disregard them. But they damage the romantic life if they occur in public, and when we find them worded in a poem or a novel, the words leap from the page and not only report the little noise or smell, but because they report it, and in and by the act of reporting it, they make much of it, and consequently cast the personage in an unfavorable light, comic or serious. For literature is always emblematic. We readers know that the author rummages in the bottomless hamper of reality, and we know that anything he lifts out has been particularly chosen for that distinction, and is therefore significant. If he chooses a belch for Hector (or something "worse"), it can only be in order to bring him down.

Thus the writer continues willy-nilly to make emblematic use of the ancient connotations. Furthermore, the wise writer does not seek to change these traditional connotations and does not want them changed. He does not want our famous four-letter word for sexual union to acquire a fragrance of innocence, delight, and romance; he needs its foul connotations for the occasions when foulness is what he requires.

The physiological realities are not all on the same level of unromantic coarseness. Some are so low and undignified that we have no words to dignify them. Describe them in plain English monosyllables or by means of Latinized terms—it does not matter; the moment an author chooses to apply them to a character, that character is lowered. But sexual intercourse is in the middle range. I have spoken of our Janus-like attitude. As a result, an author has a goodly range of words to pick from. He has Dulcinea words, Dr. Watson words, and army sergeant words. Our novels, stories, plays, and poems show the modern writer hard at work trying to efface these distinctions. He assiduously uses army sergeant words in Dulcinea contexts, for example, almost as a sort of political protest against hierarchies in language, as if low words were underpaid coal miners. Fortunately he fails. Language is more stubborn than he is potent.

Shall we ever get ecstatic unions of lipids? Will enchantment accrue to pituitary glands? Why do neon lights become Jesus less than candles? I see no conclusion to this high comedy. Our scientific ideas, with their appropriate language, are so many juniors whacking away at their romantic dads, whose blood seems to replenish itself as fast as it flows. It is a double comedy, as Turgenev understood when he wrote *Fathers and Sons*. The romantic father is always being demolished by the brutal facts, and the scientific son is always meeting a Dulcinea who forces him into a rhapsody without foundation.

THE GARDEN

The Garden

I place you in a garden
but a garden twenty times
as good as paradise,
with hordes of flowers
and grass piled on in legions
where a toadstool would get lost
if a toadstool could be found
disgracing in my garden
twenty times
as good
as paradise.

And over it an orange sun
contracted for eleven in the morning
in incessant May,
a cloud or two
for humor and trees
trees making a great windy rush
to stay precisely where they are,
near you that is,
spying out of every green and rascal leaf.

And round about
I stick a wide and nasty wall
made of the foulest foul brown stone
which looks as if it always rained on it,
besides electric wires, spikes,
and here and there a hungry dog.
As I can't fly
I add a stingy gate
locked by a ton of steel
to which the only key sits in my pocket.
The gate is smart and understands
the king and janitor is me.

First published in *The New England Review and Bread Loaf Quarterly*, Spring 1983

The rest? I'll eat my tongue.
When it is I come,
and how it is you greet me,
the weight and contour of our dialogues,
the kiss that interferes
with topics of importance,
the bodies in their moist entanglements,
you know, I know,
we spread no gospels—
although that daisy
standing by our keel its yellow eye wide open
that daisy I suspect
is learning dimly in its roots
there's more to nature
than the bureaucrats of pollen
and the sniff of lowly snouts.

— 1 —

These love poems—some sad, some joyous—I hardly seem the person to . . . yet I have written my share and more than my share of them. I shall let you guess, my imagined reader, how many of them arise from experience, and how many are literary sham, and how many display a touch of both. I do think it is difficult to write a good poem on a subject one is indifferent to, or quite inexperienced in: knowledge of the craft of poetry and ambition to succeed will go far, but the "extra thrust"—the final urge and surge of energy are provided, when all is said and done, by what used to be called "sincerity," that is to say, a genuine fascination with the subject at hand which exists and subsists outside of one's artistic preoccupations. But this does not mean that a good love-poem rests squarely on a real experience. A wish for an experience, a dream of an experience, is an experience too; the imaginative mind can make a great deal out of very little—a *Romeo and Juliet* out of three words exchanged with an *ignota.*

Still, as the world does not always know this, or keep it in mind, I find myself curiously embarrassed by some of my own works. I positively conceal them from my relatives, friends, and colleagues. My neighbor is different. She is a lady, as respectable a mother of three as I am a father of none, who writes lurid commercial novels in which the genital life is accorded all the exposure demanded by fashion today. We drink coffee together; we gossip about agents and publishers; she has a good, sober husband who could have sat for Goethe's Albert in *The Sorrows of Young Werther*. He cheerfully manages her business affairs— she obviously has no others. And she is not embarrassed at all. But I fancy there is a difference between the novel, officially fictive, and lyric poetry, known to be "from the heart." Does the sophisticated critic, who claims that "the lyric I is but a mask, a fiction, a dramatic device," *really* believe it?

For the rest, I am glad that I have paid my respects to the immemorial tradition of love poetry by adding my voice, in true Chinese fashion, neither in a slavish copying of my predecessors nor with a brattish attempt at "originality." As far as I am concerned, mankind continues to exist within the human compass, and as I see most people continuing to carry a single head on their necks, I continue to paint them monocephalically. That is to say—on the basis of this perennial monocephalism (if I may so put it) of the human race—its obstinate permanences which overwhelm its innovations (in the empty horrors of space our astronauts gab about baseball scores)—on the basis, then, of our endurances and persistences, I am deeply suspicious of experiments which seem to run miles ahead of the changes that have occurred in the human character and situation. The rhythms, words, and form of my poem are as adequate to reality and therefore as modern as I want anything to be.

The Garden as garden, however, has a parlous Moorish look. I never thought, years ago, many years ago, when I wrote this poem, that I was enacting the part of a "male chauvinist pig," as they say today in their quaint pseudo-language. A very prison-garden—the woman apparently for my exclusive use—the key to the gate in my pocket. It does not look as if this heroine will ever become a traffic cop, a senator, or a terrorist. Or even have much to say with respect to my occupations outside that medieval wall. I must have been thinking about a certain delicious little picture I once saw in Frankfurt (I believe) showing an ideal garden, the wall, orange trees, fountains, tame animals, and tamer damsels embroidering and playing music.

And yet, the wall, I bashfully suggest, is of her devising as much as mine. If my She disliked it, it would not be there. The moment she begins to dislike it truly and most truly, it will fall down. The analogy to a master-and-slave condition limps at every step. For unlike master and slave, male and female struck a secret bargain long ago. Beyond the wall, life is very exciting and variegated: that has its advantages. Inside, life is calmer and safer: that has its advantages too. Making decisions is notoriously pleasant. Having others make them for you is also notoriously pleasant. We enjoy giving commands. We also enjoy being pampered. This is what the economists bluntly call a trade-off.

On the issue of justice I yield without a struggle. Our women from China through Israel and all the way to California have proved to my satisfaction that washing dishes is not an instinct imprinted in the female's nucleic acids. Yes, women bear children, and women are not quite so strong in the aggregate as men. But since neither of these supposed impediments to equality ever prevented the gentle sex from working "like mules" in the fields, I think that the bearded hero had better leave this argument alone. And shall I, who am hardly an Achilles at five foot five and a hundred twenty pounds, strut about the streets with statistics on the weakness of women? No, madam, Nature does not instruct you to be the passive sex and stay at home minding the babies and playing the piano. You have the same right and the same power as us men to be president, banker, physician, bullfighter, artist, engineer, soldier (yes, your turn to be killed on the battlefield, madam), ditch-digger, pope, or gangster. I read in today's newspaper that a woman has at last made it as a coal miner; this is justice. And males can knit as well as drive tractors. It is only at the extreme limits of physical strength—in the region of heavyweight boxers—that women fall short; and this comprehends too minute a fraction of mankind and its travails to detain us.

I suppose, like many others, that the relegation of women to activities "behind the front lines" occurred because our race began as hunters rather than as farmers. Hunting requires speed, frequent speed. Farming demands steadiness. A pregnant girl who could hold her own in the fields almost up to the time of delivery would be at a disadvantage for months in the hunt. Besides, it is again in the hunt, and not on the farm, that the woman's smaller stature would count against her. In hunting societies, therefore, there was a sound natural basis for a division of labor which made man the leader, the aggressor, the dominant partner, and woman the stay-at-home who did the cooking. By the time men exchanged the spear for the plow, these roles had become profoundly fixed in the race, and they maintained themselves even though a woman could, and evidently did, work as effectively in the fields as her man.

But let us follow this hard-working female on the farm. I think she gets the worst of both worlds sowing, reaping, feeding, milking, and then making children and cooking too. There is nothing "feminine" about her. She has inherited the role of the led, the obedient from ages past, but instead of the relative sinecure around the campfire, waiting for the hunter to come home, and in the meanwhile nursing the babies or gathering fruit from a few trees, she works as hard as her husband, and probably much harder. Voltaire's Gengis Khan (in the *Chinese Orphan*) is struck by the difference between these sturdy females he has known exclusively up to now and the tender, gentle Chinese ladies he meets in conquered Peking:

> De nos travaux grossiers les compagnes sauvages
> Partageaient l'âpreté de nos mâles courages.

The syntax is dubious but the sense is clear: rude, crude females sharing hardship with their men in the fields, as against "la tranquille Idamé," whose words and features all breathe "the art of pleasing."

For this Chinese Idamé represents the next stage. Imagine a lucky family of farmers when our time was young. They thrive and move to the walled town; the husband sets up shop and manufactures saddles for the nobility. In his old age he becomes an alderman. Thank God, his wife can give up the hard work. She supervises the servants. She carries the keys in her pocket. Her hands become white. She hires a music teacher for her daughters. The daughters read romances. They dream of lovers under the moonlight. The ladies have turned gentle.

So we are back, you see, where we began. The men are still the leaders, but now they are doing the hard sweaty work by themselves once more, and the women are sitting around the new campfire (the hearth) or picking a new fruit off the trees (serving tea and cakes). Alas, one thing leads to another. The ladies go to school. They begin to think. It occurs to them that, apart from running after lions or boxing in a ring, they are as well equipped by Nature to be aldermen or preside over General Motors as their husbands. They rebel against spinets and moonlight. They want to work in the fields! And back goes the pendulum again: the women are sweating at the job from eight to five.

But we pay a price for everything, even justice, and I would glow with a warmer feeling for our militant feminists if they gave some sign of understanding that their victory will be, or rather is already, like all victories, tragic. For the moment, I see no evidence that equality is producing as large a volume of happiness as it is of justice. If happiness were the only "variable" to be measured, who would be able to decide, on the whole, between a career woman in New York or Paris and one of those spoiled women in some warm, retrograde country—I name no names— pudgy, with buttered skin and rosy cheeks, placid—weeping over a hurt sparrow—all mother and lace—her wars confined to securing an invitation denied to a neighbor, a box at the opera, a dress, a bauble. Her sister, instead, is intelligent, aware, disputatious, efficient, cynical, demanding. She has "been around." She is not "taking any _____ from anybody." She "knows the score." Come to think of it, however, our pretty Idamé "knows the score" too, just as the toughest *macho* may know how to darn a sock. Half of her is truly feminine, the other half plays the role of being truly feminine. What of it? The question is, how does one decide what is more desirable for the party herself? I marvel at all the confident opinions I hear.

So it goes with most social reforms. The social web is indescribably complicated. You tug one strand with the best faith in the world, but only a god can foretell what all the other strands will do when you pull. Our certainties are confined to extreme situations. Downright hunger and disease beg for bluff remedies. When you stand in front of Auschwitz, no need to feed data and queries into computers. But away from the extremes, every answer riddles us with questions. I see where even the evils of slavery in America have been questioned in an exhaustive two-volume study. If we could measure happiness by means of electrodes under our dandruff, would the average free black man come off with a higher score than his enslaved grandfather? "Happiness," you reply in your best Carlylean manner, "is not our only goal; there is human dignity, human usefulness . . ." Tear-streaked dignity? Harrowed usefulness? I don't know. Still, say that I agree with you—even so, happiness does matter, does it not? And if it does, then, before you give the social order a thorough jolt, perpend. What if justice and happiness do not always lie on the same side of a program?

Now, as to slavery, I cannot force it down my gullet, even in a diabolical mood. Not because I think men and women are too good to be slaves. Quite otherwise: I think very few of us are fit to be anything else. No, what offends me is that one set of brutes should lord it over another. The injustice of it so whips up my blood that I forget to take "scientific readings" of happiness.

Or do, at any rate, in certain moods.

But this so-called tyranny of man over woman, this supposed subjugation of one sex by the other, is another matter altogether. I say it again: I suspect a secret compact, an arrangement, a pseudo-tyranny more or less satisfying to both sides, a series of compromises across the table, bed, or battlefield, an exchange of advantages, some obvious and public, others covert, yes, even subconscious. That is why so many women have to be dragged to their victory.

"Beware of justice!" I should like to cry to women. "Here is equality for you: we men have not even the right to give it to you, for we never had the right to withhold it from you. And yet do not take it!" Too late. Once the apple has been bitten, there is no unbiting it. I must slip into the past perfect: I wish, my dears, that you had not bitten.

So too, at any rate, in certain moods.

In others, I become indignant at the thought of robbing our civilization of half of its builders. Until I twist again and wonder whether we could not do with a little less building and a trifle more living. Perhaps; but if we reduce our civilizing enterprises by half, why cut that half out of the female portion? Thank God no one is relying on me for firm answers!

One can wish a new order never to have happened, without wishing to cancel it after it did happen.

The logical result of my vacillations is that I am in love with women who have extracted for themselves the best of both worlds. They are professionals who are at the same time "feminine"; delicate yet efficient; achievers, yet tender. This is heroic juggling. I admire it to distraction. These are the saints of our time. But how many great souls can any age beget? For most women (and of course for most men) the Yang cannot be had without a certain sacrifice of the Yin. Hence, if there were a Spirit of History, and that Spirit asked me point-blank: What should it be for women—femininity by the hearth or unisex contribution to society—it would not do for me to evade the question by alleging the possibility of a balance between the two. The balance can be struck, has been struck, is frequently struck—but this is too fine a poise for an entire society—and so I would answer, at last, and with the most awful stammering, that the talent had better be wasted, on the whole, and that justice had better be left in the lurch, on the whole, and that an occasional Joan of Arc or Catherine of Russia will do, and that the femininity-masculinity polarity is more important for both partners in the end, than all the other considerations—on the whole . . . But I would stipulate a remaking of women's *aspirations* to precede the remaking of her *condition*, so that Ms X, Personnel Manager of Bethlehem Steel, would not only lose her position but would want, would long, would demand to lose it in favor of the spinet.

For here is a distinction to heed—between returning (in imagination) to an earlier social pattern and returning to the frame of mind that went with it. Most of us perform the first acrobatic act with gusto, but forget or fail to support it with the essential second. This must be taken into account when we playfully ask women whether they might not prefer to advance backward into Queen Victoria's time. They reply with an indignant negative; yet is it not because they see themselves dressed in a Victorian bustle but thinking topless? "I would hate it," they say. I? Which I?

When I speak of an occasional Joan of Arc or Catherine of Russia, I am really saying that in the Western world the femininity of women has always been enforced less firmly than in other civilizations. In our civilization bold and ambitious women have been able to push doors open. This chance for women has been a part of our "Faustian" character. We are fierce entrepreneurs in every conceivable field of thought and activity. So fierce that no class, no group has been completely deprived of the possibility to "make it big." The injustice is not that women were excluded from the buccaneering life, but that men—and women themselves!—made it ten times as hard for them to walk the deck. Yet if we consider, on one side, the enormous benefits that accrue to both sexes from the fundamental human division into two species of temperament and destiny; and on the other side, the vast benefits brought about by equal opportunities and equal contributions—when we consider this epic opposition of two desirables, we may be disposed to pay our civilization a compliment, and admire it for a rather tactful compromise. Other civilizations refused to compromise at all. They were blind to what they were missing. Ours was intent on keeping the Yang and Yin distinction too, but realized (I am writing as if a civilization were a conscious human being) that something, even something much, could be yielded to the principle of equal opportunity and contribution without at once annihilating the beautiful twoness of humanity.

And where are we now? Of course the differences between one part of the world and another are vertiginous. My own experience is of urban industrial Western society. There I see a marked fluidity. Unisex is advancing, but is not triumphant yet. While many women are clamoring for their right to compete with men equal to equal, many others prefer to remain in what I have fancied to be the hunting-gathering stage of human evolution, with its easy and coddled life for the ladies. But Justice is on the march. It is hardening our fibers year by year. I can see myself playing tennis with most of the women I meet, but coming home to very few of them. Tough! they answer.

I return to the secret complicity (now expiring) between men and women. I find it too, or think I find it, in the traditionally passive erotic role that women played in the past. How unjust, we hear today, how false to biological reality is this passivity; and how wonderful that now at last the female may, can, and does grab at anybody she likes! In the arts, too, our women have become so remarkably liberated that almost all the "explicit" poems, for example, seem to be written by them. I am no authority on these questions, and my diffidence increases with every word I write. But when I consider the sexual intermittency of most men (I leave out of account the very young and those enviable hyperphallic heroes who perform as many times in a row as a dog can bark)—and set it against the well-nigh limitless capacity of the female vessel, I surmise a sort of underground, unspoken, unwitting compensatory treaty between the sexes which corrects and equalizes these differences through the artificial cultivation of an ideal of feminine passivity and male aggressiveness. The man, who can accomplish less, is allowed to "attack" and name his terms, and the woman, who can accomplish more, yields with a secret smile. If pure Nature had its way, would not a woman go inexhaustibly from male to male, wringing each one dry for the day, the week or the month, depending on his age and constitution? *She* does not falter with age, and *she* does not worry about a sufficient stock of genital liquid. Hopelessly overmatched, the male rippled his muscles (real, they), and induced the female to sign the pact one day in the savannah. An invented coyness brought about a kind of equality between the sexes. The female secreted some of her power from view, thereby giving the male a vastly exaggerated conception of his.

This means that the present-day addition to women's power does not restore, it breaks equality. Our tough-minded ladies assert their natural sexual preeminence and drop the old restraints, and as a result we see a prodigious increase in the number of intimidated, frightened, and all but castrated males. In film, play, and novel, our typical hero today is a loser, sexually defeated and overpowered. I think, too, that homosexual recruits are queuing up as never before to enlist in the easier maneuvers of male sexuality. Women are complicated mechanisms and often difficult to set in motion; hence, as far as they are concerned, all too many men fall short. Men may gloat over their conquests, but they seldom have occasion to laugh at the clumsiness of their women. Women say little about their conquests, but they laugh a great deal at the ineptitude of their men. Every man today trembles to know that his mistress, far from worshiping or silently enduring (in compliance with the ancient pact) is picking him over with her girlfriends under a high-wattage light. I imagine that homosexuals seldom if ever ridicule each other's sexual abilities, or feel that they are being ridiculed in absentia.

The least describable benefit which humankind derived from the distinction between the masculine and the feminine personality was the *charm* this bestowed on our lives—on the lives, I insist, of both sexes. I like to stress this point instead of delving into the "profoundest psychic needs of the human species" because charm does not rank very high as a value in this earnest, drab, scientific, philanthropic, democratic, and labor-mad age. Placed on the agenda at a meeting of a cabinet or before the legislature, or advanced at one of our numberless national or international conferences, congresses, and conventions, all of them balefully occupied with the improvement of society, the idea of charm would be received with a strained smile of impatience as a diversion from the serious business in hand, like a child inadvertently crossing the stage in front of a speaker. What chance have I, pitting charm against the "equitable and effective use of all our productive forces, regardless of sex, race and nationality?" The stupendously serious determination of our official personages—from psychiatrists to economists, from social workers to legislators—to improve our lives is in large measure what keeps our lives from being improved. More precisely, they often take away with one hand while giving with the other. They give things that are concrete and measurable—like the elimination of polio—but take away (innocently enough) vital sustenance for the emotions—like the charm of psychic difference. And yet this vapory element is a "factor," and an immense one at that, in the sum of our well-being—our mental health, as it is called these days.

Still, after charm, the "deeper" issue must have its turn. The human being, whether male or female, is an active system of alternations, all of which can perhaps be summarized by the binary set stop-go. We sleep, we wake; we are cautious, we are bold; we defend, we attack; we stay home, we explore; we obey, we command. These alternations occur in each human being, but unequally. Some persons exhibit more of the "stop" features, others more of the "go." And there results a profound need on both sides to be complemented by and united with the other.

So much is platitudinous. But why should this division be carried out along sexual lines? Say that we want to preserve the psychic difference between the gentle and the strong character. Why should not half the gentle be men, and half the strong women? Have I not intimated myself that men are growing softer even now? The answer is that men are indeed growing softer, but only up to a point. I believe that more and more women will become masculinized, but I do not believe that an equal number of men will cross over to the other side. What I foresee therefore is a world whose character will become steadily more masculine. Many strong persons, both women and men, will be hacking away at the task of survival without a soft word to help. But when

I say "strong," I mean endowed with a certain aggressivity, a certain brashness, a certain knowitallsiness; I most certainly do not mean imperviousness to suffering, immunity to neurosis. Hence I see these cocky creatures suffering without exactly knowing why ("charm" will be the remotest item from their minds), while the measurable and concrete conditions of society keep ebulliently improving.

I feel it is no accident that a woman was traditionally at her most feminine during the very years when the man had to be at his most masculine—I do not mean (as you might suppose) the years of his best sexual exploits, but the years of his most intense and terrifying fight for a place in the sun—the career-building years, in short. This is the time when the need for compensatory comfort is the strongest. Whether the young woman cleverly played the proper complementary role during this period or whether it was "nature" that infused a more thrilling femininity in her just then hardly matters. What matters is the match. Many years later, when the demure young thing had turned into a shrill harridan, the old man had built himself a safe cottage and was able to dispense with the soft pillow of a gentle wife.

So it was in the past (taking a median view of life); and we must grant a certain equilibrium, harmony, and wholeness in this arrangement that we have fractured at our peril.

— 2 —

These matters of male-female complicity and male possession of the female are not at the heart of "The Garden." The poem is traveling in another direction altogether, as its conclusion makes evident. Possession is certainly in the poem, but the poem is not about possession. I am making the incidental in the poem my principal here because, upon re-reading my verses, I marveled at my abominable innocence in writing them. The boy who had written this poem was far from thinking of himself as a tyrant. Quite on the contrary. He was so modest about his ability to keep the young lady (if she existed at all) for himself "in the open market" and so persuaded of her loveliness in all the world's eyes that he trembled for his own happiness. It did not occur to him that such a trembling is precisely what makes tyrants of men.

In the poem, both *he* and *she* are presumed to have achieved security. He knows or believes that he has her all for himself, and since we find her perfectly blissful in the poem, we can suppose that she knows or believes that she has him all for herself. Our desire to possess the other, and in the other the source of our comforts, comes out of our primordial need for security; security being "the situation in which one survives." The so-called feminine way to security/survival is through submission, meekness, cajolery, renunciation of aggression. The so-called masculine way is through mastery. At first glimpse, it may seem strange that acts of aggression are conducive to survival and security. But so it goes. The man who has fought his way to the top and the nation that has conquered another's oil fields have both made themselves secure. True, they can be assaulted and deprived of their places, but flight and submission can fail as well. We are never completely secure anyhow. The point here is that the male tyranny of possession is complemented by the female's absorbing possession of that possession. They are equal and complementary once more.

"Possession" is the optimal word to use, for it brings out the connection between this spiritual act and plain gross private property. Insofar as animals "own" their territories, they clearly exhibit this connection. "As long as these acres are mine, I will survive, I am secure; therefore all others kindly keep out!" What about the baby and his shattering cries? He dominates his parents through them; he brings them running; they feed him, shelter him at his bidding; they submit; they are his private property.

Eventually, the mother and father recede from the child's life, the young adult is launched into the world on his own. Now *he* dominates and possesses no one, now *she* possesses no one through submission. It is a most insecure time. How many adolescents are happy? But given a peremptory road sign by their sexual urge—and a negative one by the incest taboo—boy and girl go out to "take possession" of a substitute for the mother/ father. They fall in exclusive love. This is infinitely more gratifying than a generalized tribal affability. "Love is a shelter." The infant's sucking, cuddling, kissing, nuzzling are restored to the adult. Sexual union intensifies this bond—and fortunately so, for the bond between any given man and any given woman is so much less instinctual, so much more adventitious, that it requires something more sensational to fix it than the cosseting of baby by its mother.

Now, as both man and woman experience the same need for security, "love" becomes a *mutual* taking possession—I possess you, you possess me—a paradoxical contract and alliance of bilateral benefit. And the feeling of tenderness which flows in both directions as a consequence of the beneficial pact is a heartfelt gratitude toward the person who has allowed himself or herself to be possessed.

This is more or less how I see the origin of our principle of exclusivity in love and marriage. It follows that I am not so very far, practically speaking, from the absurd position of a genetic basis for exclusivity. We do not need genes in this argument. Mankind is not locked into exclusivity. But a number of factors, beginning with the helplessness of the infant, make exclusivity "come easy" to us as a thing to be intensely desired. But then, what becomes of the contrary delights of tender promiscuity?

Before I return to this question—and to stray a little further yet (though I have not wandered out of sight of my Garden)—I suppose that the strange human custom of indulging in sex privately has something to do with the sense of property too. Is it not rather like "squirreling away" our favorite possession? Many animals are indeed seen running off into a corner with their catch, and burying it out of their competitors' sight. Placing garments upon alluring parts of the body, and indeed on the entire body in some societies, would answer the same purpose. In this view, human beings did not clothe *themselves*—they clothed *others*. Clothing, in short, is a wrapping up of an important and valuable property. "Hands off, my friends!" Especially if the property (one's mate) was purchased at a high price or conquered by dint of great effort. As for the sense of shame, plainly (if I am right so far) it came *after* the event. Coupling in private did not occur after and because people blushed to do it in public; they blushed to do it in public after and because they had become accustomed to doing it in private in order not to share with anybody. Likewise, people did not cover each other's private parts after and because they were ashamed of them, they became ashamed of them after and because they had had them covered. Do certain tribes go stark naked? Well, not all men, not all societies, have an equally rapacious sense of property. But I wonder, is the sexual act performed in public anywhere, as animals, even the highest primates, do it? Yes, under certain ritual conditions, here and there, and frequently as criminal actions by gangs or soldiers, that is to say, outside the permitted norm. But regularly and normally? What very odd animals we are, we and our shame! Not, by the way, that I mean to criticize it. I am not partial to Mother Nature. I am perfectly comfortable with my inhibitions.

I shall also enter a remark concerning the sense of admiration, which played so important a role in the past (and still does to some diminished extent today) in a woman's falling in love with a man. Of course, admiration runs the other way too, but for the moment let us look at such qualities as powerful muscles, skill, riches, intelligence, or dominion over others. For the woman to possess, that is to say, to bend to her wishes and needs, a personage eminent in any of the qualities I have named is of course more gratifying to the basic need for security, and derivatively to the "ego," than to command the protective capability of a ninny. That is why admiration has ever been the surest foundation of a lasting attachment, all the more because the taking possession of admired qualities "for one's own use" provokes an outpouring of tenderness whose basis is gratitude. Bluntly, as long as admiration and gratitude exist, love exists: they *are* love.

Another hesitant thought. It may be that the link between love and property gives us a hint concerning the incest taboo. I am not satisfied that Lévi-Strauss's political solution is enough. Granted that each family and each tribe wish to ally themselves with other families and tribes. But what would prevent incest from being compatible with such exchanges? Far more amazing and "outrageous" psychological combinations exist; and there is nothing unthinkable about a brother and sister mating, and even begetting a child, before either one is sent out to the neighboring tribe for a permanent partner. Such a combination would satisfy the supposed "final cause" of intermarriage, namely the enlargement of the genetic pool.

Instead, may we not suppose that the taking possession of daughter by father, or son by mother, or sister by brother, or any of these the other way around, would constitute intolerable invasions of property and thus provoke explosive jealousies within the family? The father cannot bear to be displaced by a son, even (or especially) if the initiative is not his son's but his wife's. The mother will not stand for being displaced by her daughter. The brother casting an eye on his sister will arouse the father's jealousy. And so forth. This scenario presupposes that in the typical primitive family, all the individuals have a "natural" sexual appetite for each other. Why does the taboo exist at all if this were not precisely the case? There is no need for a taboo against playing with tigers. Taboos need to be devised against the things we long for. My supposition is that our forebears were inclined to fling themselves on the partners closest at hand with no more modesty than an animal shows. The principal deterrent would have been the impossibility of coexisting under a single roof while each member of the family saw a rival in the other. As each member "owned" each other member to a certain extent, each jealously guarded his limited rights in the others and bridled at any member's suddenly making a grab for considerably more (namely sexual possession) than he had to begin with. Here at any rate is a psychological thrust powerful enough to explain the incest taboo: the sense of private property, itself grounded in our ultimate need for security.

Of course, men and women have always felt that owning is more pleasant than being owned; and this principle applies to exchanges of love as much as it does to crasser properties. The animal and the child want only to secure for themselves; the child, indeed, more rabidly so than the animal, for in the lower orders nature has implanted a few "self-less" instincts to insure that this basic egotism will not, while promoting the survival of the single animal, destroy the species. These instincts are missing in the infant. Our toddlers are supposed to learn devotion in due time—and sometimes do. In the meantime, they exhibit without compunction the creature's craving for universal possession.

This craving is one of the two motivating forces behind promiscuity. The first needs no commentary, being simply the desire for as much sensual pleasure and as many sensual pleasures as possible. The second, however, continues our rambling considerations. It is the desire to acquire as many shelters as possible. The more persons there are whose delight it is to caress me, admire me, comfort me, feed and blanket me, the happier I am. This appetite, like the first, sends men and women roving, but how

seldom they return with game in their scrips! For is it surprising
that they can catch so few true lovers, when so few can catch
them?

Fortunately, the emotion of gratitude does exist; admiration
does exist; and most important, our intelligence—and this is a
modest intelligence which nature has made available to most
members of the species—does reason out for us that an excellent
way of acquiring comfort and pleasure is to give it. That is why,
even though our primary impulse is to acquire as many possessions as possible, we are not unwilling to be acquired in turn—
sometimes—if it must be. (Restive at best.) The hunters need not
despair of finding *some* game in the woods. But by the way, my
images are not meant to convey a great deal of ferocity: their snarl
is worse than their bite.

Feminists point out that men imposed an inequality convenient to themselves in the ratio of possessing and being possessed.
Traditionally they have accumulated a royal collection of pleasures and shelters for themselves, and required their wives and
even their mistresses to be satisfied with one: the man himself.
And is this tyranny not suggested, alas, by the poem? The narrator—oh I disown him now, he is not I!—the narrator sees to it
that no one else will touch his property or enter his shelter; but
what is he doing all day long outside the walled garden? I am
sure he has given his love a thousand assurances of absolute
fidelity, for he is moderately intelligent, he knows that he must
give, or seem to give, shelter in order to be granted the same; but
can she trust him? I hope a rival has tunneled under the wall
while the tyrant was off on some plausible errand.

But this may be a wicked wish. Are not the feminists and the
egalitarians a little unjust? Can we not detect yet another secret
compact, or a compensatory advantage under one heading for a
disadvantage under the other? It may be that the man *needed*
more comforts than the woman—remember I am speaking of the
past—because, as the provider, explorer, and fighter he was exposed to so many more dangers—dangers spiritual as well as
physical. Hence the familiar image—and reality—of the sailor
with a wife in every harbor. He has as many wives, perhaps, as he
has had terrors.

For the test, are we not ignoble and childish when we refuse the
offer of shelter unless it is ours alone? When we leave it, and

prefer to expose ourselves to the rain, because we have found that someone else availed himself of it? We have a terrible anxiety lest our comfort depart from us, and the kiss bestowed on someone else seems to us, children that we are, to decree our expulsion. "First I was alone in your house; then you opened it to three or four strangers; the end must be that you will forget me, and I shall be alone in the cold world!" So goes our secret and puerile reasoning. The fact is that the mother is capable of loving several children at the same time; that we can all love several friends at the same time; and that we can be sufficiently attached to several persons at the same time to provide each one with all the comfort and attention anyone needs. Unfortunately, everyone feels that *he* can be sufficient shelter for several, but doubts that anyone else can accommodate *him* along with others. Or if he suspects that others are as accomplished as he, still he refuses: he wants to give little but take all: the childish, the normal, the human way.

The ancient longing—or demand—for virginity in the object of one's desires is a striking manifestation of this persistent puerility. It is again like the panic of a child at the thought that a rival who takes hold of the mother, or of a toy, will inevitably deprive him of the treasure. That two or more might share the mother, for example, without detriment to anyone is a notion an infant spontaneously distrusts. Why allow even the shadow of danger if a little crying and screaming might keep the picture clear? So too the man. And the woman. But here the man has made the most of the advantages granted him in the secret compact I have been sketching in these pages. Since he is the leader and the decision-maker, he has been able to enforce his desire for exclusive attention (that is to say virginity in his bride) more effectively than the woman. He has enforced it by means of tantrums, like the child, or by using the whip, like a true adult. But let us keep in mind that this is but one of the many clauses in the secret treaty, the treaty that is now dissolved or dissolving. One could spend a fruitful hour looking into the clauses which benefited the gentler sex.

A few unions are true and perfect. Admiration, pleasure, and gratitude are so intense and so equal on both sides that neither partner has any incentive to look elsewhere. Most true unions, however, are kept true by a fear of discovery. *He* (let us say) discovers by accident that *she* has a lover, and has had several before. She is no longer his property, his exclusive shelter, his absolutely guaranteed source of comfort. Shocked, angry, miserable, he announces that *his* shelter is closed to *her* from now on. But she, of course, wants this shelter along with all the others. She knew all the time that if he discovered her in other bowers, he would bar his own to her. So perhaps she roved only in her dreams. She was afraid. The story is deleted. She remained faithful.

Or else she concealed more expertly. Concealment by men and women of their "'illicit" affairs is the one human enterprise which has been unanimously damned by philosophers and littérateurs alike from the beginning of time. It is a sure topic for satire or vituperation. Murders fare better in our literature than secret affairs. For we can always think of some noble reason for killing a man, while secret trysts invariably look contemptible. Yet concealment is after all a healthy enough compromise in the face of painfully contradictory demands. Moreover, concealment is as compassionate as it is prudent. We avoid the hurt both to ourselves and to the other. The need for several pleasures and havens is acute; we know of ourselves that the haven we provide for others is spacious enough to hold several; but we also know that, our infantilism being what it is, we want the other's ministration all to ourselves, otherwise we begin to panic, and the other wants our exclusive ministrations for the same reason. What solution is more natural, and on the whole beneficient, than to give the other person the belief the other person needs, while concealing the fact that "kills"—kills, that is, because of our childishness? In plain English, this is called a lie. But are we frightened by words? If so, call it dispensing a compassionate illusion. The world has been limping along with the help of this illusion for many ages. I have spoken already of true and perfect unions; and something could be said for the free, emancipated, mature couples who manage to combine a pleasant, open, frank promiscuity with the sense of security that brings inner peace. These couples are supposed to abound in Los Angeles, where an absent-minded destiny has beached me. But I have not met them; instead I meet shoals of anchorless beings who run helter-skelter to practitioners of psychological rescue work—one of the most remunerative professions on the West Coast. It would seem that for the time being, a solid, Victorian marriage sheltered in the cove of illusion is still the best human solution for those who fall short of Baucis and Philemon.

— 3 —

My speculative predilection for "feminine grace" has its roots, I frankly confess it, in my childhood experiences. I remain undismayed by such an explanation of my thoughts. I feel quite competent, thank you, to fight the bias of experience with the weapon of philosophy. Experience is not altogether the flypaper to Reason's buzzing thoughts. Say my behavior is trapped—I am, for instance, as jealous as a pasha—my ideas are not; they are capable of excursions of their own, and I find that my speculations land in some very odd places where I, as living protoplasm, cannot follow. Furthermore, one never knows *a priori* whether a person's private history has dropped him into a sump of prejudice or elevated him to the perspective of a promontory. Mine, in any event, has afforded me a living sense of the advantages of femininity to both women and men, a sense which is denied, I think, to most urban middle-class and professional Americans.

While I was not raised wholly *à l'ombre des jeunes filles en fleur*—for I had a bevy of friends among the boys of my grade school and later in high school—yet it so fell out that all the children of my family whose age was compatible with mine for fun and games were girls. There was my sister, and for a few years a girl of my sister's age, a refugee from Germany whom my parents had taken to live with us; there were two girl cousins on one side, two on another side, and two more as occasional visitors, besides a few girlfriends of all these girls. I was the youngest of the chirruping group. I followed about, talkative, argumentative, pugnacious because safe, and was allowed to join in all the games in and out of our spacious apartments. We climbed over the furniture, dashed up and down the long corridors, chased one another in the courtyards, threw balls over nets, and laughed the afternoons away. Lo and behold, I have no sinister revelations up my sleeve, Proustian or other, concerning this little band of girls. As for the mothers, that is to say these same girlish girls grown up—they might become petulant, quarrelsome, vindictive, money-mad, ambitious (many of them remained perfectly sweet)—still their battlefield, like that of the terrifying Mme. Verdurin, was *at home,* and they continued unflagging as complements to husbands "hunting for prey," that is to say, making a living in their offices.

At home my mother and sister presented me with living pictures of unaffected modesty in speech and comportment. I have never felt the urge to rebel against this decorum, whether in my life or in my fictions; never felt the need to be the bull in the china shop. On what ground, if you please? Is eating with one's paws so much better than using fork and knife? The singularly human and in a sense anti-natural separtion of things between "ugly" and "beautiful" (animals do not find belching ugly or sunsets beautiful) is one of our most precious artificialities—precious simply because it *feels* so, no other reason, and any loss in that feeling is a loss of joy. So when ugly and beautiful become confounded in a regime of words and actions calculated to make everything uniformly normal and natural, we merely add more drabness to the already drab landscape of twentieth-century life. "Correctly" regarded, a diamond is nothing but a hard stone, and it follows that animals are smarter than men in refusing to distinguish it above any other stone. What we do, instead, is to endow this and that with a halo of preciousness, and thereby contrive for ourselves a possibility of vast elations. This may not be intelligent, but it is wise. Be that as it may, I don't wonder that when the time came for me to find a wife, I sought one who differed in a thousand ways from my mother and sister, but resembled them remarkably in the ways of femininity. All three are as incapable, for example, of telling a "dirty story" as a truck-driver is of dancing in *Giselle.*

Let me confess to that vice of modesty in myself as well and all will be out. I am deeply embarrassed by displays of sexual activity in films, in the theater, and to some extent even in literature—although the word, by interposing its symbolic self between us and the object, inevitably reduces the impact— and that is why, by the way, the freedom to display sexual activity came earlier in literature than it did on stage and in the cinema, and why literature must display more luxuriantly than film or play before making a given impact. My own

                              kiss that interferes
                              with topics of importance

and my

                        bodies in their moist entanglements

are paradigms of reticence, although I hope they show up the
useful principle that reticence and prudishness are two very different matters. To say I have never told a joke "that would raise a
blush in a maidenly cheek" would not mean very much, because
I do not tell jokes of any sort—they are contrary to my notions of
wit—but just as I would be embarrassed to witness a copulation
in actual life, so I am embarrassed by a stark representation of it
in the arts. I shall prove how independent my philosophical life
is from my personal history by refusing to philosophize over this
modesty of mine, and by recording it as a personal foible and
nothing more. It is a rather lonely foible to carry about in my
circles. My friends and acquaintances uniformly claim that they
are *bored* by pornographic films and simulated sex acts on stage.
I have never heard anyone confess to being sexually stimulated by
these naked displays. For myself, highly erotic art not only em-
barrasses me, it usually stimulates me too (I imagine that the two
responses are connected)—and I am decidedly averse to being
sexually stimulated by works of art.

Why so? To begin with, for me art is always mankind at play. If
you make theology, philosophy, politics, and sociology testify
against me, I reply: "Look at two kittens playing. They are *also*
training themselves for the serious business of hunting, but—
they are playing." So too I recognize other vital functions of art;
but they are all *also-functions*; and art remains fundamentally
mankind at play. Consequently, I object to a work of art that
whips me to the kitchen (it made me so hungry!); to a hospital (it
made me so sick!); to the trenches (it made me so furious!); or to a
brothel. *Traces* of all these emotions are welcomed—just as in the
play of kittens traces of fight, terror, and murder occur; otherwise
the game becomes boring. Traces of such emotions favor delight,
which is the only possible primary goal of art. Delight ceases
when the traces grow to a preponderance.

What is wrong with the work of art that moves us toward the
kitchen, hospital, trenches, or brothel is simply this: these are

responses to pain, not to delight. Yes, sexual craving is painful. It is a distention or insufficiency seeking relief. It is not a pleasure. It is an impulse toward pleasure. And it is an impulse toward pleasure precisely because it is not a pleasure itself but a lack of it. So then, if a work of art causes a sexual hunger in you, it is making you uncomfortable. It is, in fact, driving you away from itself (something a good work of art will never do, being in itself delightful) to seek satisfaction elsewhere.

But in all likelihood people like myself are marked for extinction. Already my views—I must call them in humble truth my inklings—make me the unwilling bedfellow of the most retrograde factions of our society. The real thinkers and movers are against me. What rubbish, these personal modesties, this dream of a world in which women would absolutely demand to return to demureness! No, the pendulum will not swing again: women will remain at the stage which I compared, at the beginning of this chapter, to the agricultural situation. Hard work with its tangle of benefits and drawbacks will be favored over the drawbacks and benefits of ease. Our economic system demands it. Better still, Justice requires it. Justice will prevail over charm; and who will be found to declaim against that armored goddess?

BEING AND JUDAISM

After Wallace Stevens: *"The imperfect is our paradise."*

I too, undoubtedly, I too
I should have ventured to conceive
this world as turquoise, aware
but softly of the streak which marred
its blue primordial. Not marred,
not so (I too, I should have said):
that darker but still blue distress
enriched the stone's peculiar price,
for blue naively blue, the lake
untampered by its island,
glib blue would make orfèvres yawn,
I too, aware, I should have said.

But could this be? I came too late.
And yet I tried. My fingers held
that delicately irritated stone,
exquisite with sin, until
the symbol failed. "Am I," a Jewess
twelve years old inquired softly
of her elders and her betters,
"the discord that beguiles the song?"

She was the flimsiest among the dead
and stinking innocently in the ditch.
A man had pushed that rod of his
between his legs between her legs.
Her skin slumped through her bones. She lay
in her own liquid filth licking
a piece of wood for succulence.
One morning she forgot her mother.
The winter froze two fingers off.
But milk and schoolsong recollections
kept her tough: she trusted God.
At last her turn she reached the ditch,

First published in *The Georgia Review*, Fall 1982, and reprinted in *The Pushcart Prize VIII: Best of the Small Presses.* 1983

she knelt, was shot, fell blood to blood,
another elbow slapped across her neck.

I trembled safe across an ocean.
Behind the barbed roses of Connecticut
El Sereno boomed his "all is well."
I could not find, oh Stevens, syntax
for this child, no jewel adequate,
no shape of nature that would tally
or be wholesome (since through rock
and thorn and tiger, symbol-making man
can anodyne his grief). And ever
untranscended, pain stands by,
there is no exile into peace:
still on my lips that excrement
successors will digest to art
but I must suffer brute and fat,
clotting paradise out of my voice.

I
— 1 —

accept the man who says, "I will not write of concentration
camps; I will write only of lapis lazuli"; but I cannot accept the
man who writes acceptingly of concentration camps. I hope I
have done Wallace Stevens an injustice in my poem. Most of the
time (if I read him right) he has nothing whatsoever to say about
evil. This Yankee child of Théophile Gautier is a master of the
sheerest sensory revels. America does not have a greater poet. He
went wrong only in thinking of himself as a thinker—and here
he reminds me, in his own way, of Robert Browning. Both are
veritable Casaubons of Intellectual Poetry: the Victorian indefatigable in his wearisome Proof for the Existence of God, the New
Englander dreary with his Function of the Imagination. Was it
the Puritan in him that whispered, "It is not enough to sing

> The skreak and skritter of evening gone
> And grackles gone and sorrows of the sun;

a man without Concepts is a sinner"? So Stevens made a Concept, and the Concept made Stevens a bore. Once in a while,
naturally, another little concept would sneak into a poem, and

this is where I think, rightly or wrongly, that I have caught him delivering himself of a thought about human evil; and I do not like what I see.

In my own literary presumptions, I have more readily grappled with concepts of ultimate horror than with the concrete contemporary horrors themselves. I do not grasp these hard in my palm because they scorch me. Before turning extermination camps into poems or stories I would have to live with them and live in them long and deep, and this is something I could do only if I possessed a secret fund of indifference—"the imperfect is our paradise"—or, on the far other side, a Messianic conviction that Art is the necessary and the only redeemer of mankind. Since I do not possess either the fund or the conviction, I have by and large kept hands off, lest they blister without doing anyone any good. There are griefs too terrible for art.

Besides, I would feel ashamed. Shall I make an *objet d'art* out of Auschwitz? Shall I turn a connoisseur's appreciative eye on the corpses of my beautiful cousins, Stella shot while trying to escape from the death train, Dita gassed to death with her mother—on them and all the others whose pitiful shapes you see in the photographs shuffling to their death in baggy clothes—on that Anne Frank whom I half-meant my poem to evoke—and cry, "Ah, here is something for my palette"—and weigh my words and my rhythms, and the breaks at the end of my lines, to find the most *satisfying* way of conveying the horror to you—and become, if I succeed, a famous writer?

You see what perplexes those of us who believe that, even though an artist may wear the garments of a prophet, missionary, philosopher, or legislator, a close look inevitably reveals, under a hem or inside a collar, a scrap of Harlequin's dubious patches. What? On Strindberg? On Kafka? On Beckett? Yes, on the gloomiest of them all.

I am no better as a reader or spectator, for I impenitently make a large swerve around "lacerating" works of art—motion pictures, plays, novels, perhaps even paintings. I do not want lacerations from Harlequin. Reality lacerates me quite enough, and I don't go begging the artist for more. I am speaking now of these "uncompromising" artifacts which only minimally perform the aesthetic operation Yeats mentions in his poem concerning shabby terrorists:

> All changed, changed utterly:
> A terrible beauty is born.

If I do approach *terrible* art, I do it on condition that the terror has been so far compromised by aesthetic constraints that I am comforted even while I am clawed. But this comfort—the comfort of all that is poetic about poetry—is a betrayal of reality. All tragic or terrible art that succeeds as art must in part enact this betrayal, since, willy-nilly, the success of a work of art turns upon the satisfaction, the pleasure it has given. Many Harlequins and most observers of Harlequins (I mean critics and aestheticians) ignore or oppose this decree of Fate, but the world itself speaks the last word, and removed *unpleasing* works of art from the roll. A mystifying dilemma results. You cannot give pleasure in a work of art whose subject is torture without betraying the truth of torture. And you cannot give torture truly without betraying art.

There is, however, no uniformity imposed on what is intolerable and for whom. I, for instance, happen to find several etchings from Goya's *Disasters of War* too horrible and need to avert my eyes. Picasso's *Guernica*, on the other hand, strikes me as very endurably grim. Stripped of its title, it might easily suggest a lunatic's nightmare and lead one's mind toward a Freudian couch rather than a mass grave. These are examples for me; you will have your own. I can endure ample infiltrations of pain into my pleasure before giving up; but in the end, at the extremity, I do give up. I do not read realistic novels concerning gas chambers, and I do not watch movies about concentration camps. As for arguing that doing so might make me a wiser or better man, might you not speculate instead that spectacles of brutality are insidiously brutalizing, even when moralized? If I had a child, I would rather have him hide in my lapels from a scene of brutality in a motion picture than nag me for a dollar to see it again.

To the extent that I myself have dealt with truths which lacerate me, I have clearly betrayed reality in the service of art. Consider lines like

> Behind the barbed roses of Connecticut
> El Sereno boomed his "all is well."

"Barbed roses"—set against the implicit barbed wire of the death camps—is a case of the purest and rankest aestheticism, designed (success or failure is another question) to delight the mind through intellectual and affective density. But observe, besides, that El Sereno is not only an allusion to that blithe mentality of Stevens which is in part the poem's concern, but also the Spanish word for a watchman. Here then is an exotic touch in Stevens's own manner, and here is the poet-watchman over mankind giving us reassurances. A "deeper" reading will bring out that your Sereno in Madrid is in fact far from reliable. Most ingenious. In the meantime the victim is rotting away in her ditch. I call this a moral scandal.

Both the pain and the moral scandal diminish as the event recedes and becomes history. Successors, says the poem, digest it to art. For the secret of tragic historical art is that the past hurts less than the present. Lucretian indifference works for distance in time even more efficiently than it does for distance in space. This is, in a way, a melancholy thought. Why should I not weep for the victims of Attila with the same brute-fresh tears I shed for Hitler's dead? On the other hand, it is a kindness of Nature to make us cruel; otherwise we would drown in tears, we could not suffer the accumulation of injustice and bloodshed over the ages. Think of those odious Aztecs at their mass murders for the sake of an imbecilic religion. Quaint images for a lovely poem, or a visit to a museum.

— 2 —

It is easy to suppose that the nausea which overcomes me when I imagine the unfathomable scurrilities perpetrated by the Germans owes much to my "being" a Jew myself—and one who came near to taking up a small place in the ditch. But the massacres commanded by Stalin, or by Idi Amin, sicken me equally. Do you suppose I could write a novel, poem, or play imitating, in the manner of Zola, certain scenes we heard of in Uganda, where prison inmates were compelled to kill their fellows by hammering out their brains?

But I want to pause in front of this much-pondered business of "being" a Jew, and to explain the quotation marks I have been using. "To be" in all its permutations is a mischief-maker if ever words made mischief in the world. Surely permanence and impermanence are opposites, and surely opposites deserve different words, and yet we will blandly say, "He *is* angry" and "He *is* bald," as if no difference existed. The Spanish language is not so guilty as ours in this respect, for it offers its *es* and its *está* as approximate responses to this difference. We simply blunder along. Granted that it is useless to keep chiding language for its notorious deficiencies and delinquencies: language seems to have done its duty whenever it has almost done it. We must take up the cudgels, however, when its laziness becomes outrageous and dangerous; and outrage and danger are ever on duty when the issue is Judaism. What do we really mean when we say, "He *is* a Jew"? As soon as we put ourselves on the alert, we discover that some are interested in giving this *being* its meaning of permanence, and others its meaning of impermanence.

Thus in the first year of Israel's independence, the Knesset defined the Jew as follows: "Everyone who considers himself a Jew is a Jew." This was clearly the impermanent view of *to be*. One might be an X on Tuesday, a Jew on Wednesday, and an X again on Thursday. I do not know in what respect this definition bothered the Parliament, because it could have given trouble for opposite reasons: allowing anyone who wanted in to come in, and allowing anyone who wanted out to depart. One can see that either of these alternatives might have displeased. Whatever the reason, the Knesset redefined the Jew in 1978 as follows: "Only a person born of a Jewish mother or who has been converted in conformity with orthodox prescriptions is a Jew." Now both meanings of *to be* were allowed: the permanent one of birth (with the extra caution of specifying the mother), and the impermanent one of conversion and adherence to a creed. This politic duplicity apparently allowed a Roman Catholic to come in if he wanted to, but prevented the son of a Jewish mother to depart if such was his wish. By implication, impermanence was conveniently attached to every other religion, and permanence, conveniently, only to Judaism.

In communist countries (instructive digression) something like the same magic is performed, whenever convenient, on being or not being a bourgeois. Is a pretext required for getting rid of an enemy? The fact that his father and mother belonged to the middle class will be dragged into the light, and it will be suggested that the condition of gentility passes ineradicably from parents to children. For one's friends, however, this is not true. Friends can forswear and drop this bad being at will, and slip victoriously out of a tuxedo origin into a present set of overalls.

Of course, communists do not make of gentility a racial taint, and nothing is said of genes or blood. Not only would such a notion be tough to apply in homogeneous societies, but Marxist doctrine, as we know, is ferociously environmentalist. Therefore, when communists wish to defame and demolish, they find that gentility is an infection one inevitably catches from one's parents and passes on to one's own children. This witty line of thought serves both doctrine and expediency. Environment, not heredity, is responsible; and this environment creates a being that is permanent or impermanent as the political situation requires.

By this detour we return better equipped to cope with the Jewish question. Not so long ago, race would have been given as the ground of a permanent being for Jews. To race/blood/genes would have been ascribed ineluctable physical characteristics (for example, a crooked nose), or unavoidable psychological traits (a pretty one like loving one's family, or a nasty one like stinginess). This racial doctrine is by no means dead, but professors no longer write treatises to expound it; it has been relegated to the crumbling slums of philosophy. Nowadays, instead, Jewish being—like bourgeois being in the Soviet Union or China— acquires its permanence mostly by inevitable infection. As you were born and raised among admitted and practicing Jews, you necessarily caught Jewishness for life. Your loyalties may be repressed into your subconscious, and your habits may wear a specious veneer, but inspection quickly detects your ineradicable being. Do you love your mother? Obviously a Jewish trait. Are you keen on education? How Jewish! Do you give to charity? Jewish to the core.

This discovery of the body under the blanket is regularly made *ex post facto*. That is to say, the sleuth already knows that the body is there when he shrewdly lifts the blanket. Dropping the metaphor: first the observer learns that his victim did indeed have a Jewish father and mother, or had been exposed to Jewish habits and doctrines, or had himself professed Judaism at one time or another; and next he astutely finds Judaic traits in his man. I recently read a learned essay on Marcel Proust in which his *verve* was authoritatively traced to the Jewish half of his 5.6 liters of blood. In *The Hudson Review* a friendly critic spoke of the "negative undertones of Jewish self-appraisal" in my verse. If I had signed myself O'Toole, he would have called my negative undertones typically Irish. A few years ago a scholar ferreting among the archives discovered that the great Fernando Rojas had been a *converso*. Presently a swarm of keen critics from the best American universities revealed that *La Celestina* could have been written by none but a Jew, an observation no one had thought of launching during the four centuries preceding the happy find in the archives. Is this any better, I ask, than the practice of biographers who speak of the "stubborn nose" in their subject's picture in the frontispiece after they have ascertained that he refused to pay his taxes for forty years?

These notions of Jewish permanence are thriving today largely because the Jews themselves cannot bear to see the roster of their tribe depleted. Christians who drop their religion never to give it another thought, or Bolsheviks who convert to capitalism, undoubtedly retain some little flavors of their past, but no one dreams of taunting them for this, assuring them that they cannot cease to *be* what they once *were*, or denying them the possibility of being what they now claim to be. And it is singularly terrifying that Nazi and Jewish fanaticism joined hands across the mass grave to agree that a man's Jewishness is ineradicable.

For myself, it now goes without much further saying that I can conceive of "being" a Jew only as a set of loyalties: loyalties to others with whom we exchange these loyalties, loyalties to certain beliefs concerning God and man, loyalties to a history, loyalties to a number of precise customs and rituals. As soon as such loyalties are dropped, a secondary or intermediate state is usually reached. The person no longer *is* a Jew (or a Rosicrucian, or a socialist, or a Cambodian), but obviously remembers the time when he was, and when he lived with his parents who were Jewish; and he usually retains some minor tastes or habits that are best called subintellectual. This stage allows for ample variations, even when we assume that the "world" does not oppose his change. How old was the man when he converted? How difficult for him was his conversion? How distant were his old creed and habits from the new ones? How well was he really equipped, psychologically and intellectually, for his new self? But this variety must not disguise the central feasibility of conversion. This is clinched a generation or two generations later, when dissolution is completed, if indeed the first of the line had not completed it himself. All of this, incidentally, was granted by some if not all of the fathers of Zionism, for they were convinced that the Jews who refused to settle in the new promised land— Palestine or Uganda—would cease to be Jews and merge into Christian Europe.

— 3 —

Against those of us who perpetuate this civilized Zionist view of free choice, the implacables, after advancing their axiom of permanent being, bring to bear a psychological weapon of which they are astonishingly fond. We who favor dissolution, they cry, are eaten up by "self-hatred." This "argument" is thought to have a devastating effect on its target. Perhaps, for all I know, it has in fact stopped short several would-be defectors and returned them shamefaced to their kin. A less impressionable subject— someone, perhaps, more responsive to ethics than to the pop psychology of the "well-adjusted personality"—might remind the implacables that the best theologians, Jewish and Christian alike, have always recommended hating in oneself that which deserves to be hated: where else does salvation lie? So that, if it is true that we hate ourselves, we can retort with some satisfaction that we have found out our sins and meekly hope to mend them. In reality, of course, this "self-hatred" is a desperate invention. The feeling is not hatred at all but aversion; and it is not aversion for ourselves, but aversion for those who would enforce upon us a being contrary to our will and our convictions. So much for "self-hatred," where little said is more than enough.

The implacables have but a single argument that deserves serious rebuttal. Even if one admits that being a Jew is as mutable "in theory" as being middle class or being a Socialist (for we do not say to a man, "Once a Socialist always a Socialist")—even if one yields this point, it still takes two (they say) to play the game. Cringe as much as you like (they say); join a Presbyterian congregation; change your name; get a nose-job; tell lies to your children; drop your old friends. But the past is always tensed like an animal ready to spring. Sooner or later one Gestapo or another will sniff you out. You will be not only a toady, but a failed toady at that. In a word, the *others* will not let you.

Recent history, imprinted with the unforgettable mark of the Nazi, makes this a poignant argument, and one must plunge through a dreadful night of emotions to recover one's reason and to grasp once again that the early Zionists were right: Jews can disappear, Jews have disappeared en masse, the *others* have in fact absorbed them. That opposition of the others is anything but a fixture of history. It was, on the contrary, an aberration of history, made possible by a new vision of the permanence of Jewish being. I am referring to the racist theories developed in the nineteenth century, prior to which the offensive characteristics of Jews had usually been imputed to alterable causes. Now, as if to prove that science too can go mad, the cause was inscribed in the "blood," in ancient and irremediable racial defects which intermarriage would only pass into the blood of Christians. The consequence was clear. If the offensive Jew is doomed to be forever offensive, even when he scrubs himself in the baptismal font, then naturally the doors of the clean must be forever barred against him. The clean may watch with amusement or disgust his abject attempts to alter his being, but when they are tired of watching, they should kick him—or gas him. Thus, in effect, spoke the science of race in its "purest" tones. It does not seem to have struck anyone as a suggestive paradox that this "scientific" theory of insuperable inferiority had failed to spread in all those dark centuries so propitious to it—when the Jews had lived in fact as squalid pariahs; and was taking hold, most curiously, *after* the Great Emancipation, in an age when a child might have realized that a Jewish and a Christian banker were peas of the same pod.

Not that these new theories were always adamant. Many a fantasist held that generations of conscientious marriage to Christians might finally clean out the dirty blood. But I am disregarding such concessions here as historical ripples within ripples because the normal spectacle of history is in any event quite the opposite; it is a spectacle of Christians begging, cajoling, bribing, or compelling Jews to convert, like those of Apulia (among many others) toward the end of the thirteenth century. This was the period when the Augustinian dispensation—which tolerated the Jews, though for reasons one may refuse to admire—was

giving way to the missionary craze of the Franciscans and Do-
minicans, guided by a bull from the quill of Pope Nicholas III:

> Summon them [i.e., the Jews] to sermons in the places where they
> live, in large and small groups, repeatedly, as many times as you
> may think beneficial. Inform them of evangelical doctrines with sal-
> utary warnings and discreet reasoning, so that after the clouds of
> darkness have gone, they may shine in the light of Christ's counte-
> nance, having been reborn at the baptismal font.

Nothing about "once a Jew always a Jew." The range of actions
spread in reality from "discreet reasoning" to solid brutality, but
the goal was the baptismal font, not the gas chamber. Three
centuries later Shylock, cursing all the way, is baptized. His
daughter marries a Christian. Everybody takes it for granted that
her children will "dissolve." More centuries pass, and Schopen-
hauer, in his *Parerga und Paralipomena*, can quietly and lumi-
nously still recommend baptism or cross-marriage:

> I am deeply sympathetic to the sensible Jew who, giving up old fa-
> bles, humbug and prejudice, makes his exit from a community
> which (exceptions aside) can afford him neither reputation nor
> profit, by way of baptism, even if he takes Christian doctrine with
> something less than high seriousness. . . . But we can spare him
> even this step and enable him to put an end to the whole tragi-
> comic mess in the gentlest way in the world, namely by allowing,
> nay promoting, marriage between Jews and Christians; something
> the Church cannot object to, inasmuch as it is supported by the au-
> thority of the Apostle himself (I Cor. 7:12–16).

Behind these words abides the imperturbable fact that, the historic aberration of racism notwithstanding, it has always seemed
evident that Jews can and do vanish into Christendom.

If this normal course is sometimes forgotten, and if we can so
easily choose to forget that the *others* have absorbed masses of
Jews in the past, the reason is that no one writes to celebrate
the apostate adventure, while libraries do not suffice to hold the
rhapsodies to and histories of Jewish solidarity, fortitude, resistance, and spiritual victory. There are words of pity for those who
were forced to convert, but no words of relief—because the tragic
story was over for them and their descendants—and least of all
words of admiration for those who had the strength of mind to

cut of their own volition the "rope of sand" which tugs so insistently at the common mind.

Quietly or not so quietly, I repeat, flocks of Jews have disappeared a hundred times since the fall of Jerusalem. Nearly everyone you meet in Spain, for instance, is the descendant of one or more Jews who were baptized (usually under duress) in the fourteenth and fifteenth centuries, led a precarious existence as "new Christians," were about to dissolve into the population in the late sixteenth century when a massive influx of Portuguese *conversos* retarded the natural process, and completed their dissolution in the eighteenth century. Completed it so well that the term "new Christian" came to be applied to the gypsies! Again, almost no one has written the history of this benign solution: hints must be extracted from all but inaccessible works of erudition, or casual asides by historians preoccupied with the more glamorous chronicles of bloody persecution and resistance.

Needless to say, Hitler would not have remembered the Jews if they had converted en masse two thousand years ago. But they would have escaped his notice too if they had allowed themselves to be absorbed, instead of merely unshackled, in the age of Napoleon and Nicholas I. The Nürnberg Laws, whose odious definitions still held when the Final Solution was being carried out, preserved anyone who could produce at least two untainted grandparents. Even the more dubious *Mischlinge* (mixed breeds)—those who were labeled as "first degree"—could hope to survive the ultimate massacre. A strange and awesome spectacle, this compromise with perpetual being, with ineffaceable racial dirt, at the very headquarters of fanaticism.

Now if we ask why, in the nineteenth century and in a Western Europe ever more alive to rational and scientific thought, a considerable segment of the Christian and indeed post-Christian world was switching, so to speak, from obliging to forbidding the Jews to convert, we must dare—all anger notwithstanding—to place much of the blame on the Jews themselves. For the masses of Jews who accepted emancipation but refused absorption played a dangerous game throughout the nineteenth century. Moving from the ghetto to the city, the orthodox traditionalists kept up a way of life singularly calculated to arouse the fury of the mob, or to make them attractive targets for persecutions

inspired by the authorities when they needed a faction to perse-
cute. Intensely tribal themselves, these Jews might have considered that others were as tribally minded as they, and that an
extravagantly conspicuous minority—conspicuous above all in
the trivia of manners, dress, and language which act, alas, as
bright signals to other tribes—a minority that competed not only
on the economic plane, but also for the sublime distinction of
being God's best-loved people—and to top it all, a minority
which their powerful hosts and neighbors still looked upon as
deicides—taking all this together, they might have considered
that their position was *biologically* untenable. The Jews, at once
helpless and high in relief, were banking on preternatural virtue
in the dominant pack. The right to live at peace which they
claimed was a platonic right: a right that lives in Cloud-Cuckoo-
Land; it was not a right on which a prudent family could sensibly raise its children.

But we must blame the so-called emancipated Jews even more.
They were about to replay a half-forgotten Alexandrian tragedy.
While the orthodox Jewish community of that city remained
content with its status as resident alien without special privi-
leges, a highly Hellenized minority attempted to enjoy the best of
two worlds by keeping the faith of their fathers but demanding
Greek citizenship. This aroused an extremist opposition and
provoked the brutal pogrom of the year 38. Now once again this
very particular sort of provocation was enacted. The liberated
Jews of the nineteenth century shaved their beards, dressed in the
best fashion, learned to speak irreproachable French and German, became physicians and professors, went to hear Rossini—
but remained Jews. They too wanted to dine at two tables. And
insofar as these Jews competed far more grandly than the orthodox for positions of wealth and power, their situation became
even more "difficult and fraught with danger," as Theodore
Mommsen wisely warned. They were displaying a perilous optimism with regard to the human species. I suppose that the Age of
Enlightenment had misled them. A cheerful trust in mankind
blinded them. They could not imagine the rabble-bullies of the
twentieth century who would supplant the polite kings and emperors of the nineteenth.

"Blame" is too harsh a word, perhaps. For indeed who could
foresee the S.S.? One might reasonably predict a century of legal

impediments, discrimination in business and the professions, trivial daily insults, social snubs, the occasional Dreyfus Affair, and sporadic violence incited by the lunatic fringe. I myself would undoubtedly have changed my name and done my best to liquidate an archaic "being," impatient with the tergiversations of my halfway brethren. But who could have foreseen the triumph of the lunatic fringe, and who could have foretold that the optimists were going to drag into the Holocaust those whose wiser course (had all adopted it) would have prevented the slaughter? The concussive events which, gathered into a sequence, finally thrust power into the hands of the anti-Semitic fringe in Germany—events, among others, like World War I, the triumph of Bolshevism in Russia, the economic collapse of Germany in the nineteen-twenties, the rising might of Bolshevism in the West—such events did not constitute a sequence attached to the Jewish situation in Europe by ties of logical or historical necessity. It was a sequence that developed externally to the Jewish situation. The proof is that it would have developed if Judaism had long ago ceased to exist. And even that which this sequence brought forth—the rise of Hitler and his gang—did not entail, by anything we can call logical or historical inevitability, the Final Solution. No wonder (incidentally) that so many of us, and even the victims themselves! remained unaware, half-aware, incredulous, or deprecating till almost the end. It remains true therefore that half-in, half-out Jewry was playing with fire, but a holocaustal fire, and all-devouring fire-storm, could have been imagined only by an emotional extremist. I blame, then, only in a manner of speaking.

It may be that in the Soviet Union today there are men and women like myself, living in something like a nineteenth-century condition of discrimination and odium without actual massacre, who curse that same shilly-shallying. Let us not forget that when the Bolsheviks triumphed, the Jews *demanded* the separate Soviet nationality which is now *imposed* on them. Once more they were proving the justice of the old accusation that they constituted a state within a state. And once more a foolish optimism with respect to human enlightenment was drawing them into a trap. Surely the Proletarian Revolution would bring about the brotherhood which the Age of Reason, and then the French Revolution, and then Napoleon had somehow failed to beget, and the Jews might remain Jews and yet be equal, equal and loved, amidst their hosts. Instead, the ancient story repeated itself. The State wanted to absorb the Jews and liquidate Judaism; the majority of the Jews offered a "splendid" and "heroic" resistance in favor of their fossil; and the regime countered with the ancient, all too natural, all too animal and human hatred.

But I am not done with the implacables who claim that the others will not let you. Their challenge must be taken up on moral as well as on practical grounds. Must I continue to look upon myself as a Jew solely because that is how the world looks at me? Let me pretend to accept the premise that the door is locked against me, in order to ask whether this is a sufficient reason for giving up the house. Socrates took himself to *be* a pious man. The majority decreed that he *was* an atheist. Should Socrates have renounced his own vision of himself?

Surely we ought to take our stand with Socrates. I am, in and for myself, what I choose to be and not to be. I choose not to be a Jew. Others insist that I am. To show how serious they are, they throw me into a concentration camp. I am still not a Jew. They laugh in my face, and for the proof that has no reply, they shoot me.

Is this an argument?

They call me dog, therefore I bark!

As others see me. As I see myself. I take it that in primitive societies this *Zwiespalt*, this split in two, hardly ever exists. There, boys and girls receive their feeling-of-themselves from their tribe, and when they are grown up they take their turn administering this feeling to the next generation. The possibility of a split between "as others see me" and "as I see myself" must have arisen as soon as the individual was placed in significant, prolonged, and (on the whole) peaceful contact with members of other groups, so that startling new ways of doing and thinking (or simply new trades and professions) offered themselves to his inspection. The possibility of eccentricity, of rebellion, of heresy was born. Perhaps such events took place now and then in the open field and in the forests; but this rubbing together of different ways is clearly a specialty of city life. And even there, it took centuries to develop. It took man centuries to comprehend this idea of freedom.

Such an idea has nothing to do with "free will." Man is not
able to invent himself any more than a chemical element is able
to choose a reaction. My freedom to be what I choose instead of
complying with the dictates of my own or some hostile tribe is
nothing but a condition of exposure to a multiplicity of causes
instead of a few or only one. It is like a vessel emerging from a
quiet channel into a turbulent, toss-vessel sea.

On this sea, prudential advice has its place. Job's friends
deserve a hearing. "Why not admit to Yahweh that you are a
sinner? Everybody knows you are. Only *you* keep denying it!"
Perhaps Socrates should have fallen on his knees and confessed
himself an atheist and a perverter of young men. Sometimes it is
not "smart" to define oneself against the police's grain. Besides,
some choices of oneself are truly mad, and they are mad even if
we grant the chooser every moral right to consider himself whatever he desires: thus the loony who calls himself Napoleon,
or a Socrates who would claim that he *is* handsome. But other
choices—like Job's or Don Quixote's—are less mad than they
seem, or mad only for a season. I, for one, have listened atten-
tively to the voice of wise counsel. I postulate that my choice of
being is not mad. (If it is, I cannot know it, being mad.) If I am
told that my choice is imprudent, or foolish, or useless (that is to
say, incapable of imposing itself on society), either I disagree or
else I bravely, yes heroically, assert it in your teeth, obstreperous
to the end.

— 4 —

I was but a child when I turned my back on the culture and
religion of my parents—long before I could formulate a single
thought on the subject. My father took me to the synagogue on
the High Holidays. He himself remained all his life deeply Jewish in all his feelings, loyalties, acquaintances, and views, and
gave perfunctory but soul-satisfying obedience to ritual. To me,
that ritual seemed odious, and downright freakish, from the beginning. I sat deep in the pew-chair, playing with the tassels of
my father's prayer shawl—I liked the silky ripple over and under
my fingers—or whispered and giggled with the boy who was
sitting behind me. In front of the tabernacle, weird bearded per-

sonages babbled and dipped their torsos as if possessed. My father showed me the prayer book and made me read the unintelligible words along with him, who understood them no better, but who felt the profound union and unction of faithfulness. The French translation on the facing pages edified me little more. The remoteness was absolute; in a word, I was bored.

If only (I hear you say) the mother and father had taken pains to make Judaism intelligible, interesting, and lovable instead of offering him their half-baked cake, their neither hot nor cold, their both here and there. Who can tell? Would Judaism have won the tug of war against Hugo and Verlaine, against the Antwerp of streetcars, bicycle rides, cinemas, and voluminous steamers docked at the quays?

Or else, would a reformed service, stripped of medieval paraphernalia, have won over the boy? It would at least have offered a simulacrum of continuity with the "real world." But here I am peremptory. If the gods have given me indeed the blessing of a clear mind, I know that the man would have quit reformed religion even more lightly than orthodoxy. Reformed Judaism is as vacuous as streamlined Roman Catholicism. When our venerable religions, which were flesh of the flesh of mankind once upon a time, perpetuate inviolate their doctrines and their ceremonies, they are so pitifully archaic that one can sympathize with inventions to bring them up-to-date. But these reforms are like updating a fish by urging him to breathe good fresh air. Modernized religions cannot make their divine right stick: they wilt; they become insipidly sociological, anemic branches of a Consumers' League. It is another dilemma without an issue.

My father had taken steps, at any rate, to make his charming little son understand prayers better than he. Once a week a Hebrew tutor appeared in our house—an advantage which my poor father, who had gone to work in a Viennese sausage factory at the age of fourteen, had not enjoyed. But never did teacher contend with a more mulish pupil. Years went by and I continued to oppose an inexorable stupidity to the alien language. At thirteen, I (*I?*) stood chanting in the center of the synagogue, declaring myself, in words I did not understand, and declared by the congregation, a grown-up male Jew. This solemn commitment exhausted all concerned, I think, for soon afterward my parents rid me of the Hebrew teacher and substituted an English master. They may have felt that *their* reputation, at any rate, had been secured by the irreproachable *bar mitzvah*. Be that as it may, suddenly the light filled my brain. The distinction between "I have" and "I am," and the conjugations of these two appealing verbs were mastered at once: and I would have conquered the English language in a year if the war had not broken out and interrupted my lessons just as "to run" was opening to me.

In the meantime I was keeping a small pad arranged in alphabetical order where I entered newly learned French words with their definitions. This miniature thesaurus meant so much to me that I hastily slipped it into a pocket on the day of our flight from Belgium and kept it with me during the entire exodus. Changing my ambition from French to English proved to be as easy as it is for a rider to leap from one horse to another when keen on his mission: mine had been, from my very boyhood, to add a posy to the grand Florilegium of the Western World.

The only object of veneration that I kept on my shelves was a chunk from the hill in the Ardennes where good King Albert the First had fallen to his death. The authorities had allowed a pious souvenir stand to be built at the foot of the fatal hill. There citizens could buy the commemorative stones, each adorned with a tiny photograph of the king and a couple of flags. How my tears had fallen on the day of his plunge! And how they fell, shortly after, when the young Queen Astrid was killed in a car accident! I purchased sentimental albums concerning my sovereigns, and made my devout, silent oblations, not to the Maccabees, but to the Saxe-Coburg.

Some of my Jewish schoolfriends came from homes similar to mine. Others were being brought up within a more earnest orthodoxy. But I do not recall that such matters were ever discussed among us. My evolution in this respect was proceeding alone, unabetted, unopposed, underground. For all I know, I was the only child of that generation to have so decidedly slipped the leash. Again it was alone, without co-plotters, that I "played hooky" so persistently from the Jewish scouts among whom my mother had enrolled me that I was brought to trial before the club's leading spirits and quite rightfully expelled. Why then was I irrevocably refusing my "Jewish heritage"? Revulsion against my family—the customary revenge of the child against his parents? Not so. I was the darling of the family, coddled and cuddling, and no one was ever less a rebel against my gentlest of parents than I. But I was a timid and cowardly child. The force operating on my unconscious mind must have been, banally enough, a desire to elude derision and blows and to draw on the strength of the dominant group by becoming one of its members. For although the Jewish minority of Antwerp was substantial, strong, and an excellent mother hen to the young, it was distinctively, even ostentatiously, a minority. Many Jews walked about in their caftans, silk hats, long beards, and curly sideburns. Certain teachers did not disguise their anti-Semitism. The Jewish minority very visibly attended the French rather than the Flemish classes in the schools of this most Flemish of cities. Many spoke with "queer" accents (my father's made my face burn red with shame). Yes, we stood out, and I did not want to stand out except to immense advantage. I did not want to be the member of a bizarre minority. If any jeering was to be done, I wanted to be the one to do it.

As it turned out, the tribe I finally joined was not precisely that of the dominant majority, but the band of intellectuals who constitute a sort of congregation within it. Of course it is perfectly possible to be an intellectual *and* a Jew, or an intellectual *and* a Roman Catholic, but it is also possible to be an intellectual *tout court*, and that evidently was enough for me. There was, fortunately, no tincture of madness in this particular "decision" of mine. The *others* did not slam their door in my face. Nor did my progenitors object. And so I quietly learned the signs, the language, the things one says, and even more important the things one takes for granted and leaves unsaid; took the decent course of initiation at the universities; learned to bleed when a beautiful monument is razed, to marvel when a scientist pokes his imagination into a Black Hole, to commune with a Japanese who loves Bach—and to write essays on Judaism or Marivaux.

The essential point, however, is not that I joined this particular band, but that the easily frightened child of a vulnerable group (one which he disliked on other grounds too, as I will presently show), sent out his "feelers"—long before he could engender a theoretical discourse about his motions—toward another group that promised, among other satisfactions, an approved-of haven.

It takes little wit to guess that these "confessions" seem un-lovely to you. They seem not so to me, who look upon mankind as an intensely social species (both for good and ill) where aberrations—what we call nonconformity—may be sometimes heroic, and sometimes necessary for progress, but must also be perilous. When I see the little monkey I was, seeking a place within the pack rather than outside it, I inquire, first, whether he was leaving virtue for vice or intelligence for stupidity; and second, whether, from within the pack, it was his intention to turn, like certain Inquisitors, into a scourge for those who were choosing to cling to the outside they loved. Since the answer is No to both questions, I can look back at the toddler with unclouded equanimity.

But let me take you down a yet darker corridor. Sometime ago, coming upon that well-known passage in *Mein Kampf* where Hitler describes the shock he received when he saw, wandering the streets of Vienna, his first East European Jew, another blow struck me by rebound: I recognized my own revulsion in his. Horrible kinship! My first impulse was to repudiate my own feelings and thoughts: change thy life!—*du musst dein Leben ändern*; the second, to conceal their existence. These then, I said, are the sensations which—carried to their pathological conclusion—led to Auschwitz. But eventually I won my way to a saner view. Were I a saint, I would still share feelings and ideas with any thug. And would Hitler snatch from his bed of dust a subtler victory than the annihilation of the Jews—namely, the extinction of reasonable discourse? Have we not seen scores of thousands discover their Jewish *being* for the sorry reason, flattering to that hooligan, that Hitler persecuted the Jews? For it has almost come to pass—because of Hitler—that we dare not criticize Judaism for a missing button, lest we be thought ready to hang every Jew for it.

Hitler's revulsion—and I shudder as I say it—was in itself normal. I repeat: every species abhors aberrations. Woe to those who deviate, who are too weak to enforce their deviation, but who ostentatiously display it: ghastly trinity of invitations to the Furies. The strange, the outlandish East Europeans Hitler saw were taunting the bull. The rest we know—from the shifty figure of this solitary vagrant, at once genius and dunce, in love with hatred, able and bold to act instead of dream, to the unimaginable luck in the historical combinations that gave him the power and the time to conduct his hatreds to their pathological conclusions.

A fraction of this, the sane fraction, was staged in the little boy's mind. Once a week it was beggars' day in the Jewish world of Antwerp. My mother prepared a cup full of coins and placed it in the vestibule. Every few minutes the doorbell rang. Mother, the maid, or I opened the door, and after the bearded personage had delivered himself of a minimal formality of wailing, we gave him his due. It was a wonderfully organized business of misery. Everyone seemed to regard it as a routine, much like the phases of the moon. For me, in that stage of my life (which could only become thought many years later), the sheer ugliness of these scenes associated itself with every other ugliness: the synagogue and its rituals, the Pelikaanstraat in which the diamond business was transacted in a whirl of high gestures, vociferations, and frantic tuggings at lapels, my Hebrew lessons, the dreary black prayer books, and the Passover ceremony over which my dear father presided in our house, leaving me mostly with an impression of inedible food and bedraggled cheer. Can you conceive, my unfriendly reader, the astronomical distance between all this and Verlaine?

Looking back, I see that this aesthetic revulsion played as important a part in my refusal of Judaism as the urge to dwell unobtrusive and safe amidst a dominant or accepted group. If Judaism had appeared to me robed in beauty, who knows? This satisfaction might have superseded the timid boy's fear of humiliation and persecution. But everything, save the love I bore my parents, worked to thrust me away from my ancestral clan.

Of course, aesthetic receptivity was a thing even less known to myself than my anxiety to conform. God knows I was not born with a "passion for beauty," nor even bred to it. At best I was born with a capacity for acquiring it. But my tastes formed slowly. In my family the tone was one of unaffected simplicity. No one talked about Culture. A few books were read, without any clear notion of Literature. For visual gratification, my parents had their glossy furniture (style Art Deco of the nineteen-thirties), a landscape or still life on the walls, and a few trinkets on the mantelpiece, preferably of a sentimental or innocently lascivious character. My sister and I were never taken to museums, palaces, or (need I say it?) churches. Recreation consisted in long middle-class walks, good hotels, a month at the beach, and many hours on the terraces of cafés. Although the drive to Knokke on the North Sea took us past cities like Ghent and Brugge, it never occurred to anyone to pause for a look at their riches. Now and then my parents went to the opera, and once—once only—I was taken to a matinee in a theater. A celebrated Dutch actor was performing in *The Miser,* and to this day I see him placing two pinches of snuff into his nostrils, sniffing zestfully away, and then prudently picking the snuff out of his nostrils to replace it in his snuffbox. It would please me to report, in the manner of inspired biographers, that "the enchantment of this first encounter with the theater had, unknown to the lad himself, marked him for life: he *would* be a playwright." The truth, however, is that I heartily enjoyed myself, and went home. I do not recollect begging my parents to let me see more plays, or pining away in silence because all I got was Laurel and Hardy at the movies. In short, no one was training me to be an intellectual or an aesthete. On the other hand, my gentle parents were not stopping me. Instead of theaters and museums, I had love—not the worst of foundations, even for an intellectual.

It is clear to me that a subtler infiltration was affecting the growing boy. I owe much, I think, to the city of Antwerp itself: its old district with its mysterious intimations, the fresh rain rubbing its parks till all the leaves shone, its harmonious avenues valanced with chestnut trees, and the cathedral bells in the distance . . . all this mingling delicately with books, with poems. Such influences are as hard to capture in words as the quality of a perfume; and if we name them, how do we know why they take hold in one person and not in another? Why was I the only boy in a large group of friends to drift into another world? Or were there others I know nothing of?

— 5 —

By now you know where I stand. The point at which all my speculations about Judaism end is that the Jews should have converted the day after Constantine changed religion and—adopting a new home, a new nest, a new cozy family—melted into the great world. An interesting chapter in man's history would have closed without harm to anyone, like a drained lake whose waters have gone elsewhere. That which Jews had contributed to mankind: several volumes of great poetry, a monotheism which (I don't know why) most people take as an important advance over polytheism, and ethical conceptions as respectable as those of the Greeks; that, I say, which the Jews as Jews had contributed to mankind *had* been contributed, and over the ruins of the Temple the Spirit of History was whispering the hint: Enough, and beware.

Because this is a psychologizing age, you may wave off this argument of mine on the ground that I myself, poor fool, have thoroughly exposed its dubious origins in my "personal emotional history." But I advise you to drop this weapon. For if it is true that a personal psychological thrust can vitiate an argument, it is equally true that another such thrust can open a man's eyes to realities concealed from his fellows. I might, for instance, be persuaded that Freud brewed his theories from a rancorous desire on the part of this ambitious but humiliated Viennese Jew to avenge himself on the Catholic Austrian ruling class. Yes, he was going to knock the monocles off Count Thun and the rest; or better, he would exhibit them—and by the majestic objective authority of Science at that—with their pants literally down. Did he not all but boast that he would in the Virgilian epigraph to his book on dreams? "If I cannot bend the higher powers, I shall stir up Acheron." Bow to me, you Gentiles, or else! This then is a picture I could readily trust; but how does it help me pass judgment on the truths or errors of the Creed? Who shall decide whether a particular psychological "bias" is benign or malign to a theoretical body of opinions? "You are misled because you were beaten as a child." "No, because I was beaten as a child I see the truth." Nothing comes, you see, of tracing an opinion back to a psychological source.

You must attack me otherwise.

"What harm were we doing by keeping the faith? What justice is there in your advising us to convert? All we asked for is a shop or a farm, the right to work hard for a living, our dear Book, and the hope for a return to the Holy Land. What people more innocent? More undemanding? More modest? More unobtrusive?"

Granted, granted, and granted. You did no harm. You were modest. You worked hard. Justice is on your side. Reason is on your side. They should have left you alone. God knows they should have left you alone. So should a tornado leave a house alone. So should a bull leave a man alone.

But I am not hardhearted enough to take my stand on Justice and Reason. I take my stand on mountains of corpses and floods of blood. Oh sons and daughters of Moses, you *did* keep the faith, and today you are stronger than you have been in twenty-five centuries: rejoice! But not I. I stagger through the corpses, I choke in the blood. Monstrous price to pay for the privilege of staying in the nest where you feel at home. Or are you telling me that your traditions—your dogma—your rites—your moral life— are so astoundingly superior to anything else the world can offer that a thousand massacres should be endured for their sakes?

For this is the lamentable theme they play over and over again, as if to shield themselves from the monstrosity of the sacrifices they chose to incur, and made others incur: the magnificent contribution of Judaism to civilization. We now leave behind us the controversies I have already touched upon. We assume for argument's sake that the Jews *could* have vanished as Jews. But now we ask whether, in consideration of that magnificent contribution, we should not rejoice that they held firm, come hunger, humiliation, or death.

Consider briefly, to begin with, what one might call intramural contributions: Judaism speaking to Judaism, and little said about affecting the rest of mankind. For instance, addressing himself to the "literary creativity" of the leaders of Russian Jewry as late as 1938 and 1939, the historian S. W. Baron exclaims with naïve admiration: "I was amazed to note that in less than two years, East European Jews published more volumes of responsa, halakhic and aggadic commentaries, homilies, kabbalistic (and hasidic) works than in any two decades of the seventeenth century, the heyday of rabbinic learning." This species of learning continues to thrive. I saw it also as a child shimmering in the pale faces of young men studying in one Yeshiva or another. Hurrying along the streets, all seemed to be thinly pregnant with yet another aggadic commentary, and impatient for delivery.

I do believe that many of those (and perhaps all) who perpetu-

ate this particular order of contribution would willingly if tear-
fully pay the tragic price: accept the hecatombs, that is, in order
to keep the faith burning in this manner. But the millions of
Jews who live outside the inner circle—inner and, let there be no
mistake, authentic as no other—need to summon, with somewhat paradoxical pride, the men and women who poured their
works of mind and hand into the stream of Occidental culture,
enriching it and altering its course beyond calculation.

Everyone will admit, I think, that the outpouring that predates
the Great Emancipation is really a trickle. Intellectual activity in
those many centuries was of the intramural kind already mentioned. Of international figures like Maimonides and Spinoza we
have not enough to help the implacables' argument. Nor will
anyone claim that the loss of Jewish art (products made by or for
Jews) would have dealt civilization an irreparable blow. Jewish
art was borrowed. The best synagogues were built on general
European models, and the aesthetics of wedding rings, embroi-
dered shawls, silver vessels, book-binding, and so forth, afford us
nothing vitally or remarkably original. For the rest, we neither
expect nor obtain a Jewish Titian or Bach. The talent, heaven
knows, was not wanting; but Jews had survival to think of, not
partitas. Indeed, their really influential inventions occurred in
the fields of finance and marketing, activities close to the problem of survival. And in the sciences, *everything* was to come.

The argument becomes genuinely weighty only when we contemplate the astonishing flood of products of the Jewish mind
and hand without which world history since the age of Napoleon
is hardly thinkable. The contention is that if the Jews had converted along with Constantine there would have been no Einstein
(and a thousand others) and no Kafka (and a thousand others).
Let us for the moment pour into the same vessel contributions
that manifest a special Jewish cast (like a painting by Chagall or
a novel by Saul Bellow); works with no discernible Jewish character (like those of Modigliani and Soutine or the discovery that
matter and energy are interchangeable), and works like Kafka's,
into which one may or may not read Jewish features. Let us call a
contribution Jewish if it has been made by a son or daughter of
Jews *and* sent (so to speak) *extra muros*. There is obviously such
abundance and such importance here that a man would be
neither a fool nor a brute for declaring that the contributions are

sufficient compensation for twenty centuries of oppression and massacre.

I promptly concede at this point that a kind of semi-oppression—something less harsh than dismal pauperization, and obviously something much less harsh than massacre—stimulates the mind as it struggles for ways of overcoming or compensating. In other words, I accept as true the commonplace notion that suffering sharpened Jewish intellects and intensified Jewish energies. If this stimulation occurred during certain periods preceding the Emancipation, it did not, as we have seen, lead to many "extramural" contributions. Only after the opening of the doors (partial and reluctant, or full and loving) could it and did it help to produce the works we are considering. I concede, therefore, that without Judaism (that is to say, if all the Jewish achievers had been born of families Christianized since Constantine, or indeed since Philip II), a distinct loss of intensity would have resulted in our world, bringing about in turn a distinct diminution in the number and power of achievers. Since the specific disabilities imposed on Jews as Jews constitute only one composite cause for major creativity, no one will claim that the Einsteins and Kafkas would have disappeared outright. But neither can anyone affirm that they would all have surged forward as before.

But if oppression is good for the soul (alas), so is opportunity. Directly we think of all the achievers produced by the pressures of Judaism and anti-Judaism, we must enter into our account book veritable armies of potential achievers since our "year zero" whose field of thought and creation was pathetically shrunk in the ghetto or the squalid village:

> But Knowledge to their eyes her ample page
>   Rich with the spoils of time did ne'er unroll;
> Chill Penury repressed their noble rage,
>   And froze the genial current of the soul.

Instead of one Spinoza, the world might have celebrated twenty; the sciences might have reached in the year 1700 the point at which they stood in 1800 or 1900; and a second Raphael might have lived and painted. This is enough for my argument; but even after the Emancipation, opportunity might have done as much good as oppression did. In short, for every Einstein produced by Judaism, I see another aborted by Judaism, and I make bold to wish that generations of pale youths had turned away from aggadic commentaries to the curricula of Oxford, Paris, or Bologna.

These calculations, distasteful in any case, lead to a blank. The only assertion the implacables can retrieve with certainty is that the especial subject matter (or coloring, or character) of products which are, to begin with, capable of being Jewish would have been lost. I doubt that any anxiety is in order concerning the sciences in which verification is practiced. Even Einstein's discoveries would have been discovered sooner or later without him —if need be by a band of lesser men doing the work of the single genius. But what would have taken the place of works of art in which the Jewish character is at least detectable and at most overwhelming? By our very hypothesis we must grant that, after replacing every Chagall and Kafka with a neo-Chagall and a neo-Kafka (or two other artists who took advantage of opportunities while the first ones sank into a lethargy of unruffled Christianity), the Jewish images and the Jewish "something" would have vanished.

To this, then, comes the loss we can be sure of, and this, in sum, is the "magnificent contribution" that would have disappeared from the world after Titus if the Jews had consented to join with Saul of Tarsus. Science and technology would have advanced undisturbed at worst. A certain number of men and women, lacking the irritant of anti-Semitism, would have lounged instead of achieving. Others, given opportunities denied them as Jews, would have substituted for them. But certain Jewish motifs, inflections, images would have been irretrievably lost to the world.

And now, make your choice. Will you preserve mankind from this loss by perpetuating Judaism and pogroms, or will you accept the loss and cancel the bloody persecutions, the forced migrations, the ceaseless exactions and degradations, and finally the colossal massacre perpetrated by the Germans? If I abolish the gas chambers, will you not let me baptize the Jews of the Roman Empire? I wish that I could ask this question of the victims themselves, "stinking innocently in the ditch"; but the dead are famous for their silence. Instead, I will take you, the living, farther with me. Let the Jewish contribution be as magnificent as you choose it to be. *Now* are you willing to pay the ghastly price?

Not I. You have been calling me coldhearted while reading these pages—I know you, my sweet reader—but who is coldhearted now? It was not from a cold heart that I cried, two thousand years ago, "Give it up! It is not worth the blood past, present and future."

Besides, the world is made neither of nor for major achievers and magnificent contributions. Plain families count too. And what does a plain family require? Health, a house, food, schools, work, security, a God to worship. Can these not be found outside Judaism? Are you abjectly "preprogrammed" animals, that you had rather die than change from one custom to another?

Or were you waiting for the world to become more intelligent, more rational, less tribe-minded than you were yourselves? I have said so before: you may as well wait for Cloud-Cuckoo-Land. No one knows better than a faithful Jew what tribal cohesion is. Who is more inclusive and exclusive than the Jew himself? Who is better situated to understand man's distrust of outsiders—that hatred of the "uncircumcised" which leads so easily to pathological conclusions? The Jews can understand that tribalism is natural, is precious, and is terrible. Yet they cry to the heavens because the Christians cannot rid themselves of it.

Let me assure you that if Judaism had been the powerful tribe, I would have cried my cry to the Christians: "Give it up; it is not worth the blood!" and urged them to file into the synagogue.

Today, of course, the Jews *are* the powerful tribe in Israel; they are, at last, a majority; and if the nation succeeds in imposing itself and, secure from Arab attack, takes up the luxurious burden of oppressing *its* minority, I hope that the local Arabs will cheerfully get themselves absorbed by their tormentors, Near Eastern like themselves: another very feasible change of being! My own view about this new nation can be guessed. Whether its repossession of Palestine is just, or constitutes an imperialist Gibraltar-like enclave—either way, for me, the price paid for it was intolerably, monstrously high, so high (I speak of twenty centuries of oppression and massacre) as to become a macabre absurdity. The price having been paid, however, and the nation being established—by means of the violence that customarily begets nations—reasonable men and women everywhere are bound to hope that diplomacy will finesse a permanent accommodation, based, one supposes, on the vast unpopulated spaces over which the Arabs dispose. If peace does settle in, a notion like mine—that the Jews would have been better off melting into the crowd than reconfirming their destiny in Palestine—becomes academic. On the other hand, it will be anything but academic if the state of Israel succumbs at last to Arab conquest—an event that will not occur without another impressive slaughter.

And outside Israel? Has Hitler's efficient work sobered the nations? May we suppose that, aside from vestigial hot spots of Jew-baiting, the Cossacks and the S.S. will ride no more? Many anxious Jews are heard to say that the bloodletting is far from over. Any time, any place, a storm of violence can fall upon the Jews again, while (short of another "final solution") the old hatred will continue to trigger the old persecutions and the old degradations. If these anxious persons are right, more of my sort should leave their other occupations and plead for the dissolution of Judaism, recapitulating my argument thus: No, the "being" of Judaism is not a permanent being; Yes, Jews can relinquish Judaism and dissolve into the circumambient culture, some in a single generation, others in two or three; and No, not religion, nor ethical singularity, nor customs, nor contributions to the general culture warrant the suffering brought about by the passion to preserve them.

Curiously, though, my own vaticinations are less grim. I think it not impossible that outside of Israel other hostilities, other problems, and other struggles will by and large deflect the attention of Cossacks and S.S. men to come. As a result of this general sense of the future, I have responded but sluggishly to my own doctrines. Coming to maturity in the United States just at the time Hitler was expiring (we hope) in his bunker, I have allowed my favorable habitat to lull me. I have not changed my name. I tell you freely who I am and whence I come. Those who smile at me, and shake their heads, and put into their voice a particular tone of confident world-wisdom to tell me, "You *are* a Jew whether you like it or not; once a Jew always a Jew," are welcome to their wisdom. And if, perchance, we have lived to witness the last hecatomb, my adjuration ends: let Judaism flourish.

— 6 —

It can flourish, I daresay, without one man's admiration. I am fond of local color and quaint old religions, but not all folkways appeal to me to the same degree. Neither Moslem nor Jewish tradition, for example, make a snug fit into my spirit. The former I know mostly by hearsay; but my distaste for the thousand prescriptions and prohibitions among which orthodox Jews live to this day derives from something approaching intimacy. Concerning these *do's* and *don't's*, Mr. Poliakov, the historian of anti-Semitism, reproduces an admirable passage from Rousseau: "To keep his people from melting among alien nations, Moses gave them manners and customs that could not be allied to those of other nations; he overloaded them with rituals and special ceremonies; he cramped them in a thousand ways to keep them unremittingly on their toes and make them forever strangers among other men; and all the ties of brotherhood that he placed among the members of his republic were so many barriers that kept them separate from their neighbors and prevented a mingling between them." An all but Darwinian explanation! And one is free to admire these strategies of survival or to deplore them. Admire them, since they enabled the group to survive through thick and thin; deplore them, since they led the group *into* thick and thin. Picture a species of animal, tightly organized and behaving according to deeply ingrained rules. The world changes all around this species but the species itself "declines" to change. As a result, its members are decimated time and time again by a number of newer predatory groups. But a few members always remain alive. They continue unchanged, almost impervious to mutation, and they multiply again, until enough of them appear for a new carnage. Is this admirable? If you wish. But since you have advised me that changing my being is impossible, I shall advise you in turn that keeping it was absurd.

For the rest, these manners and customs dumbfound me. Perhaps the Moslems are worse, but they are known to be living at an earlier stage of history, though in the very shadow of their oil wells. And besides, they live in their lands largely by themselves. Instead, a Jew who will not flip a light on the Sabbath in Manhattan, London, or Sydney is a figure almost farcical. I know a young man—a brilliant physician and musical genius—who refuses to open his refrigerator on the day of rest because the open door throws a switch that lights a bulb. At table a few weeks ago a Jewish guest spoke of a professor at Brandeis University who solves the problem of lighting his house on Saturdays by pressing the switches with his elbow, apparently with the blessing of an influential rabbi. My friend and colleague K. C. assures me that this story must be a joke. But who has not heard of a hundred similar banalities and absurdities that would shame a Papuan? K. C. herself is learned, wise, urbane, but cannot dine at my house because my dishes are polluted. Another colleague of mine is a Russian woman who fled to Israel with her eleven-year-old boy. The boy died and was refused burial because he was uncircumcised. The mother had to allow the little corpse to be put to the knife before she could get it interred. In short, as many follies, pitiful in the context of Western civilization, cover the "ethical beauty" of Judaism as quills on a porcupine's hide. These countless prescriptions and prohibitions diffuse the warmth of tradition and community, and they define the group's identity against all others so that it survives—survives to be preyed upon because so neatly identified, but survives. What is missing is sense-in-itself, I mean a present-day moral, intellectual, aesthetic, or at least economic value. A ritual kiss on the cheek among the members of a congregation might be traditional, might have survival value, and would also have moral value today. Avoiding pork chops has none.

The Darwinian perspective can also be applied to a famous Jewish trait, the love of learning. We have all been treated to emotional descriptions of centers of learning in Babylon, study houses in every Polish village, the veneration bestowed on learned boys and men (women were devoted to imbecility), and so on. But it is clear that the learning of rabbis and other masters amounted to a powerful means of sociopolitical control. The supposedly *spiritual* leaders combined in a single person the monarch, legislature, tribunal, propaganda ministry, and police force. This meant that rabbis had to provide themselves with something more than a few metaphysical doctrines concerning God, salvation, angels, etc. They must find a rationale for controlling daily actions in perpetual danger of gravitating toward the norms of the surrounding Christian communities. This they accomplished by giving religious significance to the most minute particulars of life. One could not rinse a cup without divine prescription; and divine prescription was interpreted and enforced by the rabbis. No wonder study houses were the first houses built in every new community! They were the Jewish

universities—but also the disguised chancelleries and police sta-
tions. Now we also see why so little interest was shown in the
afterlife. Cohesion here below was what mattered; and for cohesion a regulation on hair-clipping was more important than
dreams of the empyrean.

I see with a sort of stupefaction the boy I was at thirteen, when
my father took it into his head to make a mature Jew out of me. I
had just completed the ceremony of the *bar mitzvah*; now, if ever,
was the moment to make the boy wrap himself every morning in
phylacteries. I have forgotten the precise character and importance of this daily ritual, but I recollect a row of voluble prayers,
certain ribbons I placed about my arm and head, and a couple of
sinister little black boxes, which I suppose contained some incantations. I contemplate myself at a distance of almost forty years
and shake my head. They speak about Africans leaping over
twenty centuries in a single generation as they cross from anim-
ism to heavy industry. Why cite Africa? I see the tiny lad in the
Avenue de Belgique: outside his window the automobiles and
streetcars are rolling by. A short walk away is the electric railway.
Then the movie houses. The twenty-four story "skyscraper,"
Antwerp's pride. Two tunnels just finished under the broad river.
And myself muttering incantations to Yahweh. It was too wretchedly droll to last. My father struggled from a weak position, for
he was not phylacterizing himself. After two or three weeks, he
gave up, and the family returned to normal.

But the true *rite de passage* happened later. By then I was
fifteen and living in New York. When the Day of Atonement
came around, I was naturally expected to fast for twenty-four
hours along with the rest of the Jewish world. At noon, after an
hour of forced prayers in a shabby neighborhood synagogue, I
slipped out to a nearby "luncheonette," sat down on one of
its stools, and bought a solid meal. As I masticated, I searched
myself for the fatal *ayenbite of Inwit*, that is to say, the bitter
sting of remorse. I would not have been absolutely surprised if a
thunderbolt had fallen on the luncheonette. But ah, what bliss,
my conscience was clear. Not a spiculum of reproach stuck in it.
On the contrary, I fell into the marvelous elation of a youth who
has passed the test of manhood and established his right to self-
determination. In that same year I announced to my father that I
would not enter a synagogue again.

Somewhere in Germany, Hitler's despised dust is aging in some tub or pot. I too, had I not trembled safe across an ocean, would have disappeared from earth long, long ago. But in those death-camp days, if they had forced me to the ditch under a gun, I would have been executed by gangsters for a creed, and in the name of a tribe, that I had renounced two thousand years before, and for an identity foisted on me by the Nazis and the Jews alike in horrid collusion against my selfhood. Like that wretch in Plutarch and Shakespeare who—when the assassins were looking for Cinna the politician—cried out in vain, "I am Cinna the poet, I am Cinna the poet!," I would have tumbled into an inglorious, mistaken death.

ME FOR SOFT FLOORS AND
SMARTLY NOT TO THINK

Me for soft floors and smartly not to think
Vase at the window, carpet, couch, no books.
Smart in the wind a lamppost tickled
By a tree gives me a yellow, measurable wink.

I loathe the moon, and do the beauty and the stars.
Me keep me far from distance. They utter
My how dim I am how dumb I talk,
They light me naked up this mammal farce.

How can those nitwit lovers bear the sky?
Me for a chandelier hung not too high.

I am, as the fading Existentialists would have put it, in bad faith. I sturdily advocate bad faith. If death will gobble you up whether you look it in the face or not, why look it in the face? Let us huddle companionably around the fireplace instead and sing each other ditties of

Maypoles, hock-carts, wassails, wakes,
Of bridegrooms, brides, and of their bridal-cakes.

Once upon a time I wrote a book called *A Chair in the Void*. I think that image conveys all that's needed. A chair in a void is an absurdity; it does not hold; and yet we do and we must place it there—and sit on it, too—and put a cushion on the seat.

"Me for soft floors" is, if you will, a poem against Nature. My mentality is somewhat medieval in this respect. Medieval man distrusted Nature because the Devil had taken possession of it after Adam's fatal bite; and we today dislike it (when we do) for much the same reason. Only our Devil is not the cheerful sneering fellow with the pitchfork and our Hell is not that overheated club of sinners so amiably described in a famous passage of *Aucassin and Nicolette*—yet, when we think of it, with Dante

and Michelangelo it has a cozy look too; no, our Hell is the Void
itself, and our Devil is the thought of nothingness.

After Dante

My mind dwells perfectly on death's incommodation
and nothing safe. I hate noble literature
and professional wisdom: that famous Roman
calm at his blather before they broke him on the
    rack. . . .

The night I opened Hell and saw Ugolino set
his teeth into Ruggieri's head, I turned my own away,
but slow enough to catch Ruggieri's muddy grin,
and then the teeth struck bone and I was forced to look.

His hair bleeding (and Ugolino's upper lip
was pushed against his nose from biting) Ruggieri
    grinned,
Ruggieri said: "Yet I am I"; and I crouched stunned;
there is no cruelty to match no God at all.

Me for the rectangular bed and humus
my eternal coverlet, bone beneath pain,
not even crying, Someone drill a hole and thrust
a tube in mercy to periscope some sky to me. . . .

May my father and my mother die suddenly
and old, like lights switched off by accident, and not
be frightened. May I not dangle after my friends
alone to be shot like an only target in a square,

no one to hide behind and hope he will die first.
I am nervous and yet I would welcome a ghost.
I have lifted my mind, which is glory, but why?
To dwell on death without hole or consolation.

On rereading the poem, I pause before the penultimate stanza
as if to say "Oh my prophetic soul!" My father, my dear good
gentle apprehensive father, your light went out quickly, but not
so quickly as to conceal the horror leaning down on you; and you
clutched at my mother's arm (she became your mother), scolded
her bitterly and insanely for "throwing" you into a hospital,
touched and pulled at your already dead limb; and on the third
morning, calling for a trivial object, a little hand-held radio

which you miscalled a camera, on that trivial word, and expecting to hear news of the world, you fell back and died, scared. One no longer dies uttering some grand summation.

"I would welcome a ghost." It would terrify me, and yet I would welcome it as a promise of life beyond. I would die of terror but die happy. What a piece of humor!

To return to Nature: since it is held by the Devil, and teaches us the horrible lesson of cosmic indifference; yet since on the other hand it offers us relief from the city—from our daily and weekly business—from our quarrels and passions; why, the compromise is medieval again: I turn to lovely intimate gardens—the very gardens which medieval artists loved to depict. The rich men of Islam knew what I mean as well. A neatly planted garden, with a fountain in the middle, then a few orange trees and all the requisite flowers and shrubs, moreover birds chirping in the boughs and a lady playing on a cither and another embroidering: there Nature disguises its criminal nature; pretends cordial feelings toward us; and I fall in, I play the game, I relax, breathe the fresh air, and forget the message of oceans and galaxies. If I go outside the garden, kindly take me where a little brook is gurgling and looping about a meadow and I hear the cowbells in the near distance. You may also find me in some mild Spa, Bath or Baden-Baden, not drinking the waters, God forbid—first because their taste is odious, second because I do not believe in them, and third because I am in excellent health for the time being—but ambling in the park—watching a squirrel—or a goldfish—taking in the domesticated crowd—sipping coffee and forking away at a comfortable slice of pastry with whipped cream—listening to the "semiclassical" music dispensed by an amusingly inept orchestra—such are my innocent pleasures, plump out of the Victorian Age—leftovers, it turns out, of vacations in Marienbad and such places taken with my parents before World War II, when I was a child. I am, in short, a lover of Nature trimmed and inhabited—her tame edges, so to speak, as a baby fills a pail at the beach with the docile and friendly drops of that water which, pursued by the imprudent eye to any distance, quickly becomes the grim inhospitable ocean.

Most people I know crave isolation and love the absolute wilderness. They are truly happy only when they have shaken off the fatigues of social life and are breathing free under the stars in the remotest corner of some Wyoming, in no danger of meeting with another member of their species. This craving has now received official sanction in national campaigns against pollution and for the conservation of wilderness. An amusing and yet legitimate paradox sometimes arises: people must stay out of the wilderness so that the wilderness may be preserved for people. Be that as it may, I, on the contrary, shun solitude and hate wilderness. Invited to admire the ocean, I quickly turn my eye back to the negotiable shore. Now and then, when my wife and I are driving through uninhabited country at night, I switch off the car lights in order to scare myself for a moment with a clear view of all those stars, delights of romantic spirits, and oh they are beautiful, a beauty surrounded by atrocious thoughts, like a splendid woman whom we know to be a poisoner. I am not a prolonger of such contemplations.

This beauty of the stars, by the way, I take to derive from our quite fundamental affinity for light. The human being is a daylight animal, and he has every good reason—even as an infant—to prefer light over darkness. A million dots of light against a black groundcloth appeal to us as a sort of rescue and, as our sense of beauty is merely a by-product of our various senses of moral and physiological comfort, we are quick to call the night sky beautiful, even though these lights are strewn about without symmetry.

Some years ago we purchased a painting from a young artist whose way of life was to vanish for a year or two at a time in the depths of northern Canada, equipped with a rifle, a few cans of food, and camping material. All alone, except for rare excursions to an outpost two days' journeying away from his campsite, he "communed with Nature"—a far haul from Barbizon!—and painted away—very decently too. He had returned to Los Angeles to take a Master's degree at the Otis School of Art—he realized that he could not last in his Klondike forever—but he longed for the wilderness again—the crowds oppressed him—let alone the stinking freeways. Yet he was a lively and droll little fellow, and comically confessed that he was looking for a girl to take into his canoe the next time he set out, but she was not easy to find. He was in our house building a frame for the picture we had taken from him. We never saw him again, but I trust that he found the girl after all (for there are thousands upon thousands who want to dismiss themselves from civilization), and I see him happy in his tent, sharing a can of beans with his mistress, unless a bear has eaten him instead.

I recently saw these very mountains from an airplane: layer upon layer of icy monsters trooping toward the North Pole—an army of Titans—no, not trooping toward the North Pole at all— quite the opposite, they appeared to be marching in solid squadrons toward my backyard *from* the North Pole—ice upon ice, dispatched from the ice of the universe. Where shall we hide?

No, immense views do not appeal to me. From my house and no tent I want to see, beyond my garden, the guzzle and gabble of a prosperous city. Nor do I chase after those mysterious resorts "which the tourists have not yet discovered." I do not enjoy the crush of a crowd any more than—than anyone in that same crowd—but I am even less anxious to be the only human being on a beach. In his "Araby" Joyce has beautifully given us the gray, glum sense of a fair after closing time—it could be any resort the day after the season—and what sodden loneliness it impresses on the soul unlucky enough to have remained! The stores are shuttered. A waiter lounges over deserted tables. The casino's program lies hunched in a damp gutter.

No empty beaches for me. Place me instead in that famous Piazetta of Capri. All about me a colorful crowd. The homosexuals in their jewels and the tanned young things incapable, it would seem, of ever wrinkling. A cozy dimension—for the Piazetta is hardly larger than a large ballroom. Whitewashed houses—the churchlet and its belltower—the smell of good coffee—and a glimpse of Nature with her fangs concealed, all flowers. Not, mind you, that I shall be making friends with the passers-by. I am apt to sit there two months without acquiring a single acquaintance. If I do by accident fall into a conversation, it is without expecting anything new or interesting. Novelties are to be found in books, which distill them out of the mostly banal flux of life. Mostly banalities will come of these encounters. I do not avoid them, they are pleasant enough, but I do not look for them, and I am not so vain as to think that my own conversation will be a feast for anyone. Nothing of this; but I do crave the warm animation in itself—the human voices as such—they need not greet me in particular. And I recognize thereby how gregarious a beast man is, for I believe that my needs in this regard are more widespread than the urge to disappear in a solitude. There is reassurance in the mere presence of other human beings. We are in the herd, relaxed. As for the breaking of the sea against the rocks—the howl of a coyote in a distant hollow—the glacial rush of wind on a winter plain—such sounds afford us impressive and even necessary excursions from human society; but it is foolish to turn this topsy-turvy and consider our sociable life as a burdensome deviation from an uncultivated Nature where we supposedly belong.

I had rather walk with Johnson to "Messieurs Dillys, booksellers in the Poultry," than "bound like a roe" with Wordsworth over the hillside. And when I retire, I hope it will be in the heart of a thoroughly polluted metropolis, not perched atop a remote cliff to admire the ocean and lucubrate Leopardi-like on the immensity which must swallow me all too soon.

Immensity—ocean, mountains, desert, or the sky—it does not matter that on the scale of the galaxies they show hardly more than my own house—as it does not matter that within the cosmos any galaxy is as a speck of dust too. From the human standpoint, the least of these things is immensity enough to remind me that I am lost, helpless, crushed, annihilated.

Another log in the fireplace, my friends, pass the brandy around, and change the subject.

VISCERA

After running five minutes
I lie on the grass and listen to my heart.

Sometimes I feel like calling down
the well of my body
"Organs, organs! Do you hear me? Discipline!"

Lord, to be dependent on a pancreas!

If it turns off I'm dead.
Do I choose to die? Not much!
Yet this fat machinery dares run me.

Salivating with indignation
I demand to be pure spirit,
I want to boss these lungs, these kidneys, this trash.

Did you, Plato, yes or no call them my slaves?
Then why does that slave keep thumping
When I shout "At ease"?

Here is "poetic truth" for you. I truly did run for five minutes in my garden, one of my rare tussles with physical exertion. Usually an amble from one sofa to another satisfies me. Athletic activity bores me, and besides, it gives me a foolish pain in the gloomy precinct of the soul known as the conscience. Even when I have nothing else on earth to do—no book to read or write—sick to death of "intellectual work"—drifting—melancholy—not capable even of enduring music—even then, if I were invited for a swim or a round of tennis, my devil would whisper, "Shouldn't you be doing something useful, son?"—meaning, o heavenly angels, another twenty pages of literature. And yet how deadly tired I am of literature. I have long since reached the downslope of diminishing returns. The pleasures are few. The shock of ecstasy nearly impossible. I would rather pick tomatoes in the hot valleys of California than read a novel by Pynchon or

Robbe-Grillet, not to mention *Finnegans Wake*. Why then not go for a swim?

Every other summer my wife takes me to the Mediterranean, as if California had not already crammed me past bearing with sunlight, dry weather, parched vegetation, those palm trees I hate so, and oleanders which, I am told, kill you if you eat them. I am a docile husband. She lies in the water happily for hours and hours. Me, ten minutes of swimming, more than enough. Where is it taking me? Aimless flailing of arms. Bored, I return to the beach and pick up a book. I get no exhilaration out of muscular performance, nothing at any rate like the elation which lifts me out of my chair when I am skirmishing across the table with a band of sharpshooting conversationalists.

I suppose it all goes back to my timid childhood. Neither my father nor my mother exercised. In school, craven, slender, tiny, I dreaded the daily hour of physical education. The gymnasium had hanging from the ceiling certain well-polished wooden poles which all the boys were required to climb. We were all lined up in a row, and each boy had to take his turn. So exposed—all these eyes acting on me like so many spotlights—I never managed more than a foot or two up the pole before dropping miserably to the floor. The hoots which I anticipated I brought on my head by having anticipated them. For it happened that during a period of free-for-all romping in the gymnasium, I climbed unobserved to the top with perfect ease. Nor was I sluggish or clumsy elsewhere. I scrapped with my friends, rode my bicycle, ran and jumped with my cousins—but all along it was plain that I would never be the "outdoors type." In the public swimming pool I was terrified of dunkings. Both on land and water, I saw powerful bullies only too willing to torment me.

Now and then, in my adult life, I have made a half-hearted attempt to turn athlete. In one of my closets a pair of dumbbells are sleeping on the carpet. They served for a few weeks, when I undertook to build my body for ten minutes a day, until boredom exterminated my resolution. Brave dumbbells, little do you suspect that you are descended from a pair of roller-skates I extorted from my skeptical parents oh so many years ago. I rode them hard—perhaps for a year—along the pavements of Antwerp and, in the Parc de la Ville, on the asphalted road closed off for children to play in. Then they were cashiered. The ice skates did not last nearly so long. Only to my bright blue bicycle with the three speeds did I remain faithful. I loved to pump away at the pedals, loved the bicycle path on the Avenue de Belgique under the chestnut trees, and loved the bumpy cobblestones in the streets. But neither galaxies nor bicycles endure. Our concierge, who seemed so devoted to the six families living overhead, stole my *bécane* as soon as the rout of 1940 had swept us out of Belgium. That was a knickknack, of course. He plundered, denounced, and lorded it so freely, and got so far above his old station of underdog in the basement, that he was shot when the wheel of Fortune took another turn.

So I went jogging round the garden one afternoon to prove to my wife that one can be fit without exercising every day. When my heart began to thump a sound volley, I prudently stopped and lay down on the grass, panting but not unduly, and gazing at the seven cypresses that stand at the back of the garden, settled and rested, their utmost effort a concerted wagging of heads in the wind, and I listened to my body.

Poems are terribly incomplete. They record a passion (a passion of thought or of experience)—record it, naturally, in the halfway tranquillity Wordsworth speaks of—that curious mingling of emotion and cunning (one cannot write decent poetry in a whirl)—but the passion, the intensity may have been an ephemeral one: we might disown it the next day. This is all to the good, aesthetically speaking. Poetry catches its adept in any of his postures, and if a posture captivates the audience, why then the poem has accomplished what poetry was born to do. To succeed, the poem need hardly tell you the whole truth about me. Whole truth indeed! It need not even tell the truth at all, a fib will serve too, though it so happens—and here we cross into the "psychology of creation"—that most writers are unable to summon the spiritual energy they need to write a poem (and that energy is as chemically real as the energy I need to run around my garden) if the poem's matter is fundamentally "untrue" to them. But the propulsive truth of a poem can afford to be fragmentary or ephemeral. These elaborations, on the contrary, mean to be speculative tract, autobiography, meditation. Therefore they are not altogether satisfied when the poem says, "The viscera are trash." That is good enough for the poem. An interesting, a powerful, a pleasurable poem can be made out of that proposition. The proposition has "universality." One need not be a Christian or a Platonist to revile the body. Odious lump! Think of the colds that have racked you. Think of cancer. Think of the stupid resistance it offers just when we are eager to visit another museum or make love one more time.

But the philosopher, man of prose, feels compelled to complete the picture. He cries out, "Amazing mechanism!" Which is a view contradictory to the other. And yet both are solidly grounded. When I consider the complexity of the operation Man—the chemical factories embedded in each of our millions of cells—the ordered jungle of our nucleic acids—the fantasmagoria of the brain—I recover from a stunned silence either to fall down and worship Nature or accuse her of having gone berserk. Our astronomers wear themselves out to find a few organic molecules adrift in the universe. For the cosmos in its state of sanity is simple. Light atoms, heavier atoms, a few combinations, mostly a mere violent blaze and a grand flying asunder. You scan this cosmos in all its majestic dullness, you pass these novae, this intergalactic dust, these molecules of ethyl alcohol, here and there you dodge a wicked black hole, and then "out of the blue" you suddenly fall into this unbelievable luxuriance of ours, a patch of electrochemical frenzy, a soup of giant molecular tentacles. The merest microbe is a scandalous exaggeration. Well, you mark the lurid singularity, Earth drops out of sight again, you resume the endless threadbare spaces.

They tell me that the universe is teeming with living blots like ours. It must be so. The fact is mathematically demonstrated. But I do not believe it. I am persuaded that for all the zeros which you care to add to your digit when you compute the number of possible planets in the cosmos, our carnival cannot be repeated, even distantly. Nevertheless, the decree says it must be. The universe festers at intervals.

I can almost look at a flatworm without staggering. But Nature is not content with a house of ten cards; a thousand will not do; a billion only begin to satisfy it. The structure becomes so colossally implausible, you wonder how it holds together for an hour. Look around you or look at yourselves: every mother's child a sack of ailments, while physicians poison us with remedies like firefighters who rescue the furniture from the flames by ruining it in water. A truly healthy person is a wonder of nature.

The statistics are almost comical. One out of every eleven citizens suffers from disease number one; one out of every three from disease number two; one out of every six from disease number three; add the mental afflictions; and while you pity the creatures who double or triple in these roles, you are not far from wrong when you conclude that one hundred and fifteen out of each hundred human beings are physical or mental botches. Nor do I count Bangladesh and other infernos where humanity becomes a helpless magma of crawling, festering bodies, stupidly sperming and ovulating themselves into a final mass grave. We the healthy nations are sick enough: when not broken in limb or mind, when not rotting with cancers or sweating with fevers, merely feeding ourselves to death, smoking, taking vile drugs, ah what a spectacle! How many diseases are listed in the medical encyclopedias? Many more than there are saints in the Vatican's files.

I myself—half a century old—happen to have emerged a rare winner after suffering countless childhood ailments from diphtheria to nervous breakdowns. True, my five minutes in the garden took me not so very far from my limit; I thrive because I have reached a composition with a given world about me; I would be one of the first to perish under stress and deprivation; but I eat in moderation, have no vices, indulge in no excesses, am naturally mild-humored, and suffer from nothing worse than a yearly headcold. But how long will this last? I expect a horror any day: poor me, who turn faint in the *lobby* of a hospital! And then my peculiar blessedness will be that I shall be entitled to say: I had thirty or forty years uncrippled in mind and body; I ran the machine conscientiously, and conscientiously it ran: *nunc dimittis*. But elsewhere? You cannot call a friend on the telephone without hearing a tale of sickness or death. Young or old, children and adults, "the provinces of the body rebel," and it is plain that Nature, like a decadent artist, overdecorated and overcomplicated when she came to us.

At the same time, it is also an absurdity that this prodigious and overdone structure should fall to pieces after a mere sixty, seventy, or eighty years in the sun. Men would not build the humblest parish church with dead stone, let alone a cathedral, to last a miserable three score years and ten, and in steady disrepair besides!

We are like that famous church of Gaudí's in Barcelona: grotesque, yet marvelous. For marvelous, too marvelous, we surely are. Out metabolism, for instance—the journey "downward" of a slice of bread we ingest—is such as no knight-errant, led by some indefatigable Ariosto through a thousand pages of unremitting adventure, ever dreamed of; and this is matched by the correspondingly marvelous brainwork of our biochemists, who unraveled it all, from the Krebs cycle on. There we have Nature at the peak of comedy, playing on both sides of the net, on one side secretly constructing these molecular supercathedrals in perpetual organized (and ailing) movement, and on the other recording its own secret. And what shall we say when the brain analyzes the brain?

Still, the disgust clings to us. Brain having "emitted" mind like a kind of radiation, mind takes a dislike to the other molecular configurations with which it is forced to share lodgings. The mind, as the organ which, among its many obligations, desires and hates—other organs merely perform—the mind desires to survive, and it desires to travel untrammeled everywhere forever; and the other organs lime it down and eventually kill it. It is a civil war. But a civil war that does not lock us into a dualism of spirit and matter. The mind "offended" by the body is not essentially different from two other organs in conflict. A man might be building his muscles and in consequence suffer a heart attack. His biceps "offend" his heart. Likewise, our diseases and our dis-eases—fatigues, aches, aging—make themselves known to the brain which, while it seeks remedies through the agency of its "motor activities" (reaching out for a bottle of pills) also registers and expresses revulsion, since it is the organ which desires and hates. As if this were not enough, the same thinking-about-the-future that gave us, mankind, such a decisive boost in the struggle for domination over other species, this torments us with representations of diseases and pains to come, and finally with ideas of death—death which, in the only sense that matters—think of it!—only mankind endures.

So then the mind takes pleasure in the body at mealtime and sextime, and grumbles when it aches and decays, just as the heart "likes" the biceps when they promote blood circulation and "dislikes" them when they induce an infarction. I repeat therefore that the opposition of mind *to* body of which the poem speaks is not an opposition of mind *and* body; no ontological dualism is implied. "I demand to be pure spirit" is a manner of speaking. It means I want to be all mental organ, I want to be the organ that thinks and loves rather than that which digests and excretes. It is the old longing, the perished dream. In our visions of heaven, we gladly give up our kidneys and livers. Mind is what interests mind; and I daresay that if the kidneys could deliver themselves of a thought, they would beg for a survival of kidneys in the afterworld, a great Dantean rose of kidneys filtering away from all eternity, and let mind, let personality dissolve into random atoms, adieu.

I hope that the comedy of *"salivating* with indignation" while demanding to be pure spirit catches the servitude to matter which imposes itself even when we aspire to be angels. But by the way, I had better declare that I say "matter" as a shortcut. Modern Thought had drummed "crude materialism" out of the philosopher's barracks; nowadays we prefer fancy substitutes. It is more high-minded to speak of electrochemical phenomena, for instance, and every quidnunc knows how to mock those naive materialists of the nineteenth century because today we sages know that matter is but a form of energy. You understand me. Adding waves and radiations and quanta of energy to matter, or melting matter into them, makes no philosophical difference. Materialism means monism and nothing else: a universe without divinity that shapes our end. But besides, suppose that the universe is, after all, composed of two ultimate realities, one "material" and the other "spiritual." From there to God and from God to survival after death the gulf is as wide as ever, for why should not a spirit cease to be as readily as a molecule of glucose?

Metaphysics comes to me as a mood. Too often, perhaps, I sense the unspeakable cosmos behind the trivial events of the day. In my puppy times, I was frequently tormented by the thought that death would debar me forever from the secrets of the universe. I wanted to live long enough to hear the Great Solution, the final Unified Field Theory. I wanted to be present when Science had completed its work, and spoken the final words: This much mankind knows, and can know no farther; and closed its book at last.

Why has this anguish receded from my mind? It returned to me briefly just now, even while I was setting down the words, but otherwise it seldom visits me these days. Besides, I am less tortured by the thought of death plain and simple than I was ten, twenty years ago—than I was, indeed, as a child, when drops of perspiration rolled from my forehead at night as I felt the skeleton's grip waiting only for the tolling of midnight. Later, too, a terror beyond all terror often called me out before sleep; I would moan, toss, clutch face and pillow, cower, whimper as a presence of eternal obliteration, strange paradox, invaded me. These eschatological convulsions could not last long, for the ultimate consequence of such terror is to die, and to die of fear when the fear is of dying was a logical impasse from which the mind simply turned away, hoisting itself on the back of some everyday concern to ride, not toward consolation, but off into distraction.

Why, again, should I feel all this less rather than more as I grow older?—less, that is, until the day when a physician shall deliver his awful sentence after a look into my entrails. It happened too, a few years ago, that almost from one day to the next, I lost my fear of airplanes. Why? I thought then, and still half believe, that I was cured of that particular anxiety because I had just "eternalized" my plays in a book: my lifework was done, I could "twitch my mantle" and say good-bye, God be with you. Then, too, it may be that one is pulled down by a common, uncomplicated fatigue of life—I do not mean the usual discontent, disappointment, even despair, but something like the plain bone-weariness after a long, long walk. Or else our emotions age along with our viscera; perhaps this fear wanes a little along with an etiolation of our other feelings. Think (say I to myself) what an ambitious youngster you were—such a rage to "make it to the top"—oh the rapture of that first poem in print, that first article in a periodical—the desire to be celebrated, envied, caressed! Well, it is all alive yet beneath the occiput, but the fires are burning a little less hot, I care smaller, I am tired. Don't we all know that riots and revolutions, though they may be planned by old men, require boys of seventeen to get them roaring?

For a "metaphysical man" my plays, on a first inspection, look singularly political. But: in *General Audax* the hero betrays his country and goes over to the enemy; in *Island*, Demodocus betrays his nation and deserts; in *Adam Adamson* the protagonist betrays his country; Urubamba betrays his country; and so, in a way, does Gropius in *A Splitting Headache*. A few of my poems pick up the theme too:

The Deserter's Ditty

Alcaeus, Horace and Anacreon,
good cowards all (though brave in song):
I too grew nervous, dropped my gun,
and voted medals for the strong.

I favored too the bubbling of a kiss
above the tantrums of a bomb;
I did my duty to my private bliss,
Alcaeus, Horace and Anacreon.

Incidentally, it never occurred to me until years after I had written the plays that they were obsessed with this theme of betrayal. It is not, properly speaking, the betrayal of any given country or any specific cause; it is rather a despairing of political remedies, with betrayal as its consequence when the person who believed in political remedies discovers that they remedy little or nothing. So then, my plays are heavily political because they are antipolitical, and my character of "metaphysical man" is not put into jeopardy. Nevertheless, the plays do not turn to metaphysics for salvation: the ultimates fascinate me but do not console me. From the evils of the political right, and from the evils of the political left, and from the evils of political life in general, some of my heroes withdraw into solitude, but others seek the limited but comforting warmth of modest human companionship—a friend, a lover, a companion. This is expressed in a poem you have read before: "Me for soft floors and smartly not to think"— where the vertigo of the metaphysical life is exchanged for homely furniture, and the moon for a chandelier. The *divertisse-ments* which Pascal, that mighty spirit, condemned, I humbly welcome, because deprived of Pascal's God I can think of nothing better.

Keep busy is the rule of men
too shrewd to be too wise.
There is no horror in the air
but where we realize.

As for the Cyranos of Existentialism, let them explain to me why they make ugly faces at "alibis" and vociferate about "authenticity" and "good faith." First they demolish the metaphysical props which used to hold up the world of absolute values (no quarrel there), and then they beatify their own value of "authenticity" and fulminate against the *salauds* of the bourgeoisie. Fulminate on what grounds, if you please, when your very premise is that fulminations are groundless? Why is "authenticity" better than lying? If I am "free," then I am surely as free to live with illusions and make money as to face the ultimate emptiness. But why belabor Existentialism? Today is the nineteenth of September, 1975, and Sartre, though still alive, is himself aware that he is being forgotten. Other heroes of thought are sending fresh shock-notions into the field. At the perimeter, the wise man abides.

The metaphysical and the political temperaments are nearly incompatible. Mostly the political and the metaphysical man ignore each other; they live in different boroughs of the City of Intellect. It is a minor peculiarity of mine that I am a metaphysical man who visits the other part of town, stares at the bustle, and *then* shrugs his shoulders. I have before me a postcard written me by Eric Bentley, whose commitment to political life is nothing if not ardent. He is commenting on the poem entitled "Words for John Strachey's *On The Prevention of War*":

> John Strachey was his simple name.
> In Britain flew his middling fame.
>
> He thought of war. His manly spirit shook.
> To kill off war he wrote a book.
>
> The H-bomb would exterminate us all.
> Therefore (he reasoned) let it never fall.
>
> John Strachey hoped that realistic negotiation
> Would avert unthinkable obliteration.
>
> We shall (he wrote) survive, if we agree
> Upon a Super-Power World Authority.
>
> Already he detected "a new attitude of mind."
> With this the book came out and the reviews were kind.
>
> But then he died. John Strachey, looking forward, died.
> No H-bomb struck him, just the regular foul scythe.
>
> John Strachey, after all, one truth forgot:
> Man may survive, but men do not.

"I have not read Strachey's book," Mr. Bentley writes, "so cannot judge if there is a reference here I don't catch. Within the confines of the poem itself your argument is quite unpersuasive. I mean simply there is no contradiction between knowing that one will die and believing one can prevent mass murder. Did Strachey really forget the obvious?"

I replied that I knew no more about Strachey and his book than about the man in the moon. I had seen it reviewed in *The New Statesman* or *The Times Literary Supplement* and was lugubriously amused that so hearty and optimistic a political writer should have died suddenly after the completion of his tract. I hope, by the way, that I have captured in my couplets the soggy flatness of these political platitudes, at any rate as they reached me from the review. If I have been unfair to the late Mr. Strachey, we will remember that poetry must be "strong" (as Professor Bloom, always elegant in his vapors, puts it), not upright; interesting, not fair-minded.

I confessed to Mr. Bentley that his objection had a great deal of merit. *Logically* speaking, why should the metaphysical and the political temperaments clash? Plato proved in his own person that comtemplation of the Idea and fidgeting at the State can preoccupy the same person; and so, for that matter, did Sartre. And Shaw. But in general, and speaking now not logically but psychologically, your political activist does little woolgathering over ultimate realities or even his own mortality. The representatives of this opposition in our own times are Brecht and Ionesco, the latter all impregnated with the fluids of existential anguish and burdened with the anxieties of extinction, the former interested only in people getting decently fed and housed. Actually, the metaphysical man continues though he reverses the maxim of religion. The priest said to the hungry man: "Be calm, don't agitate, God will reward you after you die," and the Ionescos say: "Be calm, don't agitate, soon you're going to be annihilated anyway." Both sigh, "What's the use?" To the metaphysical man, the political man seems shallow. To the political man, the metaphysical man seems useless. The political man cries out, "In the meantime, what?" True we must die, true it is all futile in the end, but in the meantime, shall we not feed the hungry and "prevent mass murder"? This is logically flawless, and psychologically not unthinkable. But it so happens that most men lack the "psychic energy" to be both Brecht and Ionesco. Or shall we get from Samuel Beckett's pen, before he himself crumbles to zero, a play about terrorism in Belfast?

As for right and wrong, we can nag and twit the Stracheys of the world for ignoring—they are so damnably busy!—the abyss all around us; but I admit that the Stracheys can upbraid the Becketts with as much justice, and maybe more, for taking their lazy ease in the cave of metaphysical despair while Bangladesh starves.

Am I suspiciously glib when I protest that political action is mostly a knocking down of one monument to build another, or razing a slum in one place to get materials for the next one somewhere else? For when all the fine reasons are given, my political quiescence might be better explained as mere selfish caution, laziness, cowardice, and regard for my own ease. Having found my niche in the world, I have no fight of my own to take up. Bangladesh breaks my heart; but I am not flying there to help. Snug, I stay home. The thought of Bangladesh exhausts me; hopeless, I say, hopeless; why do these wretches keep reproducing? I feel with Eliot the weariness which comes of staring at mankind, cycle after cycle, generation after generation, snarling, clawing, suffering, dying, and begetting, while the political activists run to and fro "applying remedies." Behold, after all the remedies applied since the Pleistocene, behold the gas chambers, behold Bangladesh.

But as to my cowardice, why, it is no use concealing it. I am, I have to confess it, more likely to adapt myself to a tyranny, even when it bears down hard upon myself, than to join the guerrilla fighters. I will try my utmost, and let myself be reduced to dry bread, so as not to do harm to others; but I am too timid to bear arms or even carry dangerous messages. I am an odious compromiser. I want to be inconspicuous. Under threat of torture and death, I would denounce. All I can boast of is a negative virtue. I would not take high posts under a tyranny, I would not aggrandize or enrich myself at the expense of the fighters, and I would give fair warning, in one way or another, of the limits of my courage. I would say, in effect, "Count on me thus far, but no farther." On the day of liberation, I would be counted neither a traitor nor a hero.

"Giving up" is usually my first response to a difficulty, and often my last as well.

And so we clamber down from grandiose principles to very intimate weaknesses which were declaring themselves already in the child. It is hard to be a writer without pretending, if only between the lines, that one is always thinking about Mankind, the Death of the Gods, Metaphysical Anguish, and the like. And the critics are always among us to confirm these noble concerns of ours. Their own livelihood depends on it. But when I look honestly at the role this metaphysical disposition of mine plays in my emotional life, I recognize after all that Nature created thinking "the better to eat you with, my child," and not for elucubrations concerning ontological ultimates. For even though I hold sacred

> this intellectual being,
> Those thoughts that wander through Eternity;

even though I contemplate with fascinated melancholy my speck-like being, at once the "climax of creation" and a routine conglomerate of transient Lucretian atoms; even though I love to be led into the depths of matter and energy, living or unliving, by a scientist with a philosopical turn of mind; even though thoughts of mortality gnaw at my pleasures, my hopes, and my ambitions; even though I am often impatient with my daily duties and the common chit-chat of existence because the giddy depths of the Universe beckon to me; still, are the greatest emotions of my life *there*? Are anyone's? Does metaphysics ever overwhelm a life? It does, I think, but very seldom; and when it does, the rest of mankind, and the wiser heads among them, are apt to call the victim unbalanced. Granted that in the days when metaphysics meant, in effect, theology, the phenomenon of a life wholly dominated by Eternity was less exceptional and well within normalcy. But why so? Because the Ultimate had a face then; because it spoke (if I may so put it) of lollipops and spankings; it was, in short, kin to our animal. Hence we are not surprised to find ecstacy here and wanhope there, not as a "manner of speaking," or "under certain conditions," but as genuine invaders of the whole creature. But today even despair is faceless; it comes not from our live disobedience to the Father, but from the inexistence of that Father—from the sense of our extinction, and then

the unimportance even of that. This brooding is too distant from
our animal selves to take complete possession of us.

In this light, another poem becomes consistent with the rest:

Wounded Philosopher

They note that I am glum. I tell them why.
Crime is not crime. Love is self-tickle. The sun petrifies.
Try is cracked. God dissolved. Undamned I die.

Are these not cause enough? They nod, impressed, I see.
Nitwits. My woman left. I cry.

Explanatory note
Shall ontologic pain be more
Than (say) my thumb caught in the door?

This is not so different from the old and ever amusing stories
(is there not one in *Rasselas*?) of stoical philosophers who collapse into ordinary foaming-at-the-mouth humanity when ad-
versity lights on them instead of their neighbors. Nature—
again—has seen to it that a thumb caught in a door shall be more
painful than the gloomiest metaphysical conclusion, yes, than
the very death of God which involves our own. If a species is to
survive—and Nature planted survival as the direction of organic
existence as indifferently as she determined the boiling temperature of water—then a sensitivity to physical injury is of supreme
importance. So of course is mating, and the grief over the failure
to mate: cruel Amaryllis. But philosophical gloom plays no
biological role at all, therefore it makes us neither cry nor scream.

I have quite forgotten when and why this last poem got itself
written, but it must have been at a moment, in my younger days,
when I became amused at my own grief over a foiled romance. I
had walked with the success of a Tamino through the shattering
revelation that morality has no foundation; that all actions are
hedonically motivated; that the solar system must perish; that
achievement ever falls short of hope; that God is a legend; and
that even the consolation of being damned in hell is denied us;
but what I could not endure was that some Milly or Jenny should
have jilted me in favor of a biped two inches taller than I.

All the same, my aversion to homely activities such as arranging for a loan, chatting with an aunt, playing tennis, mending an appliance, investing in convertible debentures, and what have you, remains a fact of my existence. And if ever this aversion had lain concealed from my consciousness, the few years I have spent, off and on, producing plays (on a very modest scale, like everything else I do) would have brought it up to the surface. I became a playwright long ago without ever being stage-struck, and so must sign myself a son, with or without talent, of Racine rather than Molière. I may enjoy going to a rehearsal or two, I exchange many useful notes with my director, and I am elated when a line in a play, or a corridor between two lines, is made new-bright by an inflection or a gesture which actor or director has imagined. In Tennessee Williams's *The Eccentricities of a Nightingale*, which we staged in 1973, our director, Shirley Marneus, thought of having the crazy mother play a Christmas ditty on Alma's piano. She played a few bars, then began to grope, then lost her way and stopped; and the ravaging grief on the actress's face is a sight I shall never forget, though I saw it some twenty times at rehearsals and performances. Nothing of this is in Williams, yet neither was it some emptily clever imposition upon Williams by a director anxious to shine. Like all superb directing touches, it accented or developed a theme already so well displayed by the author that even an alert spectator would take it for a stage direction in the printed text. Such are the only true illuminations in the theater.

But for the rest—the set, the lights, the props, the accounts to be kept, the checks to be written, the schedules, the leaflets, the mailings—well, I have done it all, I know it is good for my soul, one must get one's fingernails dirty in this world, yet it all scrapes against my grain. Others surmise it too. They refuse to believe that I have myself, and more than once, hired, loaded, and driven a massive truck. My "image"—as they say nowadays—is that of a *noli me tangere* absentee; people are always surprised when they hear of me painting a wall or puttying a roof. Many years ago, when I was a dirty soldier stationed in Japan, a delicate Japanese girl I knew burst into tears when she caught a glimpse of me in my fatigues.

I do it, but it frantically bores me to worry about a kerosene lamp for *Ghosts*—when shall we pick it up? who will bring it over? how much deposit is wanted? And it bores me to hear the same lines rehearsed indefatigably hour after hour, week after week—when I could be dreaming of "the first and the last" of things. Not even my raging vanity serves me here; the kerosene lamps and the rehearsals for my own plays bore me too.

FROM CHIHUAHUA
TO THE BORDER

From Chihuahua to the Border

What they do out there, the mountains, is stand
stark useless; bleach (but why?) glued to the sun;
not one green hair grows on these rumps nor is heard
one woosh of a wing or grumble of a throat.
The road's a slap at them they don't know how to feel.
They wall us up (driving north) on either side of one
brown prostrate earth, we give them blank for blank,
until oh God who was it winked at them?
You, you, behind my yawn, you femurs,
ribcage, mandibles, sworn friends to me, you
plotting with foreigners, assassins in my house!

No, no, we love you, chime the bones; drive on, drive on.

"**D**riving north." That was in the year 1959, when my wife-
to-be and I spent a summer together in Mexico. The road we took
both going and returning was that grim ribbon which traverses
New Mexico and Mexico's inland center, arid, dusty, cutting
through torpid villages where now and then a policeman directs
traffic from the top of a box marked Coca-Cola.

Those were busy poetic years for me. Poetry composed itself in
my very sleep. I would leap out of bed to jot down two lines.
Altogether, if my reckoning is correct, some twenty years of
"inspiration" were granted me—and if, in spite of the inverted
commas I have prudently placed around the word, it strikes you
as fatuous, bear in mind that the mediocre enjoy the same exaltations as the gifted. The difference appears in the product, the
similarity in the invisible passion that made it. Dunces, in short,
also leap out of bed inspired. Eventually my imagination, verve

First published in *The Dalhousie Review*, Winter 1983.

and hopefulness—even my vocabulary—began to slacken and shrink, and I was virtuous enough not to beat the weary mule.

Title and landscape notwithstanding, my poem is hardly *about* Mexico. What it *is* about I have a mind to speak of at some moderate, unoppressive length. But to say "Chihuahua" without mulling over Mexico, and to mull over Mexico without grieving a while over human misery, is proving impossible to me. In a truly *human* being, ethics must precede metaphysics. The ultimates can always wait. Let them do so now the length of a few pages. . . .

I am no lover of picturesque poverty. Holland is my predilection (need I say more?)—and poverty which I cannot relieve merely breaks my heart. I like a plump, green, well-watered landscape in which no one goes hungry and uncared-for in sickness and old age, where the houses are in good repair and freshly painted, the shops paunchy with merchandise, the clothing colorful and neat. Neatness—should a poet admit it?—is my predilection too. No wonder I have not gone back to Mexico for a second visit, though I live next door to it.

I am not blind to the notorious beauties of Mexico. Once one rises onto the great central plateau and enters the realm of the Conquerors, the landscape dazzles, the clouds are arrayed in voluble billows as if to pose for a Master of the Baroque, and this would be paradise were it not for the marks everywhere upon the human settlements of misery, bad health, ignorance, and violence. In Mexico I renew, on the rebound, my (tempered) admiration for the singular achievements of that Western bourgeoisie which we accredited artists have been mauling so efficiently for nearly two centuries. How lustily we have pummeled the "commercial interests"! We men of letters can even boast of having made up a kind of collective John the Baptist to Marx the Redeemer. We preluded on the keyboard from him, and for his Apostles. While we pummel away, however, and clasp the poor to our bosoms—as metaphorically as possible—the poor have the excellent sense to use our pamphlets, money, novels, votes, and agitation only so far as these will help them up into the very middle class we love them for not belonging to. Once there, they gladly tolerate our lampoons, for they had rather be rich and pummeled than poor and patronized.

Here then is one reason why artists are so particularly fond of Mexico. The poor seem somehow more authentic to them, though why a brazier is more authentic than an all-electric kitchen quite escapes me. Not that authenticity (whatever that means) interests me a great deal anyhow. Some finer souls carry their fastidious devotion to the point of adopting these "primitive customs," shedding the "materialistic trappings of our industrial society," and learning to rejoice in crumbling walls, makeshift furniture, homespun rags, and gastroenteritis. They attract the stupefied attention of their barefooted neighbors, who, endowed with sense instead of genius, regard them as harmless loonies and continue to hope, pray, sometimes work, and if possible steal in order to buy plastic goods (long live plastic goods) and large automobiles.

The genuine beauties of Mexico, apart from its natural scenery, are mostly the legacy of the wicked Spanish occupation, dispossession, and exploitation. As happens so often, beauty and injustice go hand in hand, posing a moral dilemma which no one seems to notice but which has long bedeviled me. It is an inconvenient and unpresentable phenomenon. Good art is usually a child of luxury, and luxury is seldom a child of justice. This is apparent enough in Europe to anyone who cares to reflect upon the socioeconomic origins of almost all its beauties; but the unsavory truth is even more obvious in Mexico, where the Indians—to put it succinctly—toiled unto death in the mines so churches and palaces could be silvered over. In our own proletocracies, democratic or totalitarian, we can speak in a rough and ready fashion of a reliable inverse correlation between social justice and aesthetic achievement. The repulsive but well-meant housing blocks for the masses East and West provide the picture that stands for a thousand words.

Naturally these large human tides do not operate by clockwork, and there are, for reasons amenable to our reason, notable pockets of exception. But my heart goes out to nations or cultures in which an equilibrium of sorts came about between social justice and aesthetic refinement. In Holland, for instance, but also in colonial New England. In these and other places, extreme luxury and beauty were "renounced" in favor of such an equilibrium. Dutch and New England beauty fell short of Italian beauty, but Italian social justice fell short of Dutch and New England social justice. More social justice means less beauty, but that which remains is more wholesome for that very reason. It refreshes the mind without oppressing our thoughts with ideas of slave labor, intense poverty, disease, and Neronism. The ethical and aesthetic reach an accommodation.

I would not care to have these historical ideas of mine examined too minutely. There is something of the useful fiction in them. But also, I hope, of usable truth.

While I was conscious of the wrongdoings of the builders of Guanajuato and Taxco, this did not and does not to this day trigger in me any particular outbreak of love for their victims. I am free of that automatic twitch. We are always supposing that the oppressed are more admirable than their tormentors. But the little I know about pre-Columbian Mexico has failed to give me fits of nostalgia. The cruelties of the Spaniards but superseded the crimes of their victims. Today we hear grisly stories about the systematic extermination of the Amazonian Indians. But I do not turn instantly sentimental over these same Indians, extolling their chants and stories and customs at the expense of our own dirty civilization. A few years ago a white woman emerged from the jungles of the Amazon. She had been captured by an Indian tribe before she was ten years old, had lived with them, had married an Indian, and had remained with them until the day when, fearing for her life in one of the eternal wars which these picturesque and endearing tribes fight against one another, she had finally made her way back to civilization. The perfectly artless account of her life that she gave to some Italian anthropologists was such as to make a sentimentalist break out in perspiration. Amidst a hundred tales of truceless wars and murders in these unpolluted jungles, one episode has settled for good in my mind. A party of Indians is attacked and overpowered by some enemy warriors. The men escape or are killed in combat. The women and girls become prizes (the little white girl among them). But the boys are grabbed by the feet, swung, and their skulls smashed against a tree.

The cruelties of the Aztecs are notorious, and so are those of the North American Indians. I am not refusing to believe that "savages" can live at peace with one another. But so can the Swedes. Naked or dressed, man is an inherently irritable creature and turns amiable only under a certain constellation of external factors (have they ever been named and studied?) which can occur in the jungle, the savannah, or the city. There is, at any rate, no point in beating our civilization with a primitive's stick.

Nor did I fall into an ecstasy over pre-Columbian art. I paid dutiful visits to the pyramids, the temple sites, the ruins, the museums, always "impressed," but seldom imbued with the intense joy I require of art, whether comic or tragic. Pre-Columbian art proved too relentlessly thick, gnarled, grotesque, tormented and ferocious to suit me. These are all authentic *qualities* of course; but it so happens that, mild myself, I like them in moderation, and prefer them set off against fairer qualities—say, a gargoyle in a cathedral; while I am perfectly content when these fairer qualities beckon to me without those of ferocious power. For me, the sweetness, the pity, and the complex intellectual precision sometimes achieved in our advanced civilizations are not to be bartered for the accomplishments of primitive groups, whether in the arts or in matters of wisdom. It is good to know what they have wrought, and it would be stupid to deny that they can give us lessons (as the child can lesson the adult), for every human advance comports some losses, so that a turn of the head backward is never a waste of time—when Sèvres flood the market, an infusion of Papua is healthy—but it is sheer frowardness to hold up the primitive like a cross to lead us into battle.

While lingering among Aztec, Toltec, and Mayan vestiges, I will confess in an aside that I am not your man for even the best of ruins. You will find me walking rather disconsolately amidst heaps of stones, outlines of bathhouses, recesses for kitchens, shattered columns (unless arranged picturesquely by Chance), and segments of pavement. I do not require a few shards of pottery to grow melancholy over the leveling passage of time and the evanescence of things. In Rome look for me not in the Forum but on the Campidoglio, in the evening, when it lies in its tender lights, vunerable and harmonious above its stairs—those cascades hurrying upward to salute Marcus Aurelius. Better study a ruin in a text than sweat over it in the summer sun. After the Campidoglio you can find me with Bernini on the Piazza Navona. Aztec pyramids indeed! Think too of the unbelievable leap from those mountains in northern Mexico to the Piazza Navona. Is there a planet, among those millions of cultured and developed earths which, we are assured, wander the fearful yonders of the universe, wider and wilder than ours in its contrasts?

Many years ago I was walking along the remains of the Roman wall in England, when I met a laborer chipping away at some stones. "What are you doing?" I asked. "Mending the ruin," he replied. Mend away, friend, mend away.

As I write these pages about my summer in Mexico, I discover that I have neither the desire nor the talent to set down the dozens of intimate contours of a voyage, the flavor of a remark dropped by someone in a café, the colors of a marketplace, the juices dripping from a melon, the cry of a parrot, the reek of buses, a good diarrhea in Taxco, the night one sleeps all dressed in a hotel room out of sheer disgust, dinner among the flamingos in Mexico City . . . No, consult someone else, my patience fails me.

Still, I want to retrieve an experience, on a sunny and windy afternoon God knows where, that showed me the grain of truth in the Romantic vision of the wise, profound, genuine, unlettered therefore unspoiled peasant—a truth admissible only if we complete the picture, and are willing to add the dark colors—the brutalities, the diseases, the vicious superstitions. Be that as it may, Adriana and I drove up a hillock one afternoon, using a hazardous dirt road until it lost itself in a pile of grass; then walked to the top, which was flattened out. The height was modest, yet the prospect all around was ample. We stood on the site of some archaeological diggings into the tombs of ancient kings and their followers. The scientists were absent that day, their shack stood empty—we peeked inside and found it full of books—and the site was guarded by a native, a youngish melancholy man with an inevitable mustache, a wife whom we did not see, a vague but large number of children, and merry chickens. As my wife's Spanish is excellent, and mine passable, we had no problems with our Mexican, who was glad to see a couple of visitors. He was as true and unspoiled and perhaps noble a son of the earth as one could wish to find in a moist travelogue. He spoke in a gentle voice about the ancient rulers. When they died, their wives and their retainers were dispatched for company. He thought this admirable. "If I had a master, I would die with him too," he said (more or less) with simple artless words. Every now and then, as if coming to the end of a paragraph, he would complete a portion of a story with a "según la relación de Michoacan"—so speaks the chronicle of Michoacan—as if to give his tale a certitude which it would have lacked as one man's report. This almost sad refrain has remained with me like a music. Something out of the lungs of human history was blowing over us that afternoon. We sat on one of the funeral mounds, listening to this bard of the earth. He pointed to a cemetery in the distance, abortively surrounded by three walls. A team of officials—from the United Nations, we gathered—had been to the village; and they had scolded the villagers: "Aren't you ashamed to leave your graveyard exposed on all sides; look at the cows, look at the pigs there, grubbing among your dead!" The villagers had been ashamed. They began to build the walls. Then the team left. Three walls were completed, the fourth was never built. The cows and the pigs were still foraging among the dead. It was not very decent. Furthermore the strangers tried to keep the men in the village from drinking and shooting so much. And they built latrines. Once a little girl of his had been very sick. He made a vow to Our Lady up there, far up on another hill—he would crawl on his knees all the way from the village to light candles to her if the little girl recovered. She did. He crawled and crawled. His knees were bleeding.

The afternoon wore on. Our host dabbled in sculpture. His habit was to leaf through the books of his employers, and when he had time he hammered away at the red, porous stone of the region. What he came up with was original; he clearly did not try to copy the photographs, he allowed them to give him ideas—which were authentically Mexican, of course—not Sèvres!—strong ideas and deeply his own after all. We took two of the pieces along; they stand in our garden to this day. As for the world outside, he knew it only by hearsay. He had heard that in the cities—in the capital, for instance—people had houses on top of other people—he had trouble expressing the strange notion of houses several stories high. One day he would go see for himself. . .

So then I too have spent a few hours on an Aran island, and assured myself that there is indeed a poetry of the people, something beautiful in that it has been generated slowly, "organically," without imposition from that "above" which can be the Intellectuals, or the Officials, or Big Business—we feel it at once to be as true as the call of an animal. If we do not romanticize this poetry and this wisdom, we are allowed to say that something precious is lost when we move on, and we are allowed to turn our heads backward and sigh. But to give up our knowledge of the atom's structure, to give up Bach, to give up the Campidoglio in order to return to the folk, such a thought is monstrous. For myself, I am so far gone that I would not even give up my French sauces and wines for the beauties of primitive existence. And finally, if I admired the Mexican man on the hill, it was not in order to forget that we too counter our gas-chamber rabble with a host of "beautiful souls." Simple cultures produce them, and refined civilizations produce them.

In the capital we had rented an apartment for a month on the fourth "house above house" of a new building, never quite finished and already crumbling, like all the ambitious technological goods of poor countries. One evening a mouse jumped out of the oven door just as my wife was bending over to start the evening meal. The elevator did not work and perhaps never would. We were young and sturdy and could manage the ups and downs with ease, but we worried at first about the rubbish disposal. On the appointed day, however, a little girl appeared, not quite as tall as the trashcan and thoroughly undernourished. Filled with pity and shame, but freezing my impulse to carry the load for her, I watched her drag it painfully out the door and down the stairs. Anything else would have been impertinent. She would not have thanked me. This was her appointed task. A coin or two might be had from it, dutifully delivered to her father, the concierge. Vacationing foreigners should not break in with outlandish charities. There and elsewhere (giving half-eaten rolls to beggars and the like) I also learned the rule that where misery is the rule, the well-to-do must stiffen against compassion or be annihilated by it. Misery besieges them on every side, day after day; and what is the good of confessing, "I am one of the oppressors?" This may work in the long run, it may be historically significant and useful, it may help change the nation for the better, and therefore such recognitions should be abetted, but on a Thursday afternoon, when the hundred and fifty-fifth hungry child of the week begs you for money, what do you do in order to survive yourself? What does even a revolutionary do as he crosses the town amidst the crippled beggars, the deformed old men sleeping on benches, the mothers picking at the refuse of a restaurant? He too waves them aside. Or no longer sees them.

Here nevertheless a meanness of mine comes to haunt me again. We had dined in the company of another young couple in a restaurant where some mariachi players were performing—odious music!—and felt a crescendo of vexation at the well-organized extortions practiced upon us by the management. The charges were outrageous, the extras cropped up on every side, and when it was all over we left in a sullen mood. My car was parked near the entrance. The uniformed doorman hurried up to it and performed his minor duties. I took in his pathetically baggy trousers and ill-fitting tunic—what is more abject than a *grand gala* uniform three sizes too large?—and the look—what shall I say?—not of tragic suffering—no, simply pain and resignation when I angrily ignored his outstretched hand and drove away. The face showed in the rearview mirror for a second, perfectly void of anger. My own evaporated at once. I wanted to drive back, but could not bring myself to turn the car around, explain to my wife and friends, and issue regally to bestow a gratification on the poor devil . . . How often, and for how many years, the image of that shabby *chasseur* has come back to reproach me. Was it his fault they were cheating me inside? None of their wicked gains trickled down to him.

At the end of our summer in Mexico, we drove north out of Chihuahua one morning before breakfast, and stopped at a restaurant midway to the border. There we got our last grime and peeling walls, and took our last prudent measures—no water, no butter, no milk. Then into the desert again, the vast beautiful horror of which my poem is a memory, and then, unbelievably, Texas—I think it was Texas—or was it New Mexico? And that time only, never before and never after—an exaltation of patriotism swelled in my ribcage. I could have kissed the asphalt. We halted at a bright chromium-and-plastic "Eats," drank the water, spread the butter, poured the milk, and marveled after three months at the smiles and the cleanliness. Ah, those Indians are not a cheerful race! They are not poor in the Neapolitan way. Here was my white-toothed America again, "Hi folks, what'll it be?"

One surge of this love of America has taught me for the rest of

my life the visceral reality of such attachments; I can now reproduce the emotion of a Yank in Asia who gets news of the latest
baseball score. If I were a novelist, I would not need notebooks
filled with a hundred "real experiences." Imagination's business
is to make do with one.

Although we know how moth-eaten the ancient distinction
between the soul and body is, we cannot help continuing to feel
it, and therefore to entertain a kind of hostility toward these
bones and guts and fibers which sustain and indeed create our
consciousness, and then extinguish it. In this support and sustenance, they are at one with that portion of Nature—the earth—
which feeds and oxygenates us, and then kills and buries us. In
all strictness of thought, my poem could have chosen the green
hills of Northumberland as aptly as the brown mountains of
Chihuahua, but the feeling of death transpires more easily from
the latter, and the bones seem to be more at home there. In that
setting my spirit feels more forsaken, embedded in the body,
which in its turn is embedded in the bleak universe, than it does
where the birds give their specious gaiety to the scenery and the
saps fool us for a while into delusions of friendliness.

As I see it, we are as right to distinguish between spirit (or soul,
or mind) and body as to discriminate between lungs and stomach. I am aware that spirit is thought, that thought is (almost
exclusively) language submuttered, and that language is an "electrochemical" activity of the brain. I place that term between
slightly ironical flicks only because in another generation or two
some other word will be in fashion. The argument will remain
the same, however: mind and flesh are both made of the same
"natural stuff." But this kinship does not prevent them from
engaging in frequent civil wars, simply because each organ of
each organism seeks to maintain its own coherence, vigor, and
life. It has "its own interest at heart"—that of surviving, yes, but
more specifically, that of continuing to play its own game: digesting, breathing, squirting hormones, and the rest. The brain's
characteristic game (I mean that portion of the brain which is
most properly human) is to think, and our desire for immortal
life is little more than the brain's urge to persist in its own
inherent function. Its dislike of death corresponds to the stom-

ach's resistance to rancid food. The stomach expresses itself through certain contractions and secretions of chemicals, the brain through its alarmed and defiant thoughts.

One of these thoughts is that thinking is a product of the all too mortal brain. Another is how much lovelier it would be for our thinking if thought were an eternal, distinct, insubstantial substance (called "spirit") which only transiently condescended to occupy a room in our house of flesh. What a benefit to homeostasis that would be! Nor should we wonder that, if the brain emits thought, it also emits thought about thought, which is but another thought. Why not? The poem, in short, continues to stand under the "one substance" view of the universe: it does not imply a radical division between body and soul.

The *feelings* in which these thoughts bask take us even deeper into the "one substance" philosophy. All our feelings can be sorted out into the two categories of pleasure (favorable) and pain (unfavorable). If we translate this into a primal attraction and repulsion, we realize, perhaps with a shock, that even our most human emotions (resentment, for example) unite us, not only with the most primitive organisms, but with the entire universe, alive or unalive. For the inorganic is also constituted and agitated primordially through attraction and repulsion, the going toward and the distancing from. Step by step up the chemical ladder of complexity, this to and from becomes, in living organisms, pleasure and pain, and eventually affection and hostility—and we could write a fairy tale in which the negatively charged particles rush toward the positively charged particles with a feeling of love!

But what is the ultimate and irreducible reason for the attraction and the repulsion of two units of the universe? What is the final physical explanation? After what reason given can no further reason be asked? And: are these questions unanswerable? If so, why so?

The scientific method itself, which has my full allegiance, suggests that *any* human concept of the universe collapses at the outermost edge. The totality of the universe is not even *theoretically* apprehensible by means of the senses we possess and the equipment we manufacture to stretch our senses. We know that even though we may be wanting a few senses, having three or four more would still keep Kant's Thing-in-itself out of our reach, assuming that anything can be conceived of as being in itself. Furthermore, our radical inadequacy to the universe stares us in the face as frankly as a brick wall. Our notions of time and space lead us to a ridiculous dead end at the limits of the universe. Scientists shrug their shoulders. It is none of *their* business, they say. Well, whose business is it? Philosophers know even less about it, and surely you will not ask your local archbishop? Science pursues time, space, and causation as far as its legs will run, and then turns around and runs back. For the ultimate questions are unanswerable not because we fail to see sharply enough: not because mathematicians have yet to discover the formulas; and not because our instruments need more refinement. The ultimate questions are not in the same category as, for example, the question how many grains of sand there are in the world, which is only "technically" unanswerable. No. The ultimates take us clear across the barrier of Nature as man can conceive it forever and ever from the "prison" of his own nature. This is what I mean when I say that man is *radically* limited. From which it follows ineluctably that something in the universe is itself radically *other* than "electrochemical forces" or whatever name we choose for our "one substance."

But what if this concept of radical otherness were to be applied to our consciousness too?—strange as it may seem that otherness should give a sign of its existence not only at the confines of causation, time, and space, "where words fail us," but pat in the middle of our own "living rooms," if I may so express it.

At the heart of this supposition is a distinction which I have purposely blurred up to this point, because it is not required for the poem: the poem makes sense strictly as the clash between two members of the same ontological club—an ontological civil war, in short. But now let us make trial of another idea: *thought is other than consciousness.* Even thought about thought is separable from consciousness. We say quite sensibly that we are conscious *of* thought, whereby we correctly imply that these two events are distinct. Thought (like feeling) is the "electrochemical" activity of a specific organ and as such belongs to the world of time, place, cause-and-effect along with the rest of the body; whereas our consciousness of thought and feeling appears to escape from that universal net.

I say *appears* to escape. For concerning consciousness, the first mystery is, is there a mystery?

Sometimes I am moved by philosophers and scientists who deny the otherness, the mystery. Perhaps "consciousness" is simply a word we happen to use for yet another activity of matter— or another function of energy—for example the scanning that one portion of the brain performs upon another. But perhaps this is not enough. And then I am moved by those who feel that this "internal illumination" (the expression has been ascribed to Einstein) is *other*.

Yet to ask what this otherness consists in is futile. We know only that our human constitution leaves us helpless to answer questions which that very constitution poses. Discourse takes us to a certain faraway point, and then a black hole swallows it: it vanishes. Every conceivable geometry of space—bent, returning upon itself, and so forth—remains inside the unbreachable prison of our "categories," to use Kant's term. But these categories are not Romantic inventions of ours or accidents implanted in us. Everything we know about the evolution of living creatures implies that all of them, including man, adapt themselves to conditions laid out before any life existed in the universe. Does the earth's atmosphere happen to let certain wave-lengths through to the surface while barring others? Very well: our organs conform by seeing the ones and not seeing the others. By the same token, we do not impose the categories of time, space, and causation on the universe. The universe imposes them on us—if we want to live. We have inherited from the lowliest bacterium a humble subservience to these categories. Therefore time and space, and the chaining of events under them, can be thought of as the conditions that sprang out, with the Primal Explosion, from the radical otherness that was itself neither time nor space. Better still, they can be regarded as *constituting* the Primal Explosion, so that *they were* and *the universe was* are synonyms; while the question how that otherness sparked, or converted itself into, our very own universe must remain buried, since only our side of the tracks can be explored.

I am arguing here—with much trepidation—that a similar *otherness* faces us as soon as we separate consciousness from the thoughts and feelings which can and do exist without it, in animals, in infants, and very often in full-grown men and women. Consciousness, like time and space, seems to have one foot (so to speak) in our world of matter and energy, and the other in unutterable strangeness.

Specifically, consciousness, if it exists, is an absolute terminus. I mean: it causes nothing. It is itself obviously caused by the matter/energy of the human brain when the latter is functioning at high capacity, when we say of it that it focuses, or attends. But, uniquely among all known phenomena, it is an effect without ever being a cause. We might think of it as the useless, luxurious "humming of the machine"—provided we allow this humming to be an unutterable strangeness, since, unlike the sound waves produced by ordinary humming, it produces no effect whatsoever. Or again: we can call it the clarity in which we dwell when thoughts or feelings peak. At a certain peak of activity, the "veil is rent" (the veil that obscures the thoughts and feelings of animals, of infants, and often our own)—and the electrochemical forces are transfigured.

Remember that, even as I write these words, I remain in doubt. Is this supposed illumination but an "aspect" of neuronal activity? But all aspects of all things are co-equal perceptions that strike us (directly or through instruments) in parallel or convergently. Thus at one moment we see a rose as a beautiful flower, at another as a heap of atoms. These indeed are aspects. But while our instruments are able to catch the chemistry and electricity of our thinking and feeling, so that we can in a real sense perceive them, neither they nor our senses can catch our consciousness of these thoughts and feelings, since consciousness is incapable of acting upon any instrument. We are conscious of setting up the instruments meant to catch our consciousness, but conscious of their capturing only that which we are conscious of (namely thoughts and feelings). So perhaps this consciousness is not a mere "aspect" that we can perceive alongside other aspects. It is as though a butterfly were holding the net that is meant to catch it. Never can we get *in back* of this consciousness: it is always itself in back.

Nor is it easy to account for the oddity of consciousness by treating it as an emergence. An emergence is a quality or property of a highly complicated system which the parts of the system cannot produce *until* connected together as a system. We know that adding items to a system can sometimes do much more than merely make the system bigger. At a certain point, quite startling and unexpected properties emerge. And this seems for a moment, philosophically speaking, an adequate approach to consciousness, which undoubtedly emerges at a certain point of accretion and complication in our billions of neurons. Yet again, emergent properties *behave*; they have detectable effects; they are part and parcel of the electrochemical realities; while consciousness remains (it would seem) half in and half out of these realities. Therefore, though still teased by my doubt, I continue.

Consciousness is of thought, emotion, perception, and volition. We may think of it as their implosion, or glow, or mirror, or even receptacle, though all such terms are necessarily lame. They are lame, of course, because they necessarily belong to our "electrochemical" world; we have no "strange" terms from that "other" realm with which to describe it. We are certain only that consciousness does not disturb the world. Having no effect whatsoever, it is not subject to measurement, experimentation, alteration. We know how to snuff it out (nothing, alas, is easier), without knowing what it is. It can be left out of all scientific observations: perfectly and unalterably passive, it is incapable of modifying a result, it is never even an infinitesimal factor neglected only for practical reasons—it is a perfect zero in the world of material energy in which we move. And it has no "survival value" for the species. No wonder, says Teilhard de Chardin, that it has been ignored by science. It exists—we "see" it—but it does not behave. More: its existence is the central event of our lives. For when we say that we want the self to survive, we do not mean the mere thought, "I am I," or "I am John Doe," but the implosion of clarity in which the thought swims: the consciousness of self.

One charm of this point of view is that it does not smuggle free will into our behavior. Consciousness has nothing to do with the will except to register it. Volition, like emotion and cerebration and perception, proceeds in its world of material energy. It is subject to the ordinary laws of cause and effect, and is easily conceivable without its conscious reverberation, such as we guess it to be in animals and such as we know it to operate very often in ourselves. All one can say is that our illusion of free will probably derives from our helpless thoughts concerning our consciousness.

To argue that consciousness is perfectly passive is not to decry or deny our vaunted ability to make our minds control our bodies—to some extent. Man has always known that such control can be exercised, and this knowledge can be validated in spite of the superstitions and charlatanisms which have always polluted the "mind over matter" phenomenon. But the point is that this control refers us to thought, not to consciousness. And our thoughts are "electrochemical." So viewed, the impact of mind on matter appears as an entirely plausible interaction (within limits) of two elements belonging to the same ontological club. The stomach can act on the brain, and the brain can act on the stomach. Consciousness attends, but is irrelevant.

Does thinking exist without consciousness? It clearly does. True, our most complex cerebrations are necessarily conscious, for when the brain works above a certain threshold of intensity, it generates consciousness—what I have called the humming of the machine. But we guess that animal thinking fails to cross that threshold, we are all but sure that infant thinking is unconscious, and we know that crowds of unconscious thoughts crisscross our brains not only when we sleep but in our waking hours too. We know it—without the help of psychoanalysis—because now and then a few of these thoughts intensify suddenly enough to awaken our consciousness. As we become aware of these specific thoughts, we also grow conscious of the diffuse magma of thoughts out of which "bubbled" the important ones that sought the light. We cannot seize these lesser thoughts, but they surround the conscious ones like an aura. For the rest, our instruments confirm our individual experience, since they show a great deal of cerebral activity during certain phases of our sleep—thoughts that run helter-skelter over our sleep-loosened circuits, and most of them destined to remain subconscious.

I do not mean, however, that once our thoughts are intense enough to create consciousness, they immediately create *full* consciousness. Consciousness has its degrees; it does not obey an on/off or an all-or-none regulation. It dims and grows brighter before vanishing at one end or reaching perfection at the other—the latter when we concentrate all our thinking on the subject of ourselves: I am I. Hence I easily admit the possibility of a beginning of consciousness—a rudimentary consciousness—in the higher primates, just as it makes a beginning in the child. The guess that animals think without it when they think at all—in images, in smells, in tactile sensations, and so forth—remains reasonable, but a few beginnings of consciousness at the upper limits of primate life are not excluded.

As for computers, I am not much troubled by the question whether they will one day be conscious. Since I take our thinking as such to be purely "physical," I do not see why thinking of a sort should not be physically performed by a machine we manufacture for the purpose of thinking. But what results are to be expected from the profound chemical differences between computers and human beings? We already know that their thought-capacity is unlike ours—vastly better in some ways, clumsy in others. It remains for us to wonder whether consciousness—assuming it to be more than a word—is uniquely a property of our proteins, starches, nucleic acids and so on, or whether the components of a computer can generate it too. If they can, welcome! More consciousness can do us, or the universe, no harm. I do not begrudge it to the ape, and have no reason to be afraid of it in a machine.

Inevitably, having come this far, I need to say a word or two about the "mystical" reverberations of these views of mine, however cautiously I hold them. Scientists and philosophers who strongly feel the mystery of it all sometimes keep traveling until they arrive at positions one can call more or less religious. Their opponents suspect them of arriving there chiefly because they wanted or needed consolation. The world is full of tired scientists looking for spiritual refreshment. I, unfortunately, have no refreshment to offer. My tears do not govern my thoughts. The *otherness* we butt against simply tells me that we animals are not "adequate" to the ultimate universe. We apprehend it as the creatures we are "provincially." We can proceed to postulate that the number of such epistemological provinces is prodigious, perhaps "infinite." Furthermore they all coexist. They do not abolish one another. Now, even *a priori* we should think it unlikely that all these realities would exist merely side by side, without the least interference, like parallel slats. No, these beams into reality must cross one another now and then, and here and there—time and space must touch other "dimensions"—and where they do, the creature that stands at the beams' junction receives intimations of the reality beyond its own—or should we say athwart its own? This is where we human beings ask our unanswerable questions. But unanswerable as they are, they do not suggest—alas!—that were an answer forthcoming, it would bring us the consolations we expect from a religion, consolations without which religion does not interest us. In other words, nothing I have said opens so much as a chink through which we might catch a glimpse of a power friendly to us, or the least promise of survival after death. And I can only repeat, with a sigh: alas. I remain as I began, the fear at my throat, in love with my consciousness and cursing it all the while; loving, that is, everything in awareness except the awareness that itself will end. For I know how easily it vanishes in us even while we are alive. A minor relaxation in the physical activity of nervous tissue, an accident, an illness dim it and then switch it off. Here is an event apparently mysterious in its essence yet grossly physical in its origins. Must it die with the body that causes it, or shall we draw hope from the belief that it is in itself uncanny and other? But why should "uncanny and other" amount to an intimation of survival? In the Book of the Universe, the pages we cannot read are probably as bleak of comfort to us as those we can. My horror is intact.

Drive on, chime the bones, drive on.

SULLEN MYRMIDONS
POISON THE WEEDS

Sullen myrmidons poison the weeds
Lest an enemy survive.

In a ruin two lovers huddle.
A booted lout guffaws.

In his low brain one atom shifts.
We must love on.

— 1 —

You are free—I mean: the poem leaves you free—to stage this scene in the past, the present, or the future. We are all familiar with the spectacular prophecies of an earth reduced to rubble by atomic warfare, poisoned by the fumes and chemicals we spew into the elements, or self-devoured by the billions of famished creatures begetting billions more in a maniacal suffocation of the earth. Calmer spirits, calmer but almost equally grim, foresee a regimentation so strict as to make well-fed robots of us all. Others, more cheerful, promise that science and technology will more or less solve our problems, and spread our liberal demo-cratic ways under a docile sun trained to devote its energy to us for innumerable generations to come.

For myself, I lack the Nostradamus bump. I take global life to be so hair-raisingly complicated, and therefore so multifariously exposed to the unforeseeable—from a cure-all invention to an in-vasion from outer space by an exterminating virus—that one cannot invest one's trust in any prediction. It is true that the combination of advanced technology (which makes massive power available) and swarming populations seems to invite and even demand a rigid organization of humanity. But need it be horrible? Or will it be merely mediocre? The scenes anticipated by Dostoevsky, Huxley, and Orwell suggest that something inhuman is to be expected, and certainly something which man has never experienced before. But on the contrary. Our liberalism is the anomaly. Rigid organization is as old as mankind. Organization is in our blood. What creature is more minutely scheduled than our old friend, primitive man? If massive organization is what we are coming to, it will merely replicate, at a fully conscious and technologically refined level, the strict and complicated grammars which regulate both language and behavior in primitive societies. In our gloomings regarding a highly organized future society, we think we are frightened by regimentation when in actuality we fear *unfamiliar* rules, a far more primordial terror.

But—whether the regimentation to come, if it is to come at all, wears a cordial or a metallic face, it will probably remove both the ardent lovers and the booted louts from our world. There will be no huddled Tristans and Isoldes, no heroisms, no exaltations, but on the other hand the world will be rid of thugs running about with automatic weapons in the service of some Ugandan Caligula. One could fare worse. I, for one, might be talked into giving up the exuberances of liberty—high inventiveness, inspired fervors, the wild poetry of numberless despairs—in exchange for peace, good will, and cooled-down inventions, fervors, and poetries. Besides, when all is said and done, relying on something I make bold to call, over all objections, essential man—a something I see present in cave man and subsisting in any "brave new world"—I resist equating the regimentation of the future with an end to the old flesh and blood. The talk will not be all cybernetics, print-outs, and electromagnetic waves. The operator of a metallic monster of switches and toggles will call out forever to his passing buddy: "Make that two lumps in my coffee, Hank!"

Speculations. As I myself read the poem, it reeks of our present century. If we take these lovers, for example, to be more than boy and girl, if we think of their love in the widest sense, we can ask them to represent all that has made our century singularly humane: universal education, progressive taxation, unemployment benefits, health insurance, old-age pensions, concern for refugees, minorities, orphans, the insane, the blind, even animals—in short, our endless preoccupation with remedies for evil. Who fussed over crippled veterans in ancient Babylon? In eighteenth-century England? But on the other side stands the booted lout. The atrocities committed in our century have made it by far the most atrocious of all ages. But how can this be? How can these extremes cohabit so easily? That Western man should have become more benevolent between the Dark Ages and our own century seems normal. That he should *also* have regressed into an all but unimaginable brutality seems odd. For the moment, and altogether tentatively, I propose that a collusion of two causes is to blame: the first, that our brilliant technology had made it as easy to slaughter a million as a hundred (in the past, killing was hard work), and the second, that—how shall I put it?—the masses have been let loose, and the restraints of hereditary patrician honor, delicacy, and good taste, however tenuous they were, yet real albeit tenous, have utterly dissolved.

As the poem stands, it suggests that the presence and the endurance of love can, does, and will make a difference in the world. The booted lout is affected. But did I forget that influences work, alas, both ways? Does not an atom shift in the lovers' heads as well? Is not brutality a good teacher too? Perhaps in the end lover and lout come to a standoff. The existence of love at one end of the spectrum prevents brutal hatred from swamping mankind; the pressure of brutal hatred at the other keeps love from winning the race. In any event, there is no danger that love will ever surrender the battlefield to hate. For the louts *beget* the lovers. This is a predictable corollary of the principle according to which a reasonably satisfied society, regimented or otherwise, loses both extremes of passionate love and brutal hatred. We know that in time of war, or when a natural calamity falls on a nation, or when people groan under a regime they detest, there occurs a passionate drawing together of the sufferers: the Enemy creates an exhilarating and a vital solidarity. It is not cynicism, I hope, to point out that these increases in the "temperature" of love, these reinforcements of the almost chemical bonds among people under pressure, are useful to survival. They are, in short, adaptive. Therefore the more cruel the myrmidon, the tighter the lovers' embrace; the viler the society, the deeper the solidarities; and, paradoxically, the more favorable the social ambience, the more relaxed our attachments.

East Europeans who escape to the free, easy, and affluent pleasures of America discover to their sorrow that we are, though

friendly, indifferent to one another, and superficial in our friend-
ships. They become nostalgic for the warmth, the heroic mutual
help, the perilous generosities they experienced in the permanent
state of siege which they previously endured.

In evil countries, those who love "huddle," that is to say their
love, while more intense, is also more clannish, "us against
them." In good countries, love is less intense but more widespread; there is, *ex hypothesis*, less of a sense of menace, of the
enemy's presence, hence a larger diffusion of a lukewarm good
will.

From the beginning of the universe, every particle of matter
has had to face the threat of destruction, that is to say the possibility of being suddenly transmuted from one state to another.
Every electron can "die" and become a wave of energy. When
matter acquires the characteristics of what we—possessing these
characteristics—decide to call life, we simply remove the inverted
commas from "die." One of the defining peculiarities of this sort
of matter consists in the resistance it opposes to the irreversible
liquidation of its structure. At the racial level, this resistance to
death takes the form of systematic reproduction—the breeding of
offsprings. But I am concerned here with this resistance at the
individual level. At a certain point of complication on the evolutionary scale, the animal acquires a new weapon in his individual struggle to survive. This new weapon is *others*. I mean the act
of being rescued or helped—not only when he is a baby, but in
his full maturity—an act the obverse of which is that of rescuing
or helping. "Mutual help"—such as one finds among elephants,
for instance, is obviously a valuable instinct. And it is equally
obvious that our own refined feelings of compassion, solidarity,
love (any of these names, and others like it, will do) are firmly
rooted in our animal past. In us, of course, these feelings supersede animal instinct. They must occur before the action is performed. The hunter will not be stretching his hand out to a
comrade fallen into a ditch until he has felt the proper emotion
that will "motivate" him to help. But the survival value for the
reasoned feelings is the same as it is for instinctive co-operation.
In their nakedness, the small, vulnerable bands of prehistoric
hunters and gatherers needed all the solidarity they could muster
in order to survive, and then in order to conquer. Although
reasoned feelings were less reliable than instinct—a man might

not feel the right motivation to help his fellow—that proved to be a price which could be paid without making too many victims, in exchange for the immense benefits the creature got from the interposition of feeling and thought between stimulus and response.

The legacy of the animal world shows up again in the limits upon the radius of love. The solidarity of animals is confined as a matter of course to some sort of inner group, whose exact composition is irrelevant here. Chimpanzees happily smash the skulls of little chimpanzees who belong to *outsiders*, and eat the baby brains without remorse, licking their fingers so as to enjoy the last scrap. In man too, Nature was content to make compassion and love clannish. These feelings flowed, characteristically, to the family—where the helplessness of the human infant made it imperative and therefore very nearly instinctive—and on to the tribe; and then stopped with a slam. A neighboring tribe might even be grudged the name of human. It is as though Nature had said, "To survive, my dears, you must help each other against the cold, the heat, wild animals, disease, hunger, floods, and fires; but feel free to try to murder the clan across the river. As you are well matched, the race will not perish, and in the meantime you will be induced to favor the strong and healthy, give them all the wives they want, and so strengthen your admirable species."

Today, as a million years ago, love does not normally flow very far out, or at any rate not very far for very long. Even in the best societies, where good will is widespread, we think of the few who really care for Humanity as exceptional beings. Man evolved so as to behave effectively in cohesive groups, much as the baboons do. He was not endowed with an inherent capacity to weep because children are starving five thousand miles away. To be deeply affected by these remote cries (as if they came from one's own baby) still requires an abnormal, and extraordinary hyperalgesia: the tenderness of the saint.

To extend the radius of love is a cherishable ideal. But the pressing question is how to convert the myrmidon's brutality to a mild benevolence, even if the measures we take turn into mere mild benevolence the huddled lover's passion. My answer sends me back to my not unfriendly quarrel with my poem. Is it the example of the saints, of parental affection, or of lovers' passion, which softens Achilles' myrmidons? Well, I should not like to experiment on the world by taking the examples away. But my more deliberate notion of moral progress is that the ruffians of the world make their lives comfortable by plundering wherever and whatever possible, after which their grandchildren, basking in peace and comfort, acquire a measure of tenderness for others, five thousand miles away. A good meal and a warm bed will do more to humanize the brute than the sight of my lovers huddling in the ruin, or of a mother cradling her sick child. So says the Marxist in me, for, as on every ideology hangs at least a fringe of good sense, I can be enrolled at the fringe of any ideology. Feed the brute, I cry.

To be sure, after he is fed and invited to dwell in a nation at peace with its neighbors, much remains to be done. How shall we keep his parents, siblings, teachers, schoolchums, and girlfriends from inflicting, unbeknownst to themselves, some brutalizing "neuroses" on him? How shall we keep him from furiously envying those who are a little better fed than he? By all means, I want to feed the brute; I trust it will do us all good; but I am not forecasting heaven on earth if we do.

Shortly after print immobilized my poem, as I lay in bed in that sometimes highly productive period before sleep, when ideas, like creatures shy of daylight, venture softly out, it occurred to me that I might as well have written, and indeed ought to have written, my questionable couplet as follows:

> In his low brain no atom shifts.
> We must love on.

And I hereby grant a majestic permission to mankind to pick the couplet it prefers. The first says that we must continue to love on the chance, however slight, that we might cause a little moral light to fall on the brutes around us. The second, more somber yet more thrilling, tells us that we must persist and endure even though in vain—for our own sakes—in order to salvage what can be salvaged. I prefer the second version, but do not preclude the first. Do not preclude it as an idea, nor as an effective part of the poetic machinery. However, I prefer the other on ideological grounds, and in addition, separately, because it makes, I think, the better poem. It raises love to a sublimity it did not quite possess while it was effective and useful. A desolate defiant heroism enters into the poem: love unsupported by hope; whence a deeper emotion than before.

— 2 —

The myrmidons who populate my poem should not be thought of as members of some professional criminal class. They are your average men with average ranges of love and compassion. I evoke them briefly as they impressed me, for instance, in the years when I was a soldier comradely with them. In some societies there are fewer of them than in others, but whether West or East, in prosperous America or starving Somalia, the type is on no one's list of endangered species. I am sorry in advance if, in the pages that follow, I will be seen taking an arrogantly elitist view of the Common Man. I move among intellectuals, lovers of Common Man, and I am loath to alienate their affection and esteem. But they themselves have taught me, in their best and noblest books, to hold up Ideas like banners in battle, no matter how murderous the fire, and with especial bravery when the fire originates not, as expected, from the ignorant, but far more dangerous, from the intellectuals themselves.

I move, I repeat, among intellectuals—but not all the time, thank heaven. I often break bread with members of the solid business class, where good nature is more pervasive than among intellectuals. But I also have in my own family a representative of the "lower orders," as the majority used to be called in ages when a frankness different from ours prevailed in the language—frankness, be it said parenthetically, shifts its grounds from age to age. This representative is my Uncle Zygmunt, a seventy-five-year-old stalwart who lives at the other end of the country, but who obliges my wife and myself with an occasional visit of a few weeks' duration. When I need to refresh my mind concerning the Common Man, I refer to the anatomical chart of Uncle Zygmunt which I keep hanging in a closet of my mind.

Uncle Zygmunt is truly the perdurable brute in average man, man the voracious, cheerful, and irascible predator, guzzling all he can guzzle, roaring when in good spirits, punching those who stand in his way, using the moral precepts dropped at his feet from the eyrie of the Intelligentsia when they suit him, laughing till his eyes water at the imbecility of anything he does not understand, sure he understands everything, a great joker, a great snarler, always ready for a scrap, thieving and lying when the chance is good, and as incapable of pity as a piranha. Although Zygmunt has never (so far as I know) done harm on a grand scale, this is not due to any abhorrence of crime or compassion for the weak. Weakness attracts his contempt, and incidentally I think I have here a clue to the psychological mechanism that makes possible the average cruelty of the soldier who trains his automatic weapon on civilians, or the prison guard who executes "vermin." My uncle sneers at the weak; but he has left crime alone simply because he prefers easy fun.

When I sit at table with the old man, and he has, without getting tipsy, drunk half a gallon of red wine to my half glass, banging the table with a mighty fist at every joyous moment, I feel that I have the advantage over my *confrères* mounting assaults upon bourgeois capitalism on the Boulevard Montparnasse. There, jolly and tough, sits the everlasting Cain—Cain who remains everlastingly mysterious to the Abels of this world. For brutality as the brute feels it is as unknowable to refined weaklings like myself as is the inner life of a virus. I open my newspaper and read that two youths abducted a girl at knife point, drove her to a certain dark place, raped her, threw her out of the car, and carefully ran the car over her—six times. Please imagine this. They throw the raped girl onto the asphalt. They run the car over her. She has probably been beaten unconscious before and so does not scream or defend herself. They hear the bones crunch. Fifty feet away, they turn the car around. The girl is not quite dead. They slowly drive over her again. The car rises gently twice, and lurches a little, since only one of the front and rear wheels goes over the body. The third time, to vary the game, they decide to aim at the face, or the breasts, to obliterate the one or the others. From the window they watch the dirty pulp. Again they turn the car about. The fourth time they change the angle and run the car the long way up what was the woman. The fifth time the car hardly bumps anymore. They do a sixth run without much appetite. Nothing much can be done to the body anymore. Their semen has been ejected and they feel like a rest. They drive to the nearest bar for a drink.

And this is the species to which we belong. True, there are nice gradations, as, for instance, from slapping around to abducting, from abducting to raping, from raping alone to raping in turn, from raping to killing, and from simply killing to slowly torturing to death, or even killing, so to speak, six times. I do not know at which point I take leave of the species. At the very first, I hope. I grant you that the *six times* is as abnormal on its side as my queasiness on the other, but the area of normalcy, where the booted louts operate, is no garden of delights.

My uncle was the sore spot of a respectable and well-to-do Polish family; a ne'er do well, idler, and gallows bird from the beginning; a loudmouth beneath a simple brain within a very thick skull. The thick skull is figurative in the customary sense, but it was and remains impressively real as well. He used it (he tells me) to good purpose as a young man to butt, batter, and demolish his enemies. I doubt whether a brick falling from a five-story building could dent that skull even now. The rest of his body matches the skull; Zygmunt is powerful, rugged, impervious to sickness and almost to fatigue: a perfect survivor of the species. A cancer which had the gall to attack his nostrils in his old age retreated in confusion—it had attacked the wrong customer. Death, my whimsy tells me, can come to him only when the side of a cliff decides to fall on him.

How and why he was induced to marry my mother's sister I do not know. I suspect she was offered to him as a "good deal," and he was not the man to worry about consequences. But the mismatch between my poker-till-three-in-the-morning uncle and my nunnish aunt was spectacular. The bull wrecked the china shop and quickly hoofed his way out. For as long as they could, my aunt and her four girls made believe that their wild bull was a sturdy dray-horse. They gave some of us to understand, for instance, that when my uncle arrived in America, he became a building contractor. But the man himself had no aspirations to gentility, and did not even know that the ladies of the family had promoted him behind his back for their own sakes. When my wife and I took him for a walk in Beverly Hills one night, he stopped before an office building under construction and led us into the open, unfinished spaces on the ground floor, giving the walls appreciative taps. It turned out that he had never been anything but a lath and plaster man when he chose to work—and the unemployed cock of the walk at all other times.

Do not imagine that the women of Zygmunt's family are being satirized here. If I were a modern novelist, satire could be taken for granted. I would then choose between fervor or hilarity in exposing the manipulations of the genteel when they try to cover the sordid truth with an attractive embroidery. But remember that I am not a modern novelist. These small prevarications belong to man the social being. We live in groups, and we want to look our best in the groups we live in. I do not object to a person who tints his hair, nor to my aunt and cousins who raised their man a notch in the social scale. There is an aesthetic cosmetic, and a social one; I am more inclined to wink at either than to fulminate; and besides, I make a vital distinction between an innocuous "Make a place upstairs for me too, if you please," and a vicious kick down the stairs for one's rivals: "There's room only for me, get out of my way!" What harm was done by this particular cleansing of the shoddy truth? These ladies had the breeding, the habits of life, the expectations which gave them the right to a civilized husband and father. Wicked chance had tied them to a primitive. They were right, I say, to slip the collar.

My aunt had been a frail body fresh out of a refined girls' school. She did not like sex, she demurely confided to me a few years before she died. I suppose that her husband violated her regularly, and begot his four daughters on a conspicuously disgusted wife. It must have been threadbare fun for him; and having fun was and has remained to this day his loftiest ambition. Neither the world nor any compunctions of his own ever stood in the way of his fun, and a family would have been the last imaginable impediment for him, if any impediment could have resisted a butt, literal or figurative, from his powerful head. In Warsaw he was a minor employee in the post office. But much of the year he reported sick, filched money from his wife, and ran after women. His handsome face, his granitic body, his easy laugh, a brutal sort of distinction, plenty of cologne, neat dress, and impeccable cleanliness captivated the ladies in their "thousand and threes." Even today in his old age he comes down to breakfast with a net over his sparse hair.

During World War I he soldiered for a while in the Austrian army. All around him filth, wormy food, rain, and cold felled his comrades; he stood firm and grinned. At the front, he lingered only long enough for a bullet to dent him a little. He will remove his shirt to show you the scar on his torso any time of the day. The war was a big laugh, as it is to most people—I need not dwell on the fact, do I, that war is always secretly the best of times for most people; yes, for women too. If it were not, even the most ferocious tyrants could hardly force it on mankind. Later Zygmunt went to jail twice—but here I have drawn a blank; nudge or urge as I try, the man will tell me only that he was sent to jail; he refuses to tell me why, whence I conclude that something "mean" rather than "heroic" was the reason both times. These episodes too (it goes without saying) were put under lock and key by the women of the house: they imprisoned his imprisonment, and I would certainly have done so too in their place.

Shortly before World War II, and as a result of another infraction that he will not name, he smuggled himself out of Poland to escape from the police, namely by bribing some officers on a ship bound for New York. They concealed him and duly delivered him behind the backs of American customs officers to his relatives, among them a brother long since established in New York, who gave him employment in his construction business. This brother (whom I knew only from hearsay) was something of a bully to his workers, a violent tyrant to his family, and, like Zygmunt, a dynamic gambler; but unlike his brother he was "smart," sported a "head on his shoulders," and "made it" in America. So much so that, having absorbed the excellent American custom of starting everyone, even one's darlingest sons, at the bottom of the ladder, he gave Zygmunt the meanest job in the business, no doubt intending to promote him if he proved his aptitude in the contracting line. But before it could come to the brother's attention that my uncle had never demonstrated and never would demonstrate aptitude in any sort of steady labor demanding attendance and punctuality every day of the week (the race track was another matter), Zygmunt had thrown over the job and parted from his brother with a volley of curses and bearing, I think, the first true immitigable hatred of his life. He may have been a wastrel, but he was a proud one. In Poland, brother did not start brother at the bottom of the ladder. Zygmunt had suffered an affront of the sort men quench in murder.

I vividly recall, somehow in this connection, a time when

Zygmunt drove my wife and me to the airport in New York, but ran out of fuel midway on the turnpike. Nothing would induce him to trudge up to a filling station carrying a can, empty or full—like a peasant—or to allow nobility like myself to do it either, let alone a dainty princess like my wife. Missing the plane proved, to me, a minor event compared to the impressive scene on that highway.

The only job Zygmunt—an illegal immigrant—could find after hurling himself away from his brother turned out to be much the same the brother had offered him, but since it came to him from a stranger, he was willing to give it his best mixture of sporadic application and consistent malingering. Presently the lawyers legitimized him, and in good time he became an American citizen. Years later, out of pure hatred, his oldest daughter, my mad cousin with the thin tight lips, denounced him to the immigration service as a stowaway, but the only consequence of her remarkable action was to give another lawyer patchwork to do.

The war kept Zygmunt involuntarily separated from the five women of his family, who had remained behind, hidden in Hungary. He actually fell in love with a woman in New York who eventually died of cancer. I believe this was the only time in his life that a genuine feeling for another person crept into Zygmunt's amusement park of a soul. Not (he reported to me) that he refused himself to other mistresses at the same time. For the rest, the new war was fun too. Good money, plenty of women, blackmarket gasoline, fat dinners with torrents of wine, and endless poker games with his buddies. These may have been the years when his passion for horse racing began. But he was always too carefree and dim-witted to moderate it or to exploit it for his profit. He won little, as he cheerfully told me more than once, lost much and often, and his buoyant mania ruined him completely in the years of his retirement. In those years he was forced to steal money from his second wife, a simple, homely, nervous, gabby, and (as always for my uncle) extremely respectable woman. Zygmunt had rescued her from the kitchen of a wealthy Italian couple, emigrated to New York, who had held her in slavery most of her life—an orphan who had never dreamed that she might come into a husband and a home of her own. Zygmunt shook the tree and the apple fell; the owners' outcries were to no avail. The newly married couple set up house. Marietta became a dietitian in a hospital, brought home the money, and Zygmunt spent it.

But I do not mean to suggest that poverty ever upset my uncle. He has always been equally merry and pugnacious, wallet full or empty. His experience has shown him that before a man like himself will starve, or run out of betting money, a woman will always appear, anxious to fund him in exchange for good company and sundry little services.

The war came and went. Zygmunt, wishing perhaps to show his American circle that he had a distinguished family, made grandiose promises, bought a house in Queens, and invited wife and children to join him. This became the great mistake of his life. The family, one daughter—the one who was to denounce him—a college graduate, another preparing for a career at a university, and all accustomed to the decorum and decency of middle-class life in Europe, took one look at his boon companions and barred the door. The discovery of his sexual escapades did not endear him either. The ladies gave him hints concerning his own and his friends' vulgarities which penetrated even Zygmunt's resistant hide. For the second time in his life a really durable hatred took hold of the man. He was being insulted and derided in the very home he had made for his women! Neither he nor his wife was capable of rising to the intellectual height (moderate enough) from which one can view a situation panoramically as a tragic clash of incompatibilities of every description, all beyond anyone's control. Each party simply found the other loathsome. In the end they parted and were divorced. But on his last visit to us, Zygmunt gave out that he had decided, while they still lived together, to set fire to the house one night and rid the world of his ungrateful wife and her four uppity acolytes. It was his mistress who had prevented him—begging him "on her knees," dragging along the carpet of her apartment as he paced and raged across the room. Only her tears, he said, had saved his family. Did I believe my uncle? Not quite, for, as I have said before, I do not see flaming crime in Zygmunt's real books. But not everything that I do not see does not exist.

Either way, I can report that my uncle told me his tale in the best of spirits, neither boasting on the one hand nor exhibiting remorse on the other. His meaning was, judiciously, that "the bitches deserved it." The situation had its oddity. Good Zygmunt was letting himself be entertained by the blood relation of those he had made up his mind to murder. But such oddities are odd only for sensitive antennas. Besides, almost a quarter of a century had passed; time turns mountains into molehills, and Zygmunt was not the man to allow a grudge to interfere with a blithe visit to his nephew in California.

As for going to jail for such a crime of passion—well, he had not enjoyed his two stretches in Polish cells; but then Polish prisons are wretchedly suffocating places. "I don't give a . . . if they put me in jail here." I think he had heard comforting tales about American prisons; or else, like most of the simple-minded people who commit crimes, he lacked the sort of morbid imagination which, in more complicated beings, brings the future in a hundred horrid shapes into the mind's present, and "sicklies o'er" resolution.

Apropos of fire, my very first peek into Zygmunt's rollicking past occurred years ago when he related with some pride that he had once set fire to his automobile after dousing it in gasoline on a deserted road. He disliked the car because the ignition kept giving him trouble. With the insurance money he bought one that displayed a greater sense of responsibility toward a man of his caliber.

A true block quarried from the salt of the earth, my uncle runs headlong into every available error, hatred, and fantasy as soon as he undertakes to theorize about the world. When young men began to wear their hair long, he was for shooting them in the streets on sight. His knowledge of Polish history and culture is confined to the information that Paderewski was a great "author." Any custom strange to him strikes him as worthy of a colossal laugh of derision followed by instant death. When he watches the news on television, he accompanies every episode with cheerful snorts and snarls of contempt, for he has learned that by means of cynical dismissals a man can always get the reputation that he is too smart to be hoodwinked. As all *others* are, at best, unreal to him, the calamities of the world—air crashes, battles, mass starvation—amuse him much the way they beguile us (alas) in works of art—say a nicely lit massacre by Delacroix. When he denounces the Democrats as bastards one and all, it is only because a Democrat has appeared on the screen to make some promise or announce a fact. If a Republican had spoken, the Republicans would have been denounced as bastards one and all. My uncle will vociferate against thieves while his hand is in his neighbor's pocket. But all of this—threats, denunciations, growls of contempt—with the eyes rolling in their sockets and, at every word, that mighty fist I have mentioned before slamming a table so that I marvel that any furniture has survived his passage (my arm, by the bye, is blue from the vehement loving nudges and slaps I catch when he addresses me)—all this, I say, goes like a squall that passes in the twinkling of an eye, and is followed by a thundering series of guffaws if, for example, some corrupt official is walked up the court steps in handcuffs: Zygmunt is happy again.

One day Zygmunt observed a plump and savory woman gazing at a newly built apartment house in his neighborhood. He approached her with the aplomb learned in sixty years of sweeping savory ladies off their feet and engaged her in a learned conversation regarding the building. His deportment gave her the impression, which he chose not to dispel for the time being, that he was its manager, perhaps an owner, at least a partner, in short, a man of means. The two became kissing friends. Before long, she discovered that he had squandered not only all his own money on the horses, but also a substantial sum belonging to his second wife. Still, he was handsome, manly, "fun to be with," and she was alone, for her husband, a Norwegian sailor in the merchant marine, had been murdered five years before in a New York subway. Presently Miss Luisa (she was a Venezuelan) was bailing Zygmunt out of odd little debts, while he reciprocated by mending and painting in her apartment, taking her to Jones Beach, and performing such minor feats of sexual love as a man in his seventies—even a man like my uncle—must be content to offer and enjoy. Luisa lived on a pension. This convenience gave Zygmunt, deserted daily by his wife on account of her determination to work to the last hour of her life, a pleasant daytime home.

Eventually, to make life a little easier and more fun, he contrived an "accidental" meeting between his wife and mistress, as follows: he persuaded Marietta to finance a weekend in Atlantic City, and arranged for his girlfriend to take the room next door in the same hotel. As Zygmunt is jovial and expansive, a greeting was natural; the greeting improved into chitchat; the satisfying discovery was made that they all lived in the same neighborhood; and promises of friendship were happily exchanged.

The time came when Zygmunt decided to take his Luisa to California. Using a high moral tone in order to keep him away failed to work. He wanted to travel with his sweetheart, to show her off to us, and to show us off to her. Luisa paid for the trip. Officially, he was visiting us alone.

She too was eminently respectable, precisely in the way Lawrence and Shaw have portrayed the finicky morality of the lower classes when they aspire to a higher place. Big-breasted and heavy-lipped, with generous servings of flesh pressing hard against corsets, buckles, and laces, she was meticulously neat, proper, garrulous, eloquent as to her "excellent connections," and uneasy about the relationship. She had a son in an executive position in a large oil company; and it was perhaps an unconscious ploy on the part of Zygmunt to place my wife and myself on his side of the scale against the eminent son. Be that as it may, she made a strong point of siding with Marietta, *in absentia*, against all the vices and shortcomings of her boyfriend, inside of which, after two years of intercourse, she was thoroughly at home. On the ladder of human development she stood, and well knew that she stood, several rungs higher than my uncle. If she was not educated, as she freely, volubly, and repeatedly acknowledged, she knew at least what education was and worshiped it. It was clear to her that she lived in a dimension unknown to Zygmunt.

The visit began uneventfully with drives, walks, and conversations. One morning, however, my wife missed her most precious piece of jewelry: a bracelet steeped in diamonds, given to her (worse luck) by my mother. She had casually left it—she thought—in a drawer of our bathroom. I hasten across the panic, the ransacking of drawers, boxes, pockets, bedlinen, masses of clothing; the inquisition into corners, nooks, shelves, sofas, wastebaskets, papers, sacks of vacuum cleaners—with each failure our ideas became loonier—then the police reports, inspections by Officer Muldrew (the compleat detective from the womb of a television set), the embarrassing suspicions, the perfect absence of clues, the uproar with our Mexican maid when we delicately opened the subject to her—in short, a little poisoned cosmos. When nothing came to light, Officer Muldrew asked Zygmunt and Luisa point-blank whether he might get their consent to being strapped to a polygraph, vulgarly known as a lie detector, and interrogated. My wife and I were dismayed (although a saint could not have squashed suspicion out of his conscience)—but our guests promptly agreed. Officer Muldrew conveyed them to headquarters. Luisa, respectable to the fingertips—fingertips which had gone so far, she confessed, as to secrete into her purse a souvenir ashtray from the table of a hotel (in Atlantic City?)—was declared "clean" within ten minutes. My uncle's business took two hours. He drove the electronic equipment out of its wits. He bellowed, contradicted himself, misunderstood on purpose and not on purpose, lied, editorialized, babbled and bullied, while the foul voltages from an ample sixty years of prevaricating, cheating, pilfering, brazening, and malingering joggled the astonished needle out of any conceivable coherence. Officer Muldrew returned the old man to us with a shrug of the shoulders. The advice from the experts was to leave him alone. Above a certain age, they said, nothing certain could be defined.

Luisa, who had been embarrassed and nervous before the test (I draw the blinds on our own confusion of motives) was as happy now as a cow in clover. She failed to notice that her boyfriend had turned somber. I know today that he had not purloined the diamonds, namely for the comfort of his declining years—they were found years later in a forgotten nook—but I did not know it then, and I was surprised that in the midst of his mortification he gave not the smallest sign of resentment against my wife and myself. Apparently he took our fulsome protestations at face value, and never dreamed that we might dream that he was guilty. Nor was he troubled by the summons to the police station in itself; he was used to embranglements with the law. But he was used to coming out of them with a swagger, and possibly an obsequious wink from the turnkey himself. Now he had lost face, and lost it in front of Luisa's triumphant cheek. He clearly wanted the subject dropped, and, harboring a sense of guilt ourselves, we would have been happy to oblige, after all our reassurances and our abashed apologies; but Luisa's elation was not to be dropped into a well of discretion. She chattered and chattered: went into every detail of the interrogation, informed us once again of her respectability—her background—her affluence—her son in the oil company—her snug condominium in

Flushing—her entrenched honesty—her excellent connections in Venezuela—the gratulations of the detectives—the amazement of the lie detector operator—and grew merrier and merrier over the all too stark contrast between her own serene triumph, and Zygmunt's messy defeat in the encounter with the polygraph.

That evening my wife and I left for an engagement. At midnight, when we returned to the house, all was quiet. But a great storm had actually swept over our guest room. At breakfast we found the lovers sullen. Luisa had been too merry too long. The old man's repetition of "You talk too much" had had no effect. Direct commands to shut up had only opened the sluices wider. Dangerous subjects had begun to infiltrate the dialogue in the guest room: Luisa's eminently refined friend in New York, male by nature if not by conviction, who had warned her God knew how many times against her lout of a boyfriend; the moneys spent and the gifts purchased by Luisa for her penniless beau; her own used car given to him as a present by a subterfuge meant to delude his wife; and (I shudder as I write the words) Zygmunt's sexual diminishments—why, a woman like herself, still youthful if not young, full-bodied, lively as a filly—she could find better provender of that sort by winking twice in any public place, if she ever cared to stoop so low; then back to her success that afternoon at the police station, and forth to his discomfiture. All the while she was brushing her nails, and this casual, satisfied, and downright insolent brushing of nails stuck in Zygmunt's mind like a rock in his craw, he could not spit it out often enough in the next several days. He finally threw the question hot in her face: "Are you telling me I stole them?" to which she replied, or rather he thought she replied, "I don't know." Luisa swore to us that she had answered "I don't know" to some question she had understood quite differently. Here the truth will never be settled, for the hues of Luisa's English were not the same as Zygmunt's, and the two rudimentary languages functioned in harmony only as long as their owners were themselves at peace. My wife and I tried hard the next day to impress our guests with the possibility of an honest misunderstanding between them, but the meshes were too wide for fine verbal distinctions: nothing came of our humane attempts except a new round of invectives and threats.

But to return to the guest room. No sooner did Luisa say "I don't know" than my uncle punched her in the face, told her to pack her things, get out, take the plane, and vanish. But at night—in Los Angeles—without a car—or a sense of direction—the saber could only rattle in the scabbard. Luisa cried and sobbed, and the couple eventually took to their beds. My uncle fell asleep, but Luisa kept an eye open all night from her mattress, three feet away from his, in terror for her life.

Having failed, on the next day, to reconcile the lovers, we made arrangements for Luisa to fly back to New York on the morrow. She placed a discreet call to her refined friend in order to be picked up at the airport. That evening I went upstairs to my study to read. The house was quiet, for the antagonists had not spoken to each other all day. But all of a sudden I heard cries and grunts. I ran down the stairs and found Zygmunt pummeling Luisa again, Luisa screaming, and my tender, blossom-soft wife standing terrified and speechless to one side. She had tried once more to make peace between the lovers, but this could not be done without words, and words had led back to the fatal "I don't know." Luisa, no coward (she reminded me of some hefty saloon-keeper in a sailors' bar in Amsterdam) had stood her ground—and the blows had fallen again. Luisa squealed, my wife stood stiff, my uncle's eyes rolled like Othello's, and my own legs, I must say, began to melt like the columns of Bernini's tabernacle at St. Peter's. Still, I managed to separate the fighters, and even "tried a little psychology," as the saying goes, by taunting the old fellow with his cravenness in striking a woman. But he was immune to this sort of Arthurian psychology, for (as he told me a week later, all jolly again, on the day of *his* departure for New York), he always mauled his women, they all deserved it, and that was the only way to keep them up to the mark. When the knightly line failed me, I dredged up some expressions of authority, composed my face to suit the words, and asserted that I was the ruler of this particular house, and if he did not obey my regulations, he must leave the next day too. Whether this worked a little better, or whether (as is more likely), Zygmunt felt he had made his point, the hostile forces turned their backs on one another and the incident became history. That night Luisa slept on the sofa in our "den" (as one calls the parlor nowadays in

California), and the next morning, without another word between the two, I drove her to the airport. Our hero took her
departure as a victory for himself and Justice. He returned to his
natural mood, and became again, as Swift says immortally of a
quiescent Yahoo, "a very serviceable brute." We put him to the
banausic task of painting a brick wall in our garden, where he
demonstrated to my satisfaction that Man was made for using his
head to help his hands, and not to mend his soul. The lovers have
not seen each other since. The diamonds are smiling restfully
around my wife's wrist again.

— 3 —

We live daily and yearly in the midst of, or else threatened by,
repression or devastation: devastation the result of war among
the nations, repression the form war takes when one group seeks
to subjugate another within a nation. We, in this picture, are
those who suffer the repression or devastation; it is for this
element in the population that I speak—the huddled lovers of the
poem—yet not without an awareness, first, that an antipodal
meditation could be written from the point of view of an ethic
glorifying power and terror, and second, that the *we* among
whom I enroll myself sometimes become, almost unwittingly,
dragged by circumstances we are too weak or fearful to oppose,
myrmidons ourselves, scourges onto others.

Technological progress tenders us on the one hand a vision by
no means incredible of an amiably organized global prosperity
and a human race reasonably tamed and yet reasonably free. On
the other hand, it gives mankind the means to make devastation
more devastating and repression more repressive than ever. Obviously, however, technology does not cause Hitlers and Stalins
to appear, it does not motivate men to make war or oppress their
fellow-citizens. The truth is that much of the especial violence of
our century must be ascribed to the rise, or the attempted rise, of
the common man. This enormous historical fact has supplanted
the older if hardly venerable cause for wars among nations, to
wit, the competition for power and wealth among the ruling
classes themselves. It is a truth hard for intellectuals to digest that
the warnings of Tories long ago against allowing the "rabble" to
vote (they did not mince words in those days) were altogether

sound. Partial, but sound. Partial, in that the Tories would not admit to the *injustice* of keeping the masses disfranchised; sound, inasmuch as justice, striven for or achieved, bore disastrous results embedded in the benefits. History is a foul tangle of positives and negatives; and, of all beings, the intellectual is the one who should boldly confront moral contradictions which he would prefer inexistent. I repeat, the tumultuous and bestial violence so characteristic of our times has emerged largely as a consequence of common man in motion at last to claim his rights, but perhaps more than his rights. I assure you that the man who is writing these parlous words is no bull-headed and leather-hearted conservative who chooses to ignore starving children and jobless men weeping over the charity bowl of soup they are forced to eat. I make my friends, if not my opinions, mostly on Rousseau's side of the forum. The everyday conservative does not care how hard he sits on the common people if only Property has been safeguarded. I am a conservative who, if he had the making of history in his hands, would not consent to the building of a single mansion, or even the painting of a picture, before mankind had sworn to bring the decencies of life to the commonest of the common, suitably restricted as to breeding. But that is where, authentic paternalist, I draw the line. The decencies for all, *la carrière ouverte aux talents*, and after that, back to the hierarchies! The unsolved problem, regrettably, is how to keep the elite from sooner or later exploiting the masses, and the masses from sooner or later devouring the elite. I myself abstain from the political life because this dilemma paralyzes me. Though I sympathize with elitism, I cannot vote for it, because I fear and detest its brutality against the common man; and though I sympathize with the masses, I cannot vote for them because I detest and fear their brutality against elites.

Our sentimentalities concerning the common man began to prosper in the eighteenth century, impelled by a new, optimistic notion of essential man. Philosophers and poets who never dreamed of dirtying their hands or walking within range of a rustic's garlic-scented breath became so very fond of peasants and laborers that an unnatural alliance was eventually formed between the proletariat and the intelligentsia, an alliance which grew from literary effusion to social, economic, and political action. The Romantic enthusiast did not count it enough, as I most emphatically do, to feed, clothe, house, and doctor the poor, and to give them every chance in the world to rise in the world. The poor must be called God's children; they are the repositories of authentic wisdom; they are virtuous on the shallow ground that they are abused; they deserve not merely to join the ruling class if they are able, but to be themselves the ruling class, however unable.

I call this alliance unnatural not because it was unprecedented in human annals—it was, but that would hardly make it unnatural—but because there was nothing "in it," to be quite vulgar, for the intelligentsia. The latter had always urged rulers and magistrates to be both just and merciful to the helpless masses. That much was pleasantly easy. A landlord may suffer a loss in cash as a result of an unusual regard in governing circles for the helpless masses, but philosophers and poets remain by and large unaffected; and in that safe position a high moral tone is quickly adopted. But the cold truth is that the subjugation of the masses—benign or oppressive—never damaged the "interests" of the class of intellectuals. Why then the drastic change from an innocuous and humanitarian "Give them their daily bread" to a peremptory "Let them rule"? Many intellectuals resisted and opposed this change, and have continued as Tories of one color or another. But the "center-stage" intellectuals worked ardently for it. I consider this one of the mysteries of history, and do not know whether any historian has attempted to penetrate it. Self-interest would have dictated the same courting of the bourgeoisie as the flattery formerly heaped upon kings, princes, and prelates. What animated the intelligentsia? A compassion so sublime that it pulverized self-interest? Why then, and why not before? Or resentments the elucidation of which must be sought for in submerged psychological impulses? Imagine this scenario, blended of Marx and Freud: the intellectualized sons of the bourgeoisie "murdering" or plain murdering their fathers—and blessed by their consciences for doing it!—by unleashing the proletariat at them. Is *that* where the explanation lies?

For the oppressed, this strange alliance—the very possibility of which would have astounded a laborer in Athens or a peasant under Elizabeth I—brought welcome reinforcement. The proletariat supplied the brawn, the intellectuals the brain. The workers struck and rioted; the intellectuals led, gave ideas, organized political parties, pamphleteered, demoralized the opposition, and philosophized like the devil. The crossing was stormy, but eventually a landing was made in the Century of the Common Man. Leaving to one side the inevitable drop in the aesthetic distinction of our world (I speak of this in other chapters), we can probably affirm that in democracies and near-democracies the intelligentsia is neither better nor worse off than it had been under George III or the several Frederick Williams of Prussia. But in the countless tyrannies of the left and right, all spawned by the rise or the opposition to the rise of the proletariat, the intelligentsia has been and is being pitifully mauled. We have not marked strongly enough the stupendously ironical fate of the Russian intellectual elite: so many splendid men and women arguing and plotting for the proletariat in the century before the October Revolution; so many of them decimated by it; and so many of them, today, ardent if secret reactionaries puzzled by left-wing intellectuals in the Western World. This is—by the way—wonderfully worded by one of the victims—Nikolai Erdman, who has the following fable in *The Suicide*:

> ARISTARCH. There was once a compassionate hen that was given duck eggs to sit on. For years it sat on them. For years it kept them warm with its own body, until the young were ready to come out. Well, the ducklings crept out of their shells, they waddled out from beneath the hen, they grabbed her by the neck and dragged her to the water. "I'm your mama," the hen squawked. "I hatched you. What are you doing to me?" "Swim," quacked the ducklings. Do you see the moral?
>
> VOICES. Not exactly . . . not really, no.
>
> ARISTARCH. Who is the hen? Our intelligentsia. Who are the eggs? The eggs are the proletariat. . . . Now you tell me, why did we hatch those eggs? If we'd known, we would have taken the eggs and . . . and what, citizen Podsekalnikov?
>
> SEMYON. Made egg nog.
>
> (Translated by Peter Tegel)

This play, written in the mid-twenties, remains (need one say it?) unproduced in the Soviet world, and if Erdman died of old age, albeit in misery and I believe in exile, it was only because he cowered for nearly fifty years not writing another word.

And what about the proletariat? The intellectuals of the left were in effect demanding the substitution of a new common man, bringing peace through his happy emancipation for the old common man kept from disturbing the peace by being locked up. The first genuinely successful enterprise under this new banner—mightily assisted by the intelligentsia—declared itself with a prophetic Reign of Terror which has been fulfilled a hundred times since. Nevertheless, the intellectuals were not entirely misguided. In what might be called the British model, the seizure of power by the masses—through the suffrage and through economic betterment—occurred gradually enough, and in a context of sufficient general prosperity, to result in a difussion, a widespread sharing, of power and wealth. Not, of course, without conflicts and even bloodshed. But catastrophic upheavals were avoided, and it did turn out, on the whole, that "feeding the brute" (as I baldly put it before) was a sound alternative to locking him up. Of the two ways of taming him, this one had at least the advantage of justice as conceived by almost any system of thought. True, the now enfranchised and "educated" masses did not, as some intellectuals seem to have hoped, turn into lovers of the Well-Tempered Clavier, but that is not the issue now. My myrmidon poem is happily out of place in the nations evolved on the British model, of which there are possibly a score in the world—including, though just barely, the United States, where inequalities which produce an "average" amount of lawlessness in other nations stir up so many plunderers and killers that living there gives many citizens a feeling of huddling against the very lout of my poem.

The twenty-odd countries, and a few marginal ones, allow us to breathe for a historical moment, free, or more or less free of the rampaging myrmidon. But what happened and what happens elsewhere?

In the nations fashioned on the Bolshevik model, the unchained Zygmunts systematically eliminate the noble, the rich, the middle class, the enterprising, the dissenters. Mass upheavals breed a new class of leaders, rugged adventurers utterly stripped of the niceties characteristic of the supplanted royal houses or aristocracies. Leading the common man into battle, firing him with an ideology supplied by the intelligentsia, they take their countries into, and through, a long period of Red terror, during which millions are slaughtered on both sides. Set my poem, if you please, in the midst of such a period. When this bloody interregnum comes to an end, and the leadership monopolizes power, terror gives way to semiterror. The intelligentsia continues to tremble, the vivacious, the curious, the enterprising remain in danger, but the ruins are cleared and my poem is no longer a completely fair image of prevailing conditions. And what has happened to the common man whose aspirations set the vast enterprise in motion? He is a trifle better off than he had been under the tsar, for the party does not quite forget that it created itself for the sharply defined purpose of feeding, housing, doctoring, employing, vacationing and pensioning everybody. Against this it would be utterly unrealistic not to set a calamitous spiritual loss, for, opiate or perfume, religion is a wonderful source of happiness for those who are allowed to enjoy it. Still, let us rule that when the terror has abated, the common man is, as they say, ahead of the game, and—locked up again so as not to threaten the leaders. For this is the grand ironical ending of it all. The common man broke out of bondage on the day he stormed the Bastille, turned the world upside down, ousted a series of decorative autocrats, and returned into bondage.

The march of the masses provoked a third phenomenon which we can call the Fascist model, where the threatened elite summoned and armed a hooligan of their own: Hitler or almost any Latin American colonel. In the earlier locked up position, and in spite of an occasional local fling at insurrection (always bloodily suppressed), the masses could be held in by an hereditary leadership which, apart from its determination to keep labor cheap and weak, exhibited all manner of delightful traits that we call *civilized*. With the masses on the move wholesale, fanning out, and taking over country after country, sterner means were required, and the "polite" emperors, kings, and princes gave way to outrageous louts, balking at nothing on earth to force the masses back into their ancient pen. But history has another irony up its sleeve. After right-wing terror abates, after the dead are forgotten, and the rich feel secure once again, the common man is not infrequently as much ahead of the game as he is under communist dictators. Like his comrade under leftist dispensations, he is locked up and the policeman is never far off, but his "wage and benefits package" too is apt to sustain comparison with that of his fellow-worker or fellow-peasant on the other side. From a distance, therefore, it would appear that right or left has not been the

authentic issue. Fundamentally, because of the stiff-necked determination of the rich to give up not a penny of their hoard
without bloodshed, the common man has been obliged to cause a
series of massacres and counter-massacres in the world so as to
wrest from it a little extra for his diet.

In order not to yield to a facile cynicism, let me add to the
roster the occasional dictatorship (of the right or left or neither)
which many outside observers would agree to call "enlightened,"
in that the strong man happens—by pure historical luck—to care
for all factions and classes—for peace, economic well-being, social reform, protection of rich and poor alike, and perhaps even
for the arts and sciences. The pity is that this sort of rule is a
matter of luck. The conditions to make it last, to replicate it
elsewhere, or to guarantee an equally beneficent succession are
lacking, and no one has yet invented a method for creating these
conditions. When such rulers pass on, the country reverts to one
of the normal configurations I have sketched out.

— 4 —

As I look back at the picture I have daubed, it appears to me that I
have almost unintentionally described a vast upheaval which
may have subsided in the major countries of the world. In my
twenty-odd "free" countries, the masses neither create nor invite
a systematic application of terror. What they have instead—fig-
ured in my eternal uncle Zygmunt—is a crowd always ready to be
unleashed again, potential hooligans in their thousands, and out
of this crowd a subcrowd of active but unpoliticized criminals. In
nations on the Bolshevik and Fascist models which have run
their full evolutionary course, the locked-up masses are tame, the
potential brute is of course always present, but the murder rate is
kept low by the same efficient police that suppresses liberties in
general. Internally, there is more peace in the great nations as I
write these words in 1982 than there was in 1932. Across boundaries, there is more peace among the great powers in 1982 than
there was in 1942. My poem, alas, speaks better than ever for a
mass of smaller territories on every continent, where ferocity
armed with the best modern weapons operates within or among
countries. The major powers, instead, seem to be realizing that

total global war is unprofitable for all concerned, unlike the wars of the past, which—to be quite honest—were often smart gambles.

It turns out that I am by no means doom-ridden with respect to our historical future. One can, it seems, take a Hobbesian view of man—the everlasting Zygmunt—without despairing of the *fate* of man. If, however, the Nuclear Night makes an end of us all, lovers and louts alike, I offer, for our consolation, a concluding nursery rhyme I overheard one day from one of God's humbler creatures:

> I am a little snail
> On the green grass I sail
> Sometimes I live sometimes I die
> And in between I hear great mankind cry
> We mankind must survive
> How ghastly to deprive
> The cosmos of mankind
> Although the reason I don't find
> Being a simple snail
> On the green grass I sail.

And should the green grass fail too, and the snails of the world starve, that too the cosmos shall digest.

ROBBERS AND KILLERS

In our private and usually imaginary tangles with those who have wronged us (those whom, to be exact, we accuse of having wronged us), we are sometimes milder and sometimes harsher than the law. The law exists so as to correct these personal deviations. Thus a man may well forgive his son for forging dad's name to a check—or at least try to hush up the deed—but the law pounces on the son regardless, or almost so. On the other side, the law will keep us from personally wringing someone's neck if, in its calmer assessment, the rogue merits only twenty lashes. On reflection, there are really three claims to reckon with: what the gut clamors for—let me call this the outcry—what our moral sense (whatever it may be) preaches, and what the law of the land commands. The three sometimes coincide and coalesce, but at other times they part company, now mildly, now dramatically.

A few years ago, my wife and I were robbed in Naples. The poem I wrote soon afterward records the event and the outcry it provoked:

Robbers

In Naples a gang of experts
cracked our car in the glass eye
we were lunching standing up a block away
and they knew it
scootered off with my suitcase
leaving a dabble of blood.

The fat women were all over us
we were thumped and yanked with advice good advice
no one had seen a thing.

Now thinking of them standing that suitcase
on a dinky table and counting out my underwear
Adrienne's pearls my nice plans for another farce
my blue blazer and the rest, I see these articles

looking around flabbergasted at being pawed
by queer foreigners obviously no friends of the family.

"Where's daddy?" cries my property
spitting mad and scared to death.

Lousy gangsters,
are they laughing their heads off around that table?
No, this is business, they're serious,
one of them has a date
to go dancing tonight, Mamma is waiting
home with dinner for the two others,
they're in a hurry
and laughing their heads off.

Listen, children, listen jacket, sweater old friend,
    suits, shoes, pearls,
maybe there's hope, the blood, let's not forget
the good brown blood above the chrome
you couldn't see because you were inside the suitcase

Hey hey one of the bastards may be in (pray God)
for sensational convulsions witnessed by fainting
    nurses
maybe he'll die corroded blue and green
from messing with my underwear.

Yes but where's the satisfaction
where's the bliss
if I don't see it blue and green
with my own two eyes
or read it on page seven under local news?

If they all wind up in a Ferrari
I'm done with this damned galaxy.

I must say at once that the poem is in a sense dishonest; dishonest because its humor—which may be aesthetically pleasing
(so I paternally hope)—falsifies the very serious anger I felt in
reality that afternoon in Naples. The poem commits an act of
cowardice; it is not nasty enough. For the truth is that I was all
but wild with hatred. I would have been glad to see the robbers
lynched at the first unencumbered Neapolitan lamppost. To help
my helpless fury, I pictured them aggravating their crime by an
insulting hilarity at my expense—as if I wanted one more reason

to hang them without benefit of court or clergy. For, unquestionably, to be robbed is also to be humiliated: they have *bested* you.
For an hour or so I heard in my soul but one voice in the
trialogue of outcry, moral reproof, and legal sanction: that of my
bawling viscera.

Let me propose that this bawl should not be dismissed from
one's theoretical reflections. To begin with, I will certainly not
allow that my murderous fury placed me, for the nonce, on the
same moral level as the robbers themselves. This cannot be, since
I had suffered an *unprovoked* affront and loss. Whatever one may
urge against violence of any sort, surely the victim's revenge
cannot be ethically confounded with the predator's attack, unless
the predator had been himself the victim's victim before. But
beyond this, and in any event, even after we have granted that
morality or law (or morality *and* law) must prevail over our
outcry, the outcry must be respected too: it has its privilege, it has
even its sanctity. The truth of this comes to us more forcefully, of
course, when we substitute for mere robbery some particularly
vicious murder. Shall we not humbly efface ourselves and our
moralisms and legalisms before the clamor of parents whose
child has been raped, tortured, and butchered (as happens almost
daily in these United States)—be the aggressor as demented as
you will? This clamor, I repeat, is sacred. Its claim upon our
moral thought wanes by as much as the crime diminishes; but
even against mere robbers it retains its right—though it is a duly
diminished right—to be entered into our mature account.

Taking another line, you may object that my rage in Naples
implied an indecent attachment to material property. This sort of
argument—it can be phrased in several ways—is apt to be heard
from what, in order to be concise, I can surely call the left—even
if the voice is only that of a bushy drop-out on a public beach. We
all know that the left and Christianity are seldom friends. But
history and ideology make dreadful tangles in which inconsistencies shamelessly twine about one another. On the question of
private property, for instance, the left has taken over from Christianity the notion that an attachment to it is impure. For the
absolute Christian this attachment is so much attention stolen
from God. For the determined leftist, property is a necessity
stolen from the working man. So be it. I am disinclined to argue
over axioms, knowing full well that ultimately all axiomatic

values float in a metaphysical void. Proofs are out of the question; and I fall back on what I call *ethical provinces*, namely human groups sharing for any reason one or more well-defined values. I require no grander support to carry out useful discourse—nothing from Moses, nothing from Plato, nothing from St. Paul. Specifically, as far as the value of private property is concerned, I am the more willing to entrench myself in this populous ethical province in that my Neapolitan thieves were and remain (I dare guess) as touchy about their own belongings as the huge president of General Motors and minuscule myself.

I am not even interested in leaning upon the thesis that an attachment to private property is "natural" in that the animals from whom we descend and who have bequeathed to us our passion for fit survival almost invariably exhibit it. Animals defend their provisions and territory—and as no one scolds them for it, so (the argument might run) no one should object to our doing likewise. However, the whole point of the Moral Law is that, if need be, it is to supersede Natural Law. Christianity—and why not Marxism, Leninism, and Maoism?—all crash through our animal nature—ask us to be altruists, for instance—and will not allow us to argue from our consanguinity with animals. Useless philosophical chat. Ethical provinces function *in fact* without any foundation stronger than a community of desire and aversion. If you dislike the terrain of a particular province of mine, you do so anchored in a neighboring, hostile province whose metaphysical foundations are as imaginary as my own. You and I both float, and floating we grapple over the void.

In short, we need not *believe* in a moral order; we need only *adhere* to it.

I start off, then, with the axiom that "property is a good." Naked, this axiom permits me to rage at will against my outlaws, and to invoke against them, if not the lynching mob, at least every permissible scourge of the law. So far, therefore, the gut, the moral sense, and the appeal to law coincide. But the axiom does not remain naked very long. Property may be a good, but even in *that* ethical province, it does not become a god. How good a good is it? And when might another good take precedence over it?

Naples is all too hospitable to such compunctions. What if, contrary to what my rage imagined and my poem suggests, the mother of these robbers would have expired that night had they not rushed to the nearest apothecary with the proceeds from our suitcase? They may have tried a hundred times to earn by hard work the money to save her; could not find employment; and were driven to robbery by fell despair. This is not, in Naples, a scenario out of Hugo, Dickens, or other sentimentalists, but hard reality. Presently a hundred mitigations, a hundred heart-rending possibilities, crowd into the liberal intellect. We yield to a first vulgar anger; but presently we perpend, and a host of "factors"—psychological, political, economic, and sociological—drench our heat. We grant that not every young man trapped inside an odious social machine automatically turns into a bandit. But the thoughtful victim of rapine recognizes that such a machine *must* produce a violent faction consisting of those not patient enough to wait forever either for jewelry and pheasant, or for plain bread, or for medicine to save a sick mother. Naples inevitably, ineluctably, inexorably produces such a faction; and if Naples does, so do a thousand, so do ten thousand places on this earth beside which Naples is paradise.

What then becomes of my rage?

Several prosperous gentlemen of commerce and industry with whom it is my happiness sometimes to spend a silvery evening head off these tremulous reflections with well-tested magic formulas, such as: "I worked hard for what I've got and if they're too lazy or dumb to strike it rich, that's their lookout"; or: "Anybody who really wants to work can always get a job"; or: "They're not hard up, they're punks"; or: "Give 'em a day's wages and they'll drink it away in a tavern"; or: "The world has to have both poor and rich." And so on. A leathery conscience, applauded by other leathery consciences, is an enviable article; but for better or worse, the intellectual has thrown away that shield in favor of swift-running thoughts.

Thoughts, mitigating thoughts, duly came to me after the little crisis had run its course: after the farcical session in the police station to register one more after some fifty forced entries on this average Neapolitan day—a summary of ours being sleepily pecked out for the benefit of the victim's insurer by two fat police fingers on a senile, arthritic typewriter, well in keeping with the peeling walls of the office; after the rushed purchase of life-supporting toothbrushes, combs, razors, and the like; after a string of commentaries—also grounded in tradition—between my wife and myself regarding our stupidity in leaving the car unguarded for ten minutes; and came, finally, after a few days at Capri devoted to rites which might have fetched a comment from the thieves (supposing them possessed of some aptitude for social commentary) to the effect that robbed or unrobbed, we were still members of the ruling class. The reflections came, yet they did not cancel the first anger, nor, I propose, invalidate it philosophically.

The anger and the mitigation of the anger both deserve to stand—this is my essential point—and must make shift to co-habit in the same deontological quarters without coming to terms. The truth of this uncomfortable proposition appears most vividly when we name as victims, not gentry like my wife and myself, but the majority of any "Neapolitan" population (in Naples, that is, or in Karachi)—to wit, the men, women, and children who are not only victims of the odious social machine, but, innocent of crime themselves, fall victim a second time to the outlaws spawned by that same machine. For, as everyone knows, the predatory poor prey chiefly on the helpless poor. Since the latter have done nothing, in the large historical picture, to injure the thieves by imposing on them the inequities from which they themselves suffer, they are utterly free and clear to demand harsh punishment for the predators. They need not allow, with a tear in their eye, for the hardships the robbers have undergone, in-asmuch as they have undergone the same without becoming robbers. In short, their moral sense grants them full permission to write my poem, so to speak, without apologizing for it. From their point of view—that is to say, from an ethical province to which they may normally be expected to gravitate—the snatch-purses and motley hooligans would be better employed in politi-cal agitation, volunteer work in soup kitchens, or—frankly—plunder of the well-to-do.

But we the well-to-do reasonably argue that the specific, brute, personal act of theft is not to be measured against a diffusely un-just social system. Let us grant—unlike the leathery consciences I mentioned before—that, as beneficiaries of the system, we are fractionally guilty: the rich more so, the less than rich less so. This is a highly schematic view of social reality, of course, but if we keep reminding ourselves that a schema is all it is, we can make good use of it to avoid prolixity. Let us ascribe some responsibility for the system even to those who are most busy endowing hospitals for the poor, agitating in public bodies for reform, or even fomenting revolutions. At a certain level of ease, all of us ride on the backs of the poor, and, as a result, their attacks upon our property are never truly and entirely unprovoked. And yet we are right to condemn the specific, brute attack upon John Doe in Naples as a morally outrageous response to the complex apparatus of exploitation which John Doe did not personally create, cannot personally mend, and often barely understands. A *crime* is not an acceptable response to a "crime," even if we accept, or tolerate, the morality of an eye for an eye and a tooth for a tooth.

Then again, the complexity of the social machine insures (exceptions aside) that it purveys to its very victims a mass of benefits—many of them pocketed without a word—alongside the highly visible mass of injuries. Theft, on the other hand, is injury unalloyed.

So far, then, I am justifying my outcry. A proper preliminary conclusion seems to be that the correct response to a diffusely guilty system is the diffuse remedy of social, economic, and political reform, while the correct response to specific crime is specific punishment. The morally thoughtful citizen should therefore simultaneously "understand" the robber and "write my poem," that is to say press for social changes with one hand and crack the whip with the other. So the gut response of my poem is justified, and I should only attach to it—in order to make it philosophically sound—a second half outlining the injustices done to the robbers since their births, and the remedies to be instantly applied.

Unlike my friends in the business world—once more—I refuse to base my right to punish criminals on the principle that most of them are in fact punks who plunder because plundering is a quick and exciting shortcut to success. The reply to this argument is classic and irrefutable: it is we who made punks of them. We keep the masses poor, and that poverty invariably inseminates a number of the poor with the brutality of which we then complain.

Encouraged by this concession, however, the outlaw makes bold to counterattack my conclusions. Why should he be required to wait for a day in some remote future of which he will have no part—or indeed for a day which may never come at all—when "due process" without hold-ups, forced entries, and worse outrages will have mended the system and given all men and women at least the basic goods of life? What, pray, is he to do right now, while he is young, lusty, ambitious, and desperate? Furthermore, what if, betaking himself to peaceful political agitation, he has his nose bloodied by the police or the Mafia—or his life taken from him? What? Must he go hungry, must he go jobless, and have his bones broken besides? Say, then, that we advise him to emigrate rather than burglarize my car. Easy advice; but has he not as good a right as mine to a decent living at home? Well then, let him select his victims with greater moral accuracy and fleece rich Gradgrind instead of a middle-purse like myself. For have we not established that the richer a man is, the more he feeds upon the poor, therefore the greater his guilt? Alas, Gradgrind keeps an armed guard over his property and does not park his limousine unattended in side streets. As for sensational kidnapings and ransomings of millionaires, they are the luxury trade of crime. What is our average lawbreaker to do while waiting for the social millennium?

In all honesty, I cannot see my way out of this stalemate. My outcry seems just. So does the robber's grab. The higher resolution, the becalming synthesis—a just and prosperous social system—lies too far over hill and dale (or rather over peak and abyss) to be helpful. I grant that my right to keep my property in my own hands is tainted by my fractional social guilt. But I claim that the robber's right to seize the goods which society has not allowed him to work for is tainted by the brutality of his act. When he wins a round and makes off with my suitcase, I may in good conscience fulminate my poem against him. Should I win the round, he has every right to curse me from the dismal side of the prison bars. So goes the puzzling world.

I have already given several hints that this equilibrium which I call a moral stalemate can be broken by certain additions or reductions in the moral baggage each party carries onto the scene of the crime. The equilibrium represents the typical, the general, the normal; it refers to the mass; but we can easily explore to one side and the other of the middle mass. For instance, my right to attack the burglar (whether through the police or through a poetic explosion) takes on weight the farther we move from a

Neapolitan condition of society toward what we can emblematically call a Swiss one. This condition is summarized, a bit loosely perhaps, in the common saying: "Here, anyone who wants to work can find a job." Where this is approximately true, indignation becomes more righteous than elsewhere, for it can be safely inferred that the lawbreaker is indeed out for the "fast buck" without benefit of guilt upon our side for making him the lawbreaker he is.

I have already mentioned, too, that my moral right to anger waxes and wanes according to the degree to which I am a beneficiary of the socio-economic machine. A neutral deontologist will differentiate between a robbed *latifundista*, notorious for his exactions, and the sack of a clinic for the wretched natives of some faraway desert. And let us recall to the stage again the thief with the dying mother or the weeping child. His moral baggage gains weight; my fury is disarmed; and not infrequently the courts themselves are lenient with him. I note in passing that stealing because of an extreme hunger for drugs wins a dose of moral approval in an ethical province to which I do not belong.

The predator loses a decisive portion of his moral right as soon as he takes the next step in his aggression, and passes from the mere grabbing of property to an attack on the victim's body. If I can be forgiven for swallowing up an immense subject in a sentence or two, I will say that I have in mind here not only the everyday shooting or stabbing in home or street, but also the vast panorama of most revolutions, where diffuse socio-economic wrong is countered with bloodshed, or, in a lower bolgia, where *some* bloodshed is paid off with *torrents* of blood. This allows only for a yet deeper circle of the human hell, where the criminality of the social system loses its diffuse character; where all is exaction, brutality, torture, wanton killing; where one must kill in order not to be killed. A pit is reached at last where moral judgment disintegrates under excessive pressure. Revolution must clear the arena before moral norms can operate again.

Short of this, however, the anger of the victim of bodily violence—the outcry, too, of the witness, the reporter, the historian—takes on a weight it is hard to balance on the other side of the scale. No humor would have unfanged my poem (if I could ever have written one) had my wife been beaten or murdered before being robbed. At this level of violence, even a deep-dyed friend of the suffering proletariat is likely to demur, and to countenance punishment while working for social amelioration. Who is willing to declare bludgeoning a fair reciprocation for diffuse socio-economic injustice?

In practice, the moment we take the quantum leap from thieving to physical violence (that it to say from an assault on our property to an attempt upon our existence) the socio-economic considerations I have looked into so far tend to make way for a new line of defense: that of mental incompetence—neurosis or psychosis.

At this point, the distinction between Naples and Switzerland becomes irrelevant to the argument, for if mental sickness works, morally or legally, as a block to punishment, it does so whether or not the aggressor was one of the disinherited of society. What then, at this new level, does the gut clamor for? What does the moral sense preach? What should the law do with rapists, torturers, or murderers whom—and this is my postulate—we acknowledge to be sick or "incapable," as they say, "of distinguishing between right and wrong"?

We know what tricks the "insanity plea" plays on our judicial system in America. It barges into domestic cases of revenge, into cases of murder for rapine or amusement, into cases of mayhem under the influence of drugs, and finally, most ludicrously, into cases of political murder—because by a curious wrinkle in our complex culture, our political figures are habitually cut down by maniacs rather than ideologues. If President Kennedy's assassin had lived instead of being shot to death by a second maniac, he would have enjoyed the same scenario as did Mr. Hinckley, who tried to kill President Reagan, or Miss Moore, who shot at President Ford. Every time, out of our intellectual mists emerge our contemporary shamans, the psychiatrists. One cocksure faction declares the gunman mentally competent. The other cocksure faction declares him insane. Chance, mere chance, decides whether the subject of their analyses will end up in a psychiatric ward giving interviews, or in the penitentiary for life demanding parole.

Here is another case. A young woman by the name of Tanya Robinson is raped in her senior year at a university. At first she appears to cope with this horror. "She bought a can of chemical repellent for her purse. She got a dog and went to self-defense classes." One day she wins a prize from a radio station by calling in the right title of a popular tune. The friendly young disc jockey hands her the prize in person. Presently Tanya begins to hear the disc jockey's voice. "Robinson would be sitting, talking calmly with her friends, then would break off in mid-sentence and remark just as matter-of-factly that she would have to do something about the voices in her head. . . . She had thought her head was bugged and she couldn't understand why he was doing this to her head." By now she has a radio in every room in her apartment, and believes that every remark, every song is aimed at her by the disc jockey. Apparently it does not occur to anyone that she ought to be instantly put away; not even to the therapist whom she regularly consults in a psychiatric clinic. She often talks of suicide. She leaves town, goes far away in order to get out of the disc jockey's range, but his voice continues to hound her. Desperate and infuriated, she returns, acquires a gun, corners the disc jockey, and blasts him to death. A witness speaks: "I heard him hollering and pleading. 'Please don't, please don't.' I'll hear that the rest of my life, so pitiful, him abegging. Then two more shots."

What do we do with that harrowing cry? Is it sacred, as I suggested at the start? Does it turn—transferred to his father, mother, wife, children, you, and me—into a clamor for retribution which cannot be gainsaid? Or, reminding ourselves that we have progressed beyond the old vendetta morality, do we forgive the poor raped girl and blame ourselves, if blame we must, for not having caught her in time, and safeguarded her in an institution before instead of after the kill? In short, does insanity checkmate guilt, and are we trapped in another impasse?

If so, the prickly question arises almost every time, where does insanity end and sanity begin? What killer shall place us in this moral stalemate, and what killer are we free to kill? Let us consider a "warped personality," that of Robert Alton Harris, sitting in Death Row at San Quentin Prison. One day Robert and his younger brother Daniel spotted two teen-aged boys in the parking lot of a fast-food restaurant. The Harris brothers were planning to rob a bank that afternoon, and they wanted somebody else's car. Robert pointed a stolen 9-millimeter Luger at the boys and told them to drive to a lonely spot in the hills. The younger brother followed in the Harrises' own car. After stopping the two cars, Robert explained to the young boys that he needed their car for a bank robbery. An apparently friendly arrangement was made. The lads would wait for a while, then walk into town and report their car stolen.

As the two boys walked away, Robert shot one in the back. Then he ran after the other one, and killed him with four shots. Discovering that the first victim was still alive, he knelt down, put the Luger to the boy's head, and fired again. The head, according to Daniel, "exploded like a balloon." This done, Robert gave a laugh that "froze Daniel's blood."

The two brothers drove to a friend's house in the stolen car. There Robert ate the victims' hamburgers. Daniel became nauseated, but Robert laughed at him for being a sissy. Still elated, he drove back with his brother to the area where he had killed the boys in order to gun down some policemen, but finding no one, the two finally proceeded to the bank they wanted to rob. On the way, Robert noticed remnants of flesh on his gun-barrel. "I really blew that guy's brains out," he said, and began to laugh again. Half an hour after robbing the bank, the Harrises were arrested. Robert, it turned out, was better at killing than stealing. After his conviction, like Iago, he talked no more. A sister reported: "He just doesn't see the point of talking. He told me he had his chance, he took the road to hell and there's nothing more to say."

Our age, however, has a great deal more to say. In other epochs, the question asked of an action was, is it good or evil? Today we ask what is its cause. We intellectuals, that is. We who have relegated moral assertion to the ignorant masses like some Lovelace palming off a worn-out mistress upon the village clown. The exact sciences have all the prestige now, and so we leave it to the God-fearing Kansas farmer to fret over right and wrong, while we ask for "psychological factors that triggered the murder." Accordingly, a search into the "underlying" causes of Robert Harris's crimes quickly yielded the customary horrors. When the baby's father visited his wife in the hospital, his first words were: "Who is the father of that bastard?" Convinced that the boy was not his, the father abused his wife, who in turn began to hate her son. Money, of course, was scarce; and he was her fifth child. Again the sister: "I remember one time we were in the car and mother was in the back seat with Robbie in her arms. He was crying and my father threw a glass bottle at him, but it hit my mother in the face. The glass shattered and Robbie starting screaming. I'll never forget it; her face was all pink, from the mixture of blood and milk. She ended up blaming Robbie for all the hurt. . . ." And again: "He'd come up to my mother and just try to rub his little hands on her leg or her arm. He just never got touched at all. She'd just push him away or kick him. One time she bloodied his nose when he was trying to get close to her." The father stayed drunk most of the time. One day—there were nine children by then—he was arrested for molesting a daughter. The family survived on welfare. The father was rearrested later for the same offense. Once the reporting daughter placed a pistol to her sleeping father's temple, but failed to pull the trigger.

Young Harris began to be arrested himself from the time he went to school. He was raped several times in prison, but soon became a tough who scared the others. His brothers and sisters were aware of his "crazy instinct to destroy." He liked to torture animals. He killed a young neighbor because the latter had sent Robert's niece on too many errands. In prison the psychiatrist, like everyone else, noted his imperviousness to remorse. There, among other foul deeds, he helped gang-rape an inmate. Nevertheless, he was let out on parole, and five months later killed the two teen-agers. On Death Row he was thoroughly hated by his fellow-convicts, who were reported to be looking forward to his execution.

Everyone will recognize the typical "profile." And we know enough about "how the other half lives"—we middle-class nestlings reared with all the pieties and devotions—to be forced to trust this newspaper story in all the essentials. If the argument is advanced—as was its equivalent when we were discussing mere robbers—that many deprived and battered youngsters (including Robert's siblings) grow up nevertheless to become law-fearing citizens, we disqualify it out of hand, for it is inevitable that given certain atrocious psychological conditions in childhood and adolescence, *a number* of individuals will become criminals. That *all* do not become criminals is equally inevitable, to be sure, because the atrocious conditions vary immensely on one side, and the victims of these conditions—even when they are twins—vary immensely on the other—so complex and exceptional a psychological compound is each individual. The upshot is, at any rate, that we cannot damn Robert for being a killer on the ground that Daniel was none.

That Tanya Robinson was flatly insane even her prosecutor will admit. But do we draw the line on this or that side of Robert Harris? Has he or has he not been so brutally warped since infancy that we would be brutes ourselves to hold him accountable for his murders? And on which side of the line shall we place the drug addict? Here is a youth whom socio-economic deprivation and psychological calamity at home have driven to "the drug scene." So far he has not lashed out at the world in any newsworthy manner. Now, however, thoroughly "high," he goes outdoors, draws a gun (of course he has a gun, who doesn't in our blessed land?), and randomly kills a few people: an old lady walking her dog, a tourist from another country admiring the neat lawns in front of the neat houses, a man coming out of a store with a pint of milk in a brown bag. As usual, we have the witnesses, reporting, say, the old man on his knees before the young punk, begging to be spared . . .

Shall we again raise the question of *our* fractional guilt? How shall we answer a phalanx of Bolshevik angels and French Left-Bank spirits at the Last Judgment, when they hint that the socio-economic deprivations for which we have already admitted our participatory guilt caused the psychological warps which caused these crimes? Our reply comes in two parts. First we demand that our accusers sort out all those whose mental aberration is demonstrably independent of socio-economic deprivation. The well-to-do go mad too, and furthermore a number of insanities or warps are securely founded in chemical or electric dysfunctions which will appear in Utopia as readily as in Los Angeles. In the second part of our defense we argue that this time, at worst, our guilt is, and is admitted by our accusers to be, twice or even three times removed. We caused (fractionally) the socio-economic hardships which caused the emotional warp which caused the drug-taking which caused the murder. And the like. At worst, then, the guilt of the victim is sharply diminished, and for a moment we may think that the scale has tilted, the killer must die.

Instead, however, I fully grant the plea of mental incompetence for all the criminals I have pictured here, and all those for whom they stand. If the defense is willing to admit that a cocaine trafficker who murdered a competitor or a seductive rascal who poisoned an elderly flame for her stocks and bonds is sane, well and good. But once we enter the shadowland of the deranged, and the defense mobilizes a crew of psychiatrists, I want no drawing of lines here, or there, or a little farther yet: this man is a lunatic and must not hang, this other is just sane enough to fry, and so forth. But then, are we locked once and for all in a stalemate? Is our outcry not to be appeased? Do we make the land safe for lunatics?

How curious (I repeat) that such questions did not trouble our ancestors! Dante's evildoers are in hell, and not for a short three-score years and ten! It is the deed that counts: is it good or is it evil? Never mind the "psychological background." And yet we too apply punishment in one sector of life without inquiring into the wrongdoer's psychic history, namely when we bring up our children. We regard the act, and we regard its intention (judging that as best we can), but we do not normally regard the psychological background. We will not paddle the child if we are convinced that he intended to help the kitten he in fact hurt; but once we believe that the action answered by and large the inten-tion—he *set out* to torment the kitten—we are quick to punish. Here too a minor outcry is satisfied, for even here "something" in us demands retribution and goes hungry (so to speak) if hurts can be given without chastisement. But, more important, we feel and feel quite rightly that we are adding necessary ingredients to the child's psychological soup—a homely but useful metaphor. Our concern is for the future.

To break the stalemate, then, I make my appeal, as many have done before, to the principle of warning and prevention. Into the psychological broth of our culture must go a strong ingredient of terror at any velleity of violence. I do not need to invoke this principle with respect to admittedly sane murderers, inasmuch as the ethical weight is heavy against them to begin with. But now I make bold to ask for the same ultimate penalty against the sick, though one cannot do so without grief. Observe that it is the same grief—intensified, of course—we feel when we punish the child, knowing full well that he lacked the "mental equipment" for rational choice.

I am well aware that few liberal thinkers believe in this warn-ing principle. Beginning with the shamanistic formula "Studies show," the skeptics argue that nothing in the legal system will deter the mentally warped (or for that matter the mentally straight) from committing their crimes. It is understood that some malefactors are in fact looking for punishment: they kill in order to be killed. The rest, it is said, are operating in a medium of distorted conceptions of their fellow human beings, and driven by urges that sweep aside fears of legal sanctions as easily as an army tank disposes of twigs. All we can do is try to catch them in advance, give them psychological therapy, release them when they are cured, or keep them in asylums if their impulses continue to be dangerous.

Much of this can be granted. There is no question that *a number* of warped or insane minds will remain untouched by anticipation of gallows, axe, electric chair, inoculation, or gas chamber. But what is that number? Are there not a few, are there not *quite* a few who, foreseeing a dreadful punishment, will swerve toward another project than killing? That number—whose real size is unknown to us—is enough to break the moral stalemate. The moral sense is empowered to give satisfaction to our outcry by directing the law to exact swift, dreadful death for death, even when the killer is mentally incompetent. A truly balanced ethic forbids the law to take the plea of insanity into account. The law must present to the mentally warped—and *a fortiori* to the mentally straight—terrible images that will prevent at least *some* murders, and be of at least *some* help in pacifying society.

You see the premise underlying my stand. It is that the persons we call mentally sick are by no means exempt from cultural forces. The choices they make—and they do make choices—are not made in a cultural vacuum. That a population enjoying universal suffrage should be disarmed—that no one should be allowed to possess lethal weapons—I take utterly for granted. Tanya Robinson should have found it extremely difficult to locate a gun. But in addition, it should not have occurred to her to look for one. This particular alternative should have been missing from the menu of possible actions created in her mind by our cultural forces. When the poor creature went mad, she should have been "driven" to such acts as camping before the disc jockey's door and refusing to eat (as happens in certain cultures), or going at him with her two fists. And this, I think, might be rapidly achieved by systematic draconian retribution for violence. Punishment must be *terrifying* and *swift*. By all means let us spend money on treating the sick in time; but if we fail, and if they kill, let them remain in their death an overpowering image in the minds of the living, sick and well alike, and especially in young minds busily acquiring disposable channels of future operation.

At the same time, my program for pacifying our too irritable race demands that exhibitions of gross brutality (and only of gross brutality) be forbidden in the popular arts. This means censorship—no use waffling about it. But if the word frightens you, call it a law against the promotion of brutality. I take it as an absolute axiom that the portrayal of violence, with or without a moral tacked on, is an incitement to violence: not in you, dear reader, and not in me, but in the social aggregate. But is not censorship of any sort an odious remedy? Does it not kill our precious liberty? Liberty, I reply, is a thing of degrees. We accept thousands of encoded stops to our actions without feeling that we are squirming under a dictatorship. We do not cry out, every time an ordinance against this or that misbehavior is passed, that we are about to be ordinanced to death. Neither the domino nor the house of cards image fits the situation. Why then should a specific law directed against a well-defined category of expression so theatrically alarm us? Is expression so different a beast from behavior that the one can be safely legislated but not the other? Is not expression a species *of* behavior? It is; and therefore I am not afraid to ask that the hooligan violence of our motion pictures be outlawed. I do not for a moment believe that this prohibition will lead to others, and turn our free country into a tyranny.

The censorship of novels and even plays need not be quite so severe, for they cannot match the trompe-l'oeil realism of moving photography. In Athens of old it made sense to oblige producers of drama to report and never exhibit scenes of outrageous violence. Because the drama was the most lifelike art known, it possessed the power to influence behavior—for good and ill alike. The most lifelike art today is obviously the film. It is so lifelike as to become, for a considerable part of the mass audience, part of life itself. It teaches, it shows, or it insinuates. And I feel that we cannot forbid murder with one hand, and with the other issue to the people a flood of grisly, gory motion pictures. Gross brutality may still be reported, as on the Athenian stage, but it must either not be shown at all, or shown under such a strong light of fiction—so transmogrified by *art*—that the spectators (most of them young) can take nothing of it into their house- and street-lives.

To return to our criminals, I have no "Studies show" of my own, no experiments with "control groups," no well-funded "findings" to prove that a reign of lawful terror against terror would gut our incredible crime rate. But neither does the other side, all claims to the contrary notwithstanding. In every country where scientific studies or sound statistics are favored, punishment for murder is always uncertain, and if meted out at all, always slowly, often "humanely" (as in psychiatric wards), and at its harshest discreetly. We cannot scientifically study the effect of swift, certain, and dreadful punishment on crime deterrence because we do not inflict it. The psychological soup we feed our youngsters and adolescents does not contain the sharp ingredient we want for our studies. We give our populations the most vivid pre-perceptions of murder (especially with the help of motion pictures) but a fog of mitigations, alleviations, delays, and uncertainties with regard to punishment. The future murderer has probably a brighter vision of the penitentiary's law library than of its electric chair.

Not only do we fail to make our punishment swift, certain, and dreadful, we also studiously avoid humiliating the culprit. The electric chair has many defenders, the pillory none. As it happens, this fastidiousness of ours with respect to "human dignity" plays into the average killers' hands. We accommodate these *machos* by treating them to sanctions "tough guys" expect. This is too much consideration. Perhaps the growing-up Robert Harris required not only a vision of quick and inevitable hanging for himself, but the prospect of a more humiliating possibility—the prospect, for instance, of having his ears or hands chopped off. Why on earth (I ask) do these measures offend us more than death itself? Not that I mean to counsel outright that we chop off ears or hands. But I do recommend *some* dreadful deflation of the killer's ego. Humiliation is a perennial but underused weapon. Every society should study the psychological situation of its own time, and strike at killers with the particular demotions of the ego they fear most.

With incredulous headshakes over my armchair barbarousness, you watch me moving from an already "callous" justification of capital punishment for ordinary killers to support for the execution of the criminally insane, and thence to shockingly biblical forms of requital which even our most retrogade Fundamentalists choose to overlook in the holy texts. In truth, I am as squeamish as you are. I can advocate grimnesses on paper easily enough, but might, in a pinch, demur at voting for them in the ballot booth, let alone performing them in person. I, like you, prefer to have the cows, sheep, and chickens I devour slaughtered out of sight. And as long as it was neither my son nor my nephew who happened to be murdered by Robinson or Harris, why not embrace "civilized" mercy—to wit, lifelong care in a mental ward for the insane, and for the rational a life term in jail, eased by the possibility of parole. Sitting in one's study and analyzing all the "factors" at one's ease—son or nephew safely ordering their hamburger at the local fast-food dispenser—the gut-clamor fades, its "sacredness" wanes, and the scale begins its tilt back in favor of the murderer. We do not want to dwell on that intolerable "Please don't! Please don't!"; we do not like to think of our own mother kneeling and wailing before her brain is shattered; just as we want nothing to do with guillotines, nooses, electric chairs, or cut-off ears and tongues. But is this not altogether too much squeamishness? If I do yield to mine—and oh how easily I yield!—I do so at any rate with a deep sense of betraying my own conclusions—of evading the taxes, so to speak, of my own ethical province.

If I am strong enough to stick to my principles—and capable of weathering that sentimental, perfunctory and democratized ethic according to which there is no difference between murder and execution for murder—I must enter obvious qualifications to the rule of death for death. Perhaps I should call it the rule of shocking death for shocking death. I have already argued that the execution of the murderer must be swift and striking; otherwise it cannot deter crime and we relapse into our stalemate. On the other side of the equation, shocking is shorthand for two fundamental conditions. The murder must have been intended. And the murder must have been committed free of extreme provocation.

With regard to intention, I have implied already that it can and therefore must be imputed, nine times out of ten, to those who plead mental incompetence or insanity. The highly typical murderers we have examined can all premeditate. They plan and plot. They *set out*. This, I am arguing, is what makes them amenable to the cultural forces I spoke of before, forces which might have veered their planning and plotting in a nonlethal direction. Be that as it may, many insanities leave the reasoning power, the plotting power, unimpaired; some even sharpen it. Accordingly, having thrown out of court the problem of mental competence, we fasten on the resolvable question of intention as normally inferred from observable facts: the pistol duly loaded, aimed, and discharged at the victim. And this, whether the assailant stalked his prey for a year, or murdered him in the course of a tavern brawl. It is in fact extremely important that we do not wink at "instant murders," the sort so common in the United States, where a man responds to an insult by knifing the offender to death, or the kind more common in Latin countries, where the irate husband shoots his peccant wife, her lover, or both. Our culture must see to it that the "unthinking" actions brought about by "blind rage" be chosen, even as the rage is raging, from a repertory of nonfatal moves. Hence both the carefully planned political murder and the crime committed in the heat of passion must be decreed to be intentional.

But our humane legislators, lawyers, and judges tend to ask the prosecution that it "prove" an intention to kill as against an intention to injure or frighten. Here, for instance, is a killer, Marcelino Ramos, who orders two restaurant employees into a cooler, tells them to remove their caps, kneel, and say their prayers. He then knocks them out with a pipe, and joins an accomplice in robbing the place. The job completed, he returns to the cooler and fires. A twenty-year-old girl dies, the other is nicked by a bullet and survives. At his trial, Ramos argues that he was merely obeying orders—the Nazis' favorite argument. His partner had ordered him to kill the employees because, as he had been their fellow-worker once, they would be able to identify him. However, like many a kind-hearted servant or minister in folk tales, Ramos decided just to frighten the employees with his rifle-shots and fool his partner into thinking he had killed them.

By bad luck he misfired a little. Fortunately for him, the California Supreme Court, impressed by that nick on the survivor, resolved that the prosecution had not proved an absolute determination to kill, and reversed the death sentence a lower court had naively imposed.

For me, anyone equipped with a loaded firearm, a sharp or blunt instrument capable of killing, or a poison (and so forth)—anyone so furnished, and then *setting out* to apply his instrument with decided force, should know as he knows the sun rises in the morning that an intention to kill will be fastened on him in court, and that he will need to bring in unbreakable evidence to break that presumption. And what if he really but really did aim at the calf of the leg, but the victim twitched in the wrong direction and got killed instead? Let *him* prove that really but really of his. All *we* know (the victim is dead) is that he indulged himself in death-dealing behavior. Perhaps God knows better. But God is not telling us. The luckless killer unbosoms himself on the stand. He meant no harm, or else—a very little harm. But *we* shall tell him that from childhood on (in the dispensation I dream of) he has heard that using a weapon means deciding to kill, and that few have managed to wriggle out through the tiny hole of innocent intention. Innocent intention with a rifle or kitchen knife in hand!

The rule of intentionality rides roughshod—and, I might add, rides with some contempt—over the issue, dear to American jurisprudence, whether the offender was capable of telling right from wrong. This test is useless to the point of being bizarre. What matters is that anyone capable of planning and plotting—indeed, anyone capable of carrying on the sort of quarrel that will drive him to kill "in a blind rage"—knows that killing is *forbidden*. Whether the prohibition is right or wrong in his mind—whether his ethical perceptions are deranged or altogether lost—is his private affair. We do not in fact meddle with his ethical notions if they keep him within the law. Let him believe it is right to kill a disc jockey or a president; but let him know that it is forbidden, and let him foresee a terrifying punishment if he transgresses.

Leaving aside cases of total lunacy (the maniac in an asylum stabbing a nurse, for instance) I proceed to the only major category of exceptions, namely murders committed under conditions of extreme physical provocation. One hears from time to time, for instance, of men—personages like the father of Robert Harris—subjecting the weaker members of their household or work team to a regime of brutality and terror from which we (the jury) recognize that very nearly no issue can be found other than murder—as Robert's sister almost killed her father in his sleep. Self-defense against direct attack with a lethal weapon is of course allowed by outcry, by the moral sense, and by law, all three in harmony; but I want to indicate that less direct ferocities can also make an appeal to us as coming under the principle of extreme provocation.

Of course, we must not give the armed robber the benefit of this principle if he finds himself "compelled"—contrary, he claims, to his original intention—to kill a homeowner who has threatened him with a weapon of his own. Our procedures must so terrify prospective thieves and burglars that they will exercise their profession unarmed as a matter of course. Only then, I might add, can a society allow itself to bear down upon that same armed homeowner. He would no longer have the right to presume that the burglar is armed, and would be severely punished for killing a man who only wanted his silver.

But here I leave off. Why prolong distinctions and qualifications? I omit the thousand and one particulars and display only the large surfaces. My poem issued from a sort of magma of thoughts and feelings. I have tried to sift them and to organize them with fastidious logic. Why should not a poet be fastidiously logical? Is not extreme accuracy of vision his highest claim to the attention of mankind? But a poet thinking carefully about crime is not a criminologist writing for a law journal. I say, let us have poets (in Shelley's sense) erect the large principles to guide us, and let the specialists—criminologists among them—work out the minutiae.

Another privilege the poet enjoys is that of dreaming up rational but inapplicable solutions. He can be a pure scientist of human affairs, unconcerned with practical possibilities. Every society has at any given period of its history a feasible repertory of arguments and measures, equivalent at the social level to the menu mentioned before of available behaviors in the individual.

I do not pretend that this repertory can be exactly known, and it is bound to be especially recondite to observers embedded in the society they want to observe. Still, we can believe in its reality, and now and then, in a boundary situation, we become conscious of the finite range within which we are, happily enough, "jailed." It follows that an only or a best solution to a social problem (like the problem of crime) may be culturally unavailable to a given society even when the latter possesses the information and the technical means to apply the solution. A neighboring society, or a society of another epoch, may instead enforce this solution without compunction. Saudi Arabia is capable of cutting off your hand for stealing, but America is not. Or: one nation practices infanticide in order to reduce population, another perishes rather than commit this "abomination." Or (to illustrate philosophical rather than behavioral taboos): American partisans of the right to abortion must argue, ludicrously, that the fetus is somehow less than alive, because they *cannot* argue that an unborn life is less sacrosanct than the life of a schoolchild. Similarly, I have no doubt that a reign of terror against violent criminals—a lawful cutting through the ever-thickening layers of legalisms we have packed between murder and punishment—is "forever" culturally excluded in the United States. Yet I would argue that no other solution is "correct"—including the obvious one of equal and general prosperity to which all liberals cling, and which is at any rate unachievable.

Fortunately, behavioral limits have their compensations, for one never knows what *other* deviltries will be let loose upon the land in the process of stamping out a social affliction. I have said already that I do not believe in the domino image with respect to censorship. Nor do I believe that a draconian dealing with crime would turn us into a Central American sort of republic. But—who can be sure? Sometimes it is better to hang on to familiar devils. Besides, some of the cultural forces that paralyze us vis-à-vis our hordes of rapists and murderers deserve our praise and respect. They are excesses of virtue. What then is my conclusion? Nothing at all. Every society dies with a load of unsolved problems on its hands, even though some of these problems were "technically" amenable to solution. We, I believe, are destined to go the way of all national flesh beset by a crime rate that makes us a wonder to other advanced societies. Our only comfort, then, is to reflect that no simple judgment can be pronounced on our failure. The failure is scandalous, yes; but viewed all around, it also presents an honorable side.

The Poetry of Our Climate:
Slouch, Bric-a-brac,
and Decayed Statement

Berceuse

The prisoner falls down a ditch
and clutching at his pain he sighs
"I'll stop a bit." A soldier shoots,
the prisoner tips over, dies.

The soldier jumps into a hole,
an airplane sees him where he lies.
The bullets make a dotty line,
the soldier bleeds a pint and dies.

Home goes the pilot up the wind,
alas a shell bursts as he flies.
He thinks of mother and himself,
dives into the ground and dies.

Beside his head a daisy stands,
the night spreads out the stars;
a blade of weed leaps round her stem,
the daisy chokes, death is no farce.

I rise and strut and din at God
"Pity! Comfort! And denounce!"
God says, "I note your claim," and winks,
and all the stars, applauding, bounce.

I am not all quatrains, I have even written free verse, but my lines keep declaring their will to be music. Good music? Bad music? That is not the question here. All I am saying is that the

First published in *The New England Quarterly and Bread Loaf Review*, Autumn 1983 words willingly arrange themselves in rhythmic rows, the lines group themselves in equal clusters, the rhymes and the near-rhymes often chime in, and now and then a particular sound in the vowels or consonants speaks out. This never came of any program—some premeditated aesthetic system that I had decided to obey at the age of eighteen when I began to versify. I wrote first and reasoned later. It is only now, looking down and back from a dry altitude of years, that I take pleasure in naming the weapons I chose on temperamental grounds, and those I left hanging in the armory unused. Pleasure, but along with pleasure some sober instruction, mostly by contrasting these more or less "instinctive" methods of mine with the procedures of other poets. How far my instruction is true and how far false the next few pages will candidly allow you to conclude.

Am I mistaken in thinking that out of the music of a poem emerges its *dignity*? I am even disposed to use "music" and "dignity" interchangeably. For the absolute tunefulness of lyric poetry—of letters, words, and measures—is really so far beneath the most rudimentary ditty that, when we say "music" in a poem, we are all but speaking metaphorically. Whether we listen to the soft sounds of Tennyson's

> Breathing like one that hath a weary dream

or to the harsh ones of Browning's

> Irks care the crop-full bird?

how far does either melody take us into genuine music—the simplest song, a passage on the violin or tuba? As for rhyme—can anything be more primitive? To keep returning to the same note every few moments! No: the music of poetry is better thought of as another *structural* element. It is, like all structures, a round won against entropy, an elevation above ordinary disorder. A poetry that rhymes, or a poetry that uses a steady rhythm or a recurrent meter, is a poetry that walks erect. It is organized. It bears itself with dignity. It has pride. And that is why, when we proceed to its propositions, we discover that they too tend to reveal a degree of substance, of importance. Unless humor is intended, these propositions usually decline to be feeble. Good posture in the "form" tends to marry good deportment in the "content." As for tunefulness in itself, all that remains—listen to Tennyson and Browning again—is some trifling with vowels, or labials, or sibilants, or percussives—nothing that makes or breaks a poem—and nothing that carries any weight unless we know the meaning beforehand. Take Tennyson's eeees and make up a sentence concerning the flaying alive of infants: suddenly the music that was supposed to convey a sense of slumber turns sinister. Or else, read a contract for a shipment of lumber to a person who knows no English. He will hear as much or as little music in that as he would if you read him the purest Spenser. For in the lumber contract we will hand him pleasing sounds, repetitions of vowels and consonants, iambs and anapests, anything. Again: what we call music in a poem is above all a major principle of organization, and organization is dignity, is elevation, is pride.

And that, at bottom, is why we hear so little rhythm, meter, and rhyme in the verse of our epoch. We get this music in "ages of confidence"—that is to say, in the entire recorded past of mankind—when poets and readers believed in God, in Nation, in Man. And we lose it when the self-assured stiffness has gone out of man's thinking, and all the creeds have gone limp. The communist world has different problems, but in our own cultural parish, because so few poets care to encourage us, like Tennyson again,

> To strive, to seek, to find, and not to yield,

few are willing to use even the bare rhythm of such a line. In the broadest terms, form follows ideology, and the decay of form follows the decay of ideology.

Granted, we see all kinds of poetry nowadays. Think of the hair-raising thousands upon thousands of men, women, boys, and girls who court the Muses (as they used to say) in this supposedly materialistic country of ours. You will find music (*somebody* is bound to be writing villanelles: the statistics demand it) and you will find the confidence that goes with music—something, perhaps, like Theodore Roethke's

> She was the sickle: I, poor I, the rake,
> Coming behind her for her pretty sake
> (But what prodigious mowing we did make).

Bold voices are still singing; but they are not typical. The most genuine voice of hamburgerland—or our cultural dependency overseas—doles out the likes of

> me, milk bottles by bike
> guernsey milk, six percent butterfat
> raw and left to rise natural
>   ten cents a quart
> slipped on the ice turning
>   in to the driveway
> and broke all nine bottles.

And so on. Who made this? I opened an anthology called *A Controversy of Poets*, opened it anywhere, and fell on page 430. The lucky man was Gary Snyder. It could have been almost anyone.

This is the most native of native voices; and it is so very native above all because it slouches. For the textbook American, slouching begins at the legs and arms but ends with philosophy and politics. With philosophy, as I have just now pointed out, in that he has lost confidence in the old "noble" abstractions and all he has left is a feeling that it's nice to be nice to everybody (a worthy feeling, to be sure), or that life is hell. With politics, in that music, erect posture, pride—the rising above something that is low—all this suggests detested class distinctions: the patriciate with its spine straight, chin high, eye imperious. The music in poetry signifies a patrician order of words victorious over words as amiable rabble. The poets of a nation which has abolished the elite along with the longing for it, and whose passion for psychological debunking has given it the cynical conviction that men are swine and women sows, the poets of such a nation instinctively abandon stern structure and high music and adopt a casual method—feet on the table, shirttails out, jeans with patches, popcorn—that will fit the modest or discouraged propositions they still care to handle, like Allen Ginsberg's

> Go fuck yourself with your atom bomb.
> I don't feel good don't bother me

—two lines that neatly render the sequence "let's be nice" (and not kill each other) and "life is hell."

When I speak of high confidence and erect posture, I do not naively mean "positive thinking." The "Berceuse" makes this plain, I hope. The question I am raising is not one of optimism versus pessimism, but of the deportment with which either is carried. Nor am I making a foolish equation between music and excellence: tools are but tools; it is the wielding that counts. I may not think highly of

> I don't feel good don't bother me,

but I am no enthusiast of Coleridge either when he sings,

> My genial spirits fail;
> And what can these avail
> To lift the smothering weight from off my breast?

What can music avail here? Nevertheless, when all other things are equal (to be sure, they never are), a musical poem will give more pleasure than one which rests its case, so to speak, on the commonplace sounds and pacings of the routine language. In other words, music is so much gained. It will not amount to much if all else is foul; but it is something at worst, and a great blessing at best.

To find the slouchers at home, we open any issue of *The American Poetry Review*. Here the curious inquirer will bag as many examples of this most authentically native poetry as he can possibly wish to collect. A sampling follows:

> Dear Dick: you know all that pissing and moaning
> I've been doing, feeling unloved, certain I was
> washed up with romance for good.

x

> Crunch of leaves, a step off the porch
> makes, covering small gravel.
> Wearing shoes now, feet-heels
> of summer, gradually
> leather softens.

x

> so that when you took me
> in that small, spare room
> we rented at a stopover

it would not be
rape, or mutual
transference.

x

my father was a derelict
you know
was having an affair
with his friend's wife
the three of them
went on a binge
returned to the apartment
to sleep it off.

x

I stand and listen, head bowed,
to my inner complaint.
Persons passing by think
I am searching for a lost coin.
You're fired, I yell inside
after an especially bad episode.

x

This way of "moseyin' along" indefinitely—this democratic absence of form—attaches itself with the utmost naturalness to a subject matter consisting almost exclusively of a list of things and actions. The Imagists taught this lesson, but they were themselves responding to the "wind of history," so that it is perfectly safe to say that our poets would have found their way to listing things and actions all by themselves. Of course, there are things and things, and there are actions and actions. The alliance that formlessness sought was, inevitably, with low things and abject actions—or what used to be thought low and abject in the days of sturdy morals. The nine bottles of milk illustrate my point. Our landscape is littered with these bric-a-brac poems—poems like Frank O'Hara's, for example, with their

I just stroll into the PARK LANE
Liquor Store and ask for a bottle of Strega and
then I go back where I came from to 6th Avenue
and the tobacconist in the Ziegfeld Theatre and
casually ask for. . . .

anything you please, all but ad infinitum. Or John Berryman's

> I wrote a strong exam, but since it was Mark
> a personal friend, I had to add a note
> saying of the 42 books in the bloody course
> I'd only read 17.

A baleful quasi-doctrine of *omnism* seems to underlie this sort of poetry: anything goes, everybody can do it, everything is as good as everything else—the curious effect of which is to make sound, democratic Americans of these poets even when they appear to themselves to be arrant rebels, firebrands. Did you notice a chip in your cup this morning? Make a poem of it. That chip is as good as the Crucifixion. Did the rain soak your newspaper? Make a poem of it. Did the girl at the lunch counter smile at you? Make a poem of it. Her smile was sour, was it? Another poem. Is your beat-up station wagon blue? Did your shoe come unlaced? Did a ray of sunlight fall on your geranium? Poem, poem, poem.

In short, an orgy of *mimesis*. For we are asked to receive pleasure from a perfect, uncensored, unscreened, wholesale, and minute imitation of reality. There is something of Wordsworth's doctrine here too, because these poets "choose incidents and situations from common life"; they draw upon a "language really used by men"; and they attend to "humble and rustic life"—especially if we update "rustic" and call it "proletarian" or simply "pop." But if they are pupils of Wordsworth, they are corrupt ones, for Wordsworth calls for a *selection* of "language really used by men," he demands that "a certain coloring of the imagination" be thrown over ordinary incidents; and these are elitist policies that do not commend themselves to our best sans-culottists.

This poetry debases Walt Whitman as well. Whitman is its undeniable grandfather, but he is not responsible for his progeny. Whitman is *all* elevation: he tries, oh how he puffs and puffs and even succeeds now and then!—he tries to pull low things high: everything is noble, lofty, divine with him; while the epigones pull down—nothing is noble, lofty, divine. They resemble Whitman in that they are levelers; but they are levelers at a vastly different level. Whitman democratized Romanticism. The epigones merely democratize. Their clutter is devoid of exaltation. It is produced by quivering sensitivity to anything and everything that exists.

On the other hand, these poets have taken a logical and necessary measure that completes Whitman's achievement. Whitman had brought into the orb of poetry the innumerable humble objects of daily life, but his language had remained behind, drawing heavily on the mandarin British tradition. And no wonder. Since he wanted to elevate, to "heroize," these common objects, he had no inducement to apply a demeaning vocabulary or an erratic, insulting grammar to them. When the low-level leveling occurred, it simply found its adequate language. Thus Whitman stands strikingly midway between a "Johnsonian" aesthetic (derived from the French, to be sure) in which the common object is banned from poetry and the poet devotes himself to high thoughts nobly expressed (A X B), and our native contemporary poets who have banned high thoughts nobly expressed, and devote themselves to common objects listed in a demotic language (C X D). Whitman, in between (B X C), invited the common objects but exalted them by dipping them in the ennobling diction of classical poetry.

It may be thought that the poetic language has been immensely enriched in our times, inasmuch as, at long last, nothing that can be uttered is excluded. But this is not entirely true. While all the "low" words were gaining admittance by one door, a large number of words or expressions intolerably "noble" or "poetic" were being drummed out by another. If we counted words, we might discover that our poetry does avail itself of a larger vocabulary than that which sufficed, say, a Dryden or a Wordsworth; but a more important observation is that our vocabulary has *shifted*—shifted from the patrician to the populist range of the spectrum—and, incidentally, from a "polite" (that is to say general/elitist) vocabulary to a learned/technical one, for our poets are not afraid to combine demotic lingo with all manner of graduate-school pedantry.

Once again I feel the need to explain that I am groping for trends, typical phenomena, statistical preponderances. In the United States especially, the combination of huge population, drastically different backgrounds, and unhampered freedom of speech necessarily results in a flavorful variety of poetic expression. True, the "wind of history" does keep blowing in a given cardinal direction, so that certain preponderances are bound to occur. But they allow for all manner of permutations. Into my own collection, for instance, history has blown a substantial number of poems that slouch. It has also, I find, led me to embrace a full, modern vocabulary and to drop the "poeticisms" of another age. I am a child of my time when I begin a poem with:

> In Naples a gang of experts
> cracked our car in the glass eye
> we were lunching standing up a block away
> and they knew it
> scootered away with my suitcase
> leaving a dabble of blood.

But I have never been tempted, even when I slouch with the best and the worst, and even when I partake expansively of the modern vocabulary, to write bric-a-brac, that is to say egalitarian poetry. My mind functions hierarchically; it discriminates between chinks in cups and crucifixions; it calls one thing unimportant and the other important, and composes poetry accordingly. Here is an example of slouch, plain English, but no bric-a-brac, called "Impatience":

> Slow, oxen hours, witless muddy animals,
> I sit astride you
> Shoving you with my buttocks,
> I shout at you with the sweat in my face or
> Beg you beg you to get forward with my best furious
>   cajoleries
> And then again give you a knock between your ears
>   with my fist,
> But nothing.
> You take your insolent time, of course.
> I have to rejoice
> You lift those paws of yours at all
> And now and then we leave a tree behind.

The point of this illustration is that the elements making up the most native of our native poetry can and not infrequently do come uncoupled. History does not turn us into robots. "Impatience" displays the characteristic slouch of our times, inasmuch as it dispenses with all the musical enticements of the "Berceuse," but there is no list of clutter in it, and it rings out with a clear, confident statement. Or take the granitic propositions of Robinson Jeffers (our great neglected poet): they do not require the dainty precision of meter and rhyme in order to move counter to our native vein:

> God is here, too, secretly smiling, the beautiful power
> That piles up cities for the poem of their fall
> And gathers multitudes like game to be hunted when
> > the season comes.

In other poems, high statement or vituperation may do wonders with bric-a-brac. Or the reverse may happen. Poems may render listless or hesitant thoughts, or lists of trivia, in the most formal of forms, leaving us to guess whether such forms have the power to suggest, after all, a confidence which the surface seems to forbid. I repeat: all sorts of permutations are available. But I look upon them all as untypical cultural compounds. The typical compound that I am pursuing stabilizes itself as a combination— perhaps fusion is the better word—of slouch in the form, bric-a-brac for the matter, and decayed statement in the message, if any. These are elements which *seek* one another, and statistically they therefore prevail.

Before saying more about decayed statement, let me modify the trinity I have just named. For our culture admits in fact of *two* typical and stable poetic compounds. In the second of these, the element of itemized trivia is replaced by extravagant images. Long ago, in a paper on poetics, I made my feelings about this curiosity clear by calling it "galloping metaphoritis." Here, a little more soberly, I shall speak of surrealist imagery.

My own verse tells you beyond a doubt that I am a "meat-and-potatoes" citizen who keeps his images on a short ration of stimulants. All the greater my amazement and comic terror when I see an army of hypergifted poets advancing on their clientele with a garish assortment of figures, accompanied, more often than not, by syntactic and rhetorical pranks. If I am not mistaken, we owe this phenomenon too to the French, those specialists in intellect detached from meat and potatoes. And if we can name Walt Whitman as the founder of bric-a-brac verse, we can perhaps ascribe to Arthur Rimbaud the paternity of surrealist imagery. That Rimbaud was also, in his poetic avatar, an arch-

rebel against the Second Empire respectabilities of society is no
historical accident, for surrealist imagery, syntax and rhetoric
constitute together a drastic gesture of *désolidarisation*. This fact
in itself endeared Rimbaud's "invention" to generations of poets
to come, and will, I suppose, continue to make that invention
serviceable until they regain the old comradely desire to partake
of Second and other empires. In the meantime, surrealism works
so well because it "binds" without difficulty to slouching form.
Furthermore, it combines so readily with decayed statement as to
be characteristically indistinguishable from it. Nine times out of
ten, surrealist imagery *amounts* to decayed or vanished statement. In short, any poet who dislikes the ultra-native vein of
trivial mimesis for its imaginative poverty has had at his fingertips a deceptively contrary and colorful alternative fully responsive to the wind of history.

Surrealist poetry is not without ancestors. We can think of it as
a sort of twentieth century baroque, spiritually descended from
Italian Marinism, Spanish Gongorism, French preciosity, and
the Metaphysical school of English poetry. But just as our most
native slouchers represent the traditional *plain manner* of poetry
in a final collapse, so our surrealists practice the *fancy manner*
gone berserk. Still hostile to music and good posture, still nig-
gardly of frank, candid intelligence, they scatter images suggestive of hallucination and delirium, frequently abetted by bedlam
grammar and rhetoric. While every hack in Pope's lifetime was
able to tick off yet another couplet, today every poetaster knows
how to enact the surrealist madness with an

>   Elephants and helicopters mated all night

or

>   I know it's morning by silk
>   straining small gold curds of sun
>   into the black borsht of my slumber,

or of the sea (believe it or not)

>   Taking itself too seriously
>   all the time
>   like the close friend
>   of a famous detective.

I take these illustrations by opening any literary quarterly—here, as it happens, the Fall 1973 number of the *Ohio Review* which is lying for no apprehensible reason on a table near my typewriter. A good custom has corrupted the world, as King Arthur says. It is true that surrealism is distinctly more entertaining than bric-a-brac verse, but only because it constantly flashes lights at us. In the end one grows weary of being flashed at. Intellectual force and moral value are exiled in favor of rank sensory drama. Rank sensory drama is something, but it is seldom enough. The dazzling perpetual carnival may even send us back for relief to the other side:

> After an hour I frantically
> stuff the garbage down the drain,

etc. But notice how, in spite of the fancy manner, surrealist verse keeps us in the province of omnism. Every item in the universe is now free to mate with every other so as to produce a supposedly powerful metaphor; every rhetorical thrust is permitted, often in the name, made holy above reason, of the dream; and everything in the world is promoted or demoted to equal significance or insignificance. Can democracy go farther? Here again is an edifying exemplum for the dependence of culture on the political life. So overwhelming is this dependence that the greatest haters of the "system" can renounce it only through the agency of its own fundamental leveling gestures.

I have been speaking of low posture in form, and the choice between bric-a-brac or extravagant figures in the matter, figures that lead spontaneously to a variety of extraordinary effects in punctuation, grammar, juxtapositions, sequences, and layout on the printed page. (E. E. Cummings is the chief magician here.) But the bric-a-brac method binds in its turn quite easily with such effects, and you may consider this new combination—slouching form, mimetic trivia, surrealist rhetoric, eccentric layout, and decayed statement—as a variant of our typical cultural compound.

"Decayed statement" is of course useful shorthand, but I hope I have already more than suggested what I mean by that expression. It is worth repeating that I do not mean negative, life-denying, or desperate notions. Obviously I do not regard my

"Berceuse" as an instance of decayed statement, though its message (a word I do not fear) is gloomy enough. A decayed statement is simply on the opposite side of one that "rings clear as a bell," as the useful phrase has it. Provided, however, that we do not confine this faculty of ringing clear as a bell to oratorical, declarative, sermonizing poems. Implied propositions can "ring" too, as a poem like "My Last Duchess" proves. Poems of vigorous statement can be complex, and resonate into multiple meanings, one of them dominant, the others ancillary, "thickening" it, sometimes ironically. I must place some stress on this last point, lest I be thought to advocate that poems reveal a simple statement naked all at once to the first reader hastening across the printed page. Vigorous statements can indeed be very simple; but they can also be chordal, and sometimes dissonant; and they do not preclude the unparaphrasable halo of which criticism makes so much, forgetting perhaps that the unparaphrasable is inherent in nearly all human expression—in a journalistic report, in a painting, in "body language."

Like surrealist imagery and syntax in particular, so in general the literature that flirts with unintelligibility is carried into our midst by the wind of history: that curious collapse of the traditional solidarity between artists and the lay audience which produced Arthur Rimbaud and all that followed in his wake. Rimbaud was a rebel—but so was Milton. However, Rimbaud the rebel and Milton the rebel are obviously creatures of two utterly different species. One speaks commandingly to a large population of non-poets and non-intellectuals who are minded like himself—a settled, known, reliable, and *cherished* public—the other is an irrecoverable loner. And this new species of rebel appears (as everyone knows) at a specific turn of time's wheel: the moment, so to speak, when the artist discovers, to his chagrin, that his buyer is no longer the Duke of Urbino but Monsieur Bouvard or Pécuchet.

This process is completed when critics decide to dissolve the public itself. Intelligibility is a dream anyway, they cry. Everyone interprets everything every which way, and every interpretation is worth as much as every other. The world is made up of fragments blind to each other. What a scene! Fortunately, these overheated critics are making a mountain out of a molehill. The rest of us can quietly continue to conceive of an intelligentsia (the traditional reading public) which remains remarkably—some might say depressingly—cohesive; as cohesive as any other group—that of factory workers, for instance. A member of this public may "hate" Shelley's poetry; but, unlike the factory worker, he will not confuse the level at which Shelley operates with the level of Sunday-supplement versifying. A similar cohesiveness obtains within this public when the question is one of interpreting a particular text. Here again critics run amock, positively gloating over the supposed chaos which pervades the world of "decoders" of the "encoded" message—not only from generation to generation ("each generation must reinterpret, or reinvent, the old texts")—not only from culture to culture—but within a generation and culture—in the very halls of any congress of literary critics. From this viewpoint, my love-song to vigorous statement seems as faded as some Irish melody by Tom Moore pitted against an Alban Berg vocalization. But courage! For the mighty critics are wrong; and again their wrongness would show up in distinctest outline if they spoke more often—of poetry, that is—with members of other groups (factory workers, for instance, but with physicians, with engineers too)—for then they would soon realize how very deeply they agree with one another. Their agreements have simply become part of that world of the unspoken and the taken-for-granted which every professional group inhabits, and they quite forget that their grand "hermeneutic" battles take place not in the heartland of literature, but at the edges. Needless to say, I do not claim that confident intelligibility signifies for me a frozen, universal consent. It signifies not a point, but an area of consent, an area in which many a studious battle can be fought, indeed an area in which a number of meanings can coexist, but which remains finite.

It is, then, within this area, and with reference to a sufficiently coherent social group, that I evoke the fault of "decayed statement." "Decayed," because "abolished" statement, or perfect unintelligibility, is probably as impossible to come by in anything we call literature as the absolute zero in temperature. Besides, our difficult poets seldom try for that absolute zero. They normally operate in the regions where we find, for instance, John Ashbery's "The Other Tradition":

They all came, some wore sentiments
Emblazoned on T-shirts, proclaiming the lateness
Of the hour, and indeed the sun slanted its rays
Through branches of Norfolk Island pine as though
Politely clearing its throat, and all ideas settled
In a fuzz of dust under trees when it's drizzling:
The endless games of Scrabble, the boosters,
The celebrated omelette au Cantal, and through it
The roar of time plunging unchecked through the sluices
Of the days, dragging every sexual moment of it
Past the lenses: the end of something.
Only then did you glance up from your book,
Unable to comprehend what had been taking place, or
Say what you had been reading. More chairs
Were brought, and lamps were lit, but it tells
Nothing of how all this proceeded to materialize
Before you and the people waiting outside and in the
    next
Street, repeating its name over and over, until silence
Moved halfway up the darkened trunks,
And the meeting was called to order.
                                    I still remember
How they found you, after a dream, in your thimble hat,
Studious as a butterfly in a parking lot.
The road home was nicer then. Dispersing, each of the
Troubadours had something to say about how charity
Had run its race and won, leaving you the ex-president
Of the event, and how, though many of those present
Had wished something to come of it, if only a distant
Wisp of smoke, yet none was so deceived as to hanker
After that cool non-being of just a few minutes before,
Now that the idea of a forest had clamped itself
Over the minutiae of the scene. You found this
Charming, but turned your face fully toward night,
Speaking into it like a megaphone, not hearing
Or caring, although these still live and are generous
And all ways contained, allowed to come and go
Indefinitely in and out of the stockade
They have so much trouble remembering, when your
    forgetting
Rescues them at last as a star absorbs the night.

Professor Marjorie Perloff comments as follows in her authoritative work, *The Poetics of Indeterminacy*:

"The Other Tradition" presents a series of arresting visual images, akin to Reverdy's "living phenomena," that don't seem to add up. Who, to begin with, are these people who "came" late in the day to this setting of "Norfolk Island pine" and what are they doing? The "endless games of Scrabble" and "celebrated omelette au Cantal" suggest that the "event of line 27 is some sort of house party, but a house party is of limited duration whereas this happening is characterized by "The roar of time plunging unchecked through the sluices / Of the days, dragging every sexual moment of it / Past the lenses." Perhaps the "event" is an Encounter Group session? A religious retreat? A stay in a sanatorium or mental hospital? The "stockade" which "They have so much trouble remembering" suggests a prison. The forest setting—"branches of Norfolk Island pine," "fuzz of dust under trees," "darkened trunks"—implies that some kind of ancient rite is taking place. At the same time, the forest borders on "the next / Street," and "More chairs / Were brought, and lamps were lit," as "the meeting was called to order." Perhaps this is a political rally; on the way home, the "you" speaks into the night "like a megaphone." But in that case, why are the participants of the "event" called "Troubadours"? Dozens of provocative and possible stories suggest themselves.

What suggests itself to me when I read this and all other "indeterminate" poems written since Rimbaud was a teen-ager is that each constitutes, willy-nilly, a *mini-anthology* of poetry. This mini-anthology is held together by its external ossature (line-length, for instance) and by something like a tone—here, namely, that refined weariness, that delicately articulated discouragement, which T. S. Eliot has bequeathed to a legion of epigones. But then, anthologies are always held together by *something*. The point here is that our attention is captured by a collection of images and propositions—statements or subunits of statements—which are intelligible in themselves, and which exert their individual aesthetic pressures upon us, the latter summing up in our minds as a judgment upon the poem as a whole, in the same way as we like or dislike on the whole an ordinary anthology.

As I inspect "The Other Tradition," either allowing myself "provocative" associations of my own, or obeying those suggested by Professor Perloff, I find myself admiring

all ideas settled

In a fuzz of dust,

but wishing that Mr. Ashbery had left out the rest of the clause. I am of two minds about the Stevenish image of

> the sun slanted its rays
> Through branches of Norfolk Island pine as though
> Politely clearing its throat—

too fancy a *concetto?*—and I find

> Studious as a butterfly in a parking lot

perfectly execrable. So you and I advance across the little anthology sampling like connoisseurs, admiring here, doubting there, and making our exits in a glow of summed-up like or dislike.

The examples I have given so far consist of two well-rounded clauses and one incomplete but perfectly intelligible semiclause. Presently, however, it comes to our notice that the mini-anthology has yet shorter poems, and that the decay of statement has farther to go. Intelligibility often fails us *within* a clause or phrase. Notably (as with many precious poets) almost every "they," "its," "this," and the like remain unclarified by the rest of the statements to which they are attached. In the opening line, for instance, "they" leads its own life, almost like a Sapphic fragment on a tatter of papyrus. Elsewhere the fragments are a little more generous but equally unattached. I, for one, make nothing of the clause ending in "Past the lenses," for as I scan the various meanings of "lenses" that I am acquainted with, I fail, for each meaning—even the camera-meaning—to connect this three-word phrase to what precedes it. And I experience the same difficulty with the section of the poem beginning at "More chairs" and concluding with the meeting called to order.

Since Mr. Ashbery's poem does not deliver dramatic grammatical insults to the language, it should be remembered that this species of disorder, one of the most flourishing in the poetic industry of our century, brings about the same result of fragmenting statements and sending subunits to independent mental patterns of ours.

This leads to the general point that poems of decayed statement ("hymns of possibility," Mr. Ashbery calls them) invite an anarchical series of private readings, since the intelligible units and subunits are not directed by an indexing master unit (the theme) which forces them to become attached to one of the given mental patterns that we share with most or all of the members of our culture. The possibilities are not "infinite"—so much is true—but all thought of a community of poets and readers is necessarily dissolved, and each reading is as good as the next: another victory for democracy!

If it is argued that these poems do enforce a public meaning in that the very method they utilize is a representation of the "absurdity" of the universe, the crushing response must be that *any* jumble of words will perform this particular trick—indeed, a jumble of letters and signs will do it even better—and then we can all be great poets.

Indeterminate poems remind us so strongly of surrealist or abstract paintings—depending on whether "something" or "nothing" is made of them—that a word should be said about this seeming parallel. The fact is that a Magritte and a Mondrian have an immense advantage over the poet. The visual experience (often reinforced by the quasi-tactile experience of texture) is nonmediated, direct, and explosive. From a text, instead, all we receive directly is a row of black markings on a white background. Those made by the Chinese or the Arabs have the virtue of being directly beautiful and thus competing very favorably with the Pollocks or Hartungs; but the scribbles in our Occidental books give us scant pleasure as visual events. All they can do is evoke traces (memories or imaginations) of things seen, touched, or heard. This explains why the painter could afford to jettison intelligibility: he had so much left! whereas the poet or novelist dropped his best "weapon" when he gave up bold meaning. It also explains why the public, after a brief period of resistance and distrust, began to flock to the Magrittes and Mondrians in their tens of thousands, but could not be talked into reading *Finnegans Wake*. Indeed, clear, vigorous statement is to the literary artist what line and color are to the painter.

A final word about Mr. Ashbery's poem. What if a *very* specialized specialist demonstrated to our satisfaction that its statements do hang together and can all be made to "go home" to one of our culturally shared mental patterns? Perhaps (for instance) the poem is little more than a devious restatement of the hoary, sentimental confrontation of sublime nature with petty urban man. But a clarification of this sort would not induce me to remove my tag of "decayed statement" from this any more than from thousands of other and more famous poems scholars have been reading for us these several generations. Decay in statement is diagnosed precisely *because* a professional class of specialists in "hermeneutics" is seen palpating all that verse. With so many doctors assembled, is there not bound to be a disease?

Undoubtedly, if a new classicism were the rage today, I would urge that poems, or parts of poems, which defy our understanding can give us a strong delight, since language remains irreducibly resonant. But the voice most needed in our times is the one raised in support of public intelligibility, simple or complex, in healthy antiphon to the current tune. To this response I am also naturally prompted by my own poems, which expect their parent to defend, if not them, at least their kind. Let me argue therefore that indeterminacy is likely to sap the vital energy of a poem, for when the intelligible units hopelessly separate among our mental patterns, our interest in them becomes dispersed and tentative. Drifting is usually less satisfying than delving. Admirers may praise the "evocative" power of such texts as much as they like; but I submit—once again—that the most evocative poems are those possessing a firmly intelligible center, around which further possibilities of meaning revolve. In such poems, focused energy cohabits with evocative complexity.

Indeed, the prestige of irrationality is so high today in Western intellectual circles that we should beware of turning into dupes of a swollen critical language made up of "hymns of possibility" and "profound inner journeys" which introduce rhetoric in discourses where none should be allowed: poetry about poetry is good or bad poetry, but it is always wretched criticism.

These discourses are impalpable in the extreme, as they must be since they attempt to describe in words realms of experience alleged to be closed to language, or at any rate ordinary language. The poet is said to dip into his subconscious, his buried life, the deepest layers of his being—but why not quote directly? Here are a few phrases from a critical study of Rimbaud:

> "the vision of the unknown hidden self"
> "contemplating the absolute"
> "an absolute of expression"
> "the mythic self, discoverable in the deepest recesses of earliest memory and primal fears"
> "the deepest self"

"the unseen possibilities of memory before our life "
"a unique kind of truthfulness, not to be confused or contaminated
with historical truth "

and so forth. What we catch here—whether this rhetoric comes
from the poet himself or from the awe-struck critic—is the secu-
larization of the mystic experience. Our superstitions change
their costume; the critic no longer believes that Saint Teresa of
Avila saw an angel, that she was pierced through the heart by
that smiling numen, or that she rose off the ground, holding on to
the matting (as she recounts); but he devoutly trusts that the passionate, violent, rebellious, delirious, or hallucinated poet has
dredged up a vision pregnant with more truth, or a higher
reality, than the notions which we plodders, afflicted with our
dreary syntax, are capable of possessing or uttering. Clinging to
my syntax, I call this doctrine a heresy, diabolical or childish as
the mood inclines. But like all assertions concerning mystical
experiences, those which report on the profound visions of the
irrational poets (*profound* being one of the most abused words in
the language) are unverifiable and unfalsifiable. If we are shallow enough to ask in what the vision of the unknown hidden self
consists, or what the absolute is made of, we are told that language cannot convey it. So be it. But for my part, I like to be
prudent with words. I know that the world is in fact full of
visionaries, a few of whom happen to be poets, among them a
few with authentic talent. I know that they all believe they have
had especial visions, of which it is their privilege to give no explanation: "je réservais la traduction," as Rimbaud slyly writes.
But it is the *boy* Rimbaud (albeit boy-prodigy) who wrote in a
famous letter, "Il s'agit d'arriver à l'inconnu par le dérèglement
de tous les sens." A boy may be allowed to hope that a turmoil of
the senses will land him into the unknown; but a critic has no
right to assert the *interest* or *importance* of this same unknown
without furnishing a sample of its content that will satisfy our
minds. I think that the *man* Rimbaud would have agreed. He
seems to have realized one day that the "dérèglement de tous les
sens" keeps one not only poor, but also stupid. There was more
to be learned from the countless technical manuals he came to
read—on topography, trigonometry, industrial chemistry, and
even the *Manuel pratique des poseurs de voies de chemin de fer*,

than from the "hallucination des mots" of his adolescence. Always extreme, to be sure (Verlaine spoke of "ta perpétuelle colère contre chaque chose"—the most accurate insight into Rimbaud on record) he swung disastrously from the intellectual bankruptcy of delirious poetry to the poetic barrenness of those otherwise unimpeachable manuals. Be that as it may, until I am brought to bend the knee, I shall make it my sturdy belief that the verifiably profound utterances of mankind have always been products of the imaginative, the far-leaping *reason* of mankind.

Accordingly, genuinely significant poetry concerned with the irrational is never the poetry which speaks irrationally, but the poetry which speaks rationally *of* the irrational. Such a poetry can be passionate, violent, and moreover the irrational can in part invade the utterance itself. But ultimately the poet explores the estranging experience with a powerful effort to represent it (an effort similar to that which mystics who wrote of *their* experiences used to make)—and then, like poems about love, or the constellations, these texts are more or less profound depending upon how intelligently they have delved into this particular sector of reality.

Let me confess that when a Gertrude Stein sort of irrationality deranges the text, a malevolent suspicion arises in my mind. Has the author just possibly renounced confident statement because he has nothing of consequence to say? It may be that riffling his intellectual cupboard, all he found standing there was a collection of déjà-dits.

La chair est triste, hélas! et j'ai lu tous les livres.

Unable to energize anew the old concepts, the old states of mind, the old emotions, and unable to forge new ones, he may have been driven downward into the irrational in order to obey Baudelaire's command (parroted by Ezra Pound) to *innovate*. The innovation, however, resides nine times out of ten in superficial expression, not in thought or emotion. Hence we should be on our guard against swollen critical language that ladles out "hymns of possibility" and "profound inner journeys" and "contemplations of the absolute" with gullible self-satisfaction. We live in an age of high prestige for the irrational—it is bread and butter for numberless artists and critics daunted by the spectacular successes of positive science. A few of us remain, however, to suspect arcane poetry of being a choice haven for threadbare minds.

Shall we consult the wind of history again? Other ages have had their arcane poets—a Lycophron here, a Blake there. But they are always exceptions. In ages of high ideological confidence and solidarity, even the poets who liked to amuse their patrician readers with a few brain-teasing conceits would have hated to veil their urgent messages. More important, they *could* not have skulked very long, for they lived face to face with "consumers" not at all timid, and wrote without the mediation and support of a professional class, namely the priesthood of professors of literature. If they had been enigmatic in the Mallarméan manner, they would have found literally no one to listen to them—and, sentimental fictions notwithstanding, poets are ambitious and crave listeners. The priesthood in question reached the scene just in time to provide a small but applausive audience for poets at the historic moment when the "serious" artist and the Establishment were consummating their divorce. A bustling coalition was formed and has remained in place to this day—of artists in league with exegetical professors and related experts under the professorial spell.

Under these auspices, and furthermore set free and let loose by indifferent political regimes, poets give way to their moral perplexities, their experimental ambitions, their sense of the bankruptcy of all the old doxies, or simply their wish to be singled out. Inevitably, given our political axioms, they feel this freedom as a wonderful emancipation, a door miraculously open on infinite opportunity. I, however, choose to give this freedom another valuation. I believe that perfect artistic freedom is as pernicious to art as perfect moral license is fatal to morality. The heart of darkness tale of Mr. Kurtz serves me as a useful allegory of the emancipated writer, painter, or composer.

In any epoch and in any place, the fraction of poetry that is destined to last is infinitesimal, and every epoch, every place enjoys or endures its peculiar order of inferior verse. All I have done, therefore, is to define as best I can our own peculiar badnesses. What remains is brilliant. The traditional superiority, in Great Britain, Ireland, and the United States, of literature to the other arts (I am tempted to say, to all the other arts combined) has fully maintained itself into our times: and, for obvious historical reasons, the vital center has moved westward across the ocean. American poets have beautifully advanced and enriched the art. Are we enjoying a Silver rather than a Golden Age of poetry? If so, Silver Ages are rare and precious enough in the history of mankind. But I contend that our poets are memorable when they extricate themselves to a degree from all too typical combinations of elements. "To a degree" is not casually thrown in here. A complete extrication would be the equivalent of a barren antiquarianism—"writing like Tennyson." But to some extent the poet should have the force and the sense to resist being overwhelmed by his own time and place. Two hundred years ago we would have been wise to urge writers to withstand the tidal pressure of sentimentality. Today they should be encouraged not to yield entirely to slouch, bric-a-brac, galloping metaphoritis, and decayed statement. Not, of course, that the mere act of partial extrication or resistance guarantees great poetry—far from it. But I question whether without it, a poet can elbow his way above the cluttering common talent, clear a grand space for himself, and taking flight, prove himself what we vaguely but so importantly call a genius.

THE ARTIST AS PIERROT

Yours Truly, Ph.D.

I cannot build the house where I'm alive.
I do not understand the car I run.
And when I flick my lamp don't ask me how
A turbine wires me respectful light.

I walk in unintelligible shoes
Across a bridge that hangs I don't know why.
I give my TV set a witless stare;
I turn the knob, my science ends.

I'm dumb to vinyl, spoons and bevatrons.
How do they make a nail? A submarine?
What moves the waves that thrill my telephone?
I cannot build the house in which I thrive.

But imbecile and talented I go,
Familiar, chipper, treading on your toe,
Blinking through the glasses I can't grind,
And more than glad to speak my parasitic mind.

— 1 —

The self-adulation of the man of letters. Even today he beats his immodest drum: here comes the bard, make way for prophecy! It is an ancient rat-tat-tat, of course. It was ancient when Sir Philip Sidney, though smilingly, crowed over "the sacred mysteries of poesy," and admonished his readers "to believe, with Clauserus, the translator of Cornutus, that it pleased the heavenly Deity, by Hesiod and Homer, under the veil of fables, to give us all knowledge, logic, rhetoric, philosophy, natural and moral, and *Quid non?*" That is to say, *What not?* What not indeed? Since the man of letters is an architect (whose bricks are words), can you wonder at him for building himself temples and palaces instead of a hovel? With so many lovely trumpeting words at their disposal, and so much skill in putting them together, can poets remain modest? Are they made of ice? If tailors surveyed the cultural landscape, they, their Clauserus, and their Cornutus too, would make tailoring the compendium of all knowledge, logic, rhetoric, and what not. But in order to do so, they would have to stop their sewing machines and take up the typewriter; which they cannot afford to do, and if they could, would do it blunderfully. But the writer has nothing to stop or lay aside. Words are his business. Why then should he tolerate the sneers of princes or manufacturers? Why should he endure to be called an entertainer? Out come the words. The words, that is, about the words. "Poetry," Wordsworth decreed on the worth of words, "is the first and last knowledge."

This self-regard was not so foolish before the twentieth or before the nineteenth century—before whenever it was that the scientists very distinctly (but without beating their drums) left the rest of us behind. In 1800, when Wordsworth published his "Preface," he could begin a sentence with a most instructive conjunction: "IF the labours of Men of science should ever create any material revolution, direct or indirect, in our condition, and in the impressions we habitually receive. . . ." Such an IF made sense in 1800, and it stands where it does like a pillar in history, looking immensely backward, and looking immensely forward. So we know now; or rather, this would have been known a generation or two later, when no thinking man would have placed that monumental IF at the entrance of his speech. But in 1800 Wordsworth was still at home in the "poetic" phase of human history, without realizing how precariously.

In that habitat, stretching to the beginning of the human enterprise, a man of letters could take in a rare discovery—the motion of the earth, the microscope, gravity—with an easy, comradely admiration. "Well done, brother!" Pope to Newton. Natural and moral philosophers, poets and divines, arm in arm, and indeed expressing themselves in much the same magical language. One might without arrogance believe, and it was in fact comfortably true, that a disclosure about Man and the Universe made in a work of art matched any addition to knowledge contributed by a chemist or an engineer. For that matter, a Voltaire and a Goethe could even wage a little science on their own. There was a rough parity among intellectuals, whatever their specialty might be. It was not grossly evident that one class was treading water while the other was swimming on. If a few natural philosophers did give notice that a swimming on was intended, a plausible chuckle descended from Montaigne's tower, or a cackle rose from Swift's writing table.

But this intellectual parity is gone to the moths. My poem tells you that I take a modest view of myself as man of letters, and of anyone else who practices the craft with me, above me, or beneath me. And note, if you please, that aside from mentioning the bevatron my poem does not presume upon the mysteries of charmed quarks, the compression of time, black holes, the prowesses of nucleotides, and even relatively pedestrian adventures like voyages to the moon and beyond. For I wanted to humble myself still more. I am a baby not only in the presence of a mathematician, but in that of a toothpaste maker. If I do not gape or faint dead away when someone flicks on the television set, like an Australian aborigine suddenly dropped into Times Square, it is only because habit has made this world of mine familiar to me, and familiarity is the imbecile's substitute for knowledge; it gives me, instead of understanding, the warm feeling of nothing waiting to be understood.

"I turn the knob, my science ends." *My* science ends (allow for a little hyperbolical fun). Others, I enviously admit, do better. Others are at home in the upper reaches of mathematics, computer technology, astrophysics, molecular biology, and the like. Most of these educated writers, however, indulge in popular science fiction, a new sort of fairy tale in which laser guns and black holes can boast of no higher philosophical standing than the magic wands or flying carpets of old. But this leaves us with a number of extremely ambitious artists—artists who have every right to aspire to Jamesian or Joycean fame and who attempt to make of the concepts of science the essence rather than the paraphernalia of their works. They are to Einstein what Dante was to Aquinas. Unfortunately, their novels tend to make discouraging sounds:

> She began to rise, cigarette in mouth, as Billy went through the handwritten notes she'd left him. The first phases of communication would center on the integers. The symbols that compose Logicon will eventually have to be recoded in the form of suitable radio signals. What we have then, he read, is English to Logicon to

radio-pulse idiom or systematic frequency fluctuations. The statement "every number has a successor" becomes asterisk-N (or some such) in Logicon; this in turn, pending advice from the technical end, becomes something like pulse-pulse-gap, the point being that with a few key modifications, a juxtaposition here, a repetition there, we can establish a scheme of affirmation and negation, assent and denial, giving simple "lessons" in number and following up with some kind of basic information as to where we are in time and space.

Making predictions comes perhaps too easily to the prophet at his typewriter, but I cannot help vaticinating that *serious* writers in this category will remain members of a very small minority. Most serious writers will continue as Zulus among the scientists and engineers, and because most serious readers will rise no higher, half the really knowledgeable writers will probably renounce their scientific expertise and choose rather to stoop to their readers with more of "She began to rise, cigarette in mouth," than soar with science to realms of "systematic frequency fluctuations." My conclusion, therefore, is unchanged. The most exciting thought of our age belongs to science and technology; and, as a clan, we are not there.

Alas again for my pride, I do not belong to that band of critical ephemerids who, regarding words as little more than signs pointing at other words, all but detach human expression from the "out there" which we call Reality. "Fictions are windowless to the world," they write in the most forbidding journals. But underneath the sheer idiocy of this doctrine (there is, remember, an idiocy peculiar to intellectuals, as there is an idiocy peculiar to the illiterate) can one not detect a curious attempt at self-consolation? These critics and writers are simply taking literature out of the competition with science: a maneuver that did not occur to their ancestors, in ages when they felt they were competing to very good purpose with science and all other branches of learning. Well, that consolation is not for me. All words carry on, whether they would or not, a continual commerce with the "out there" in the sense that all of them, even the most abstract—even the *word* abstract!—are rooted, some directly, others ultimately, in our animal nonverbal experiences—those which commence in our foetal condition, long before language has installed itself in our brains. For me, then, literature is very much in the running, as far as explicating and badgering Reality is concerned. Neither do I solace myself by advancing pseudoclever arguments concerning our human inability to know anything certain about this Reality. I cannot conveniently dissolve those very terms, "to know" and "Reality," and persuade myself that the physicist, for instance, is as impotent as you and me, or that "the earth is a sphere" is as fictive a proposition as "the earth is a cube." There is a most pertinent reality-for-us "out there"; it functions whatever its connection may be to that final reality which would be in the mind of God were there a God; and it is inside the reality-for-us that I see the dispiriting difference between one discipline and another.

Were I stranded in some Amazonian forest, like a child in a tale by Grimm, a million years of human achievements would instantly drop from me, and I would turn into something much lower than a savage, since these achievements have bereft me of the talents a primeval forest requires for survival. In that forest it would quickly be borne in on me that the accomplishments of my civilization have been so many presents made to me, not cloth of my own weaving. I would stumble among the apes and the parrots, all but unable to light a fire, kill an edible mammal, or build a nest for myself, and perfectly incapable of reinventing the gas or electric stove, the rifle, or the rivet. At nightfall the first-come jaguar would make a trifling meal of me. If, by chance, I were rescued by a band of Indians and suffered to become their errand-boy, I could regale them with brilliant stories about bath-tubs and skyscrapers, but not take them a single step closer to that world of twentieth-century Western man in which I swagger as if I had made it, as if I knew its springs. These are, I assure you, thoughts that daunt and humble me.

True, the idea might come to me of teaching these Indians a few moral or logical notions, such as "Love thy neighbor even if he belongs to another tribe," or "Do not count on spells to kill him" (missionaries are handy for either moral), but the likes of me have had these notions for thousands of years. The thought of possessing such thoughts does not exhilarate me.

I have said a few words regarding certain authors who belittle the connection between literature and Reality. But they are still a minority, one with a special tactic that appeared late in the game of esoteric literature. Most of the efforts of enigmatic writers from

Mallarmé to the latest randomizer of teasing fragments I take to be disreputable insinuations of equal standing with science. "Experimental," these writers significantly call themselves, or allow others to call them, borrowing the scientist's favorite banner without a blush. When scientific experiments were in their infancy, and wits could laugh at the Royal Society, no one dreamed of creating "the experimental novel." Experimental literature and theater "labs" dawned on our intelligentsia at the moment, so to speak, when the sciences took to heading the parade. Joyce became their answer to Planck.

However, the literary intelligentsia were making a mistake. They behaved as if, because they produced a labyrinth, it must house a Minotaur. Unfortunately, a labyrinth is sometimes vacant. It is *usually* vacant. At the center of *Finnegans Wake* you will discover no "monster" of thought to requite the extreme difficulty of your exploration, but, instead, a few familiar notions which Tom Hardy could have laid out in his yeoman manner. *Finnegans Wake* and its innumerable brood resemble particularly tough Chinese puzzles, or Rubik cubes, miserably hard to solve, but banal when solved; they are monuments to mere intricacy, and it is an absurdity to compare their "vision" with, say, the clarification of the DNA molecule, a task also miserably difficult every turn of the way, but vastly rewarding for its results—an admirable concurrence of labor and product.

With the few high-tech exceptions I have already mentioned, literary works—experimental or otherwise—are "condemned" to deal with common human experience. Wordsworth is again edifying. Continuing his IF sentence, he blithely predicts that the Poet "will be ready to follow the steps of the Man of science," and not only in science's "indirect effects," but "carrying sensation into the midst of the objects of the science itself." Wordsworth naively lists three sciences in his next clause: chemistry, botany, and mineralogy!—but I suppose we will do him no injustice if we lengthen the list for him *sub rosa*, and then read on to find that "the remotest discoveries" of the scientist "will be as proper objects of the Poet's art as any upon which it can be employed." However, he qualifies at once by means of another pregnant IF: "—if the time should ever come when these shall be familiar to us." Again an IF that was reasonable in 1800. Mineralogy was not on everybody's lips in that year, but it seemed that the time might come; and it might come for chemistry, and for physics.

We know now that it failed to come, and that these sciences keep receding from us, like the galaxies themselves. I foresee no abundance of literary works concerning "systems theory," the dramatic intricacies of quantum physics, or electron transfers at synaptic junctions. Only when the mathematical narrative turns into a cooking appliance or a bomb does the poet, along with the social scientist, stand ready to take matters into his hands, and to fulfill one half of Wordsworth's prophecy—the easy half—in that the discoveries of science have then "put on a form of flesh and blood"—still in the poet's words. Here poetry can operate, and science fiction too. We poets excel at filling volumes with our indignations at the effects of nuclear warheads—nothing is easier than the poetic progress from pikestaffs to missiles—but we remain dumb to their fabrication, and dumb to the laws behind the fabrication.

To be sure, some of my friends in the sciences shake their heads at me. They are so very tired of the endless fussing in the laboratory. Here is one who tells me in confidence that he would give up his quarks to rove forever among the Romanesque churches of Spain. Yes—but he has something to give up! Having conquered and reigned—a Carlos Quinto of physics—he feels like withdrawing to his Yuste. But for myself, I have no choice in the matter: it is either those cloisters, or nothing.

The physicist understands me, more or less; but I do not understand him, neither more nor less. A rancorous Caliban sort of envy steals into my heart, followed by a Bad Angel breathing advice. Shall I not do like my colleagues in the scribbling trade and produce "experimental" literature too? Away, plain speech! We poets have secrets too. Away, profane readers! We'll strike the physicists dumb this time. It is hard to be another Joyce—but no need to despond. Puzzling Einstein is surprisingly easy. An Ashbery sort of talent, and much less, will do the trick.

But I have a Good Angel at my side too. He teaches me honesty, he counters rancor with good will, and, to conclude, he subdues me with a potion of modesty. I return from the cellar to open daylight, admitting I do not possess any secrets about man, beast, and minerals that would puzzle Einstein, or anyone who can read Homer. Happy enough if I can make a commonplace notion sing. Besides, I marvel at the products of science and engineering too much to snarl at them, whether through impenetrable poetry or in legible denunciations. And remember that I admire not only the outer reaches of scientific thought, I also respect its humbler practical products. Oblige me, will you, by looking again at the images I have used in my poem. Nails, telephones, television sets, shoes, spoons . . . Without satirical intent, if you please, for they are satirizing *me*. This must be stated and underlined, because few artists mention the products of science and industry without a point of sarcasm in their voices—the pauper's sarcasm for the tycoon. Not I. I cannot bring myself to use my electric typewriter for sermons against the age of electric typewriters. I would rather know what makes it work than mumble elegiacally about quills. Obscenely impotent and ignorant myself, I admire that foaming torrent of creation. I take my hat off to a flashlight battery. I salute a transistorized circuit. And do so without knowing to what I have made my bow; pronouncing the word—transistorized!—the way the old women in black shawls murmur mysterious Latin in church. They do not resent the officiating priest. They know their places; and I know mine. This human fertility astonishes and delights me. Fabulous digital computers! Splendid hurls into space! Cunning glass filaments where speech travels as light! I well remember as a child standing by the railway tracks in Antwerp's Central Station, a terminal in the grandest Iron Age style, and gazing dumb with admiration at the wheels of the steam locomotives. I was a dwarf to each wheel, but that was nothing: I could not believe that human beings had invented and assembled that methodical jungle of hoops, pistons, spokes, rods, and ratchets, and *quid non*? I saw thousands of pieces, each interlocked with every other, and each doing its appointed work at precisely the right moment, when, responding to the whistle's signal, the hissing, the heaving, and the tugging began, and that colossal metallic mass, pulling a dozen contemptibly passive coaches, yearned its bulk out of the station. Never, never, I realized, would a dunce like me invent so many metal mannikins, much less Napoleonize them into a marching army.

These locomotives were good instructors, for they showed the machinery to the naked eye. I know that they were primitive toys compared to our space shuttle today. But for a child, at any rate, the space crafts, and even the jet airliners, conceal their secrets: they are smooth shells and discreetly enclose their incredible viscera. They cannot astonish a ten-year-old boy like those ostentatious mastodons.

As for the evil which all these manufactured beasts have inflicted—the pollution, the ugliness, the violence—why, if I can be nostalgic for the Middle Ages in spite of the bubonic plague (and I am), I can also pay homage to my six-cylinder in spite of the noxious emissions (and I do). I do not feel the need to rush into the unpolluted wilderness. Wildernesses bore me. Nor do I look to the tabescent East—their contemplations, their fantasies, their rituals—for "spiritual strength." These renunciations of our amazing and—when all the accounts are in—our glorious West, can only be quaint, like Marie Antoinette in her rustic cottage on the grounds of Versailles. Welcome steel, welcome polyester! Welcome children of the human intellect! You do an enormous amount of harm, my dear engineers, my dear chemists, and I doubt whether you have added one drop of happiness to the universal tank which contains that volatile juice; or rather, for every drop you have added, another drop has evaporated or spilled. But I admire you all the same, you and all the others, I salute you humbly, my cap brushes the dust of the road as you pass; and, clutching my fiddle, I think a venomous thought against myself before my serenity returns.

— 2 —

That venomous thought—the thought of my imbecility—recedes a little when, hurrying down another road, I join, fiddle in hand, the company of men and women who practice the metaphysical, social, and personal branches of learning. I am much less daunted by the Oedipus complex or the rise of trade unionism than by a swarm of three-natured, zero-mass neutrinos. Here are cozier disciplines among which I can feel at home. I even strut a little among them. The critics encourage me to, for they ask questions of literature that are by no means suited to a Punch and Judy show. Let me give you a brief example from a practicing critic:

I want then to explore the "logical geography" . . . of postmodern poetry by showing how the basic ontology leads to characteristic positions on topics like the ego, language, history and mythology.

This is flattering. If my own verse (poor neglected thing) ever gains admittance to the best critical circles, my "positions" will receive attentions highly gratifying to the minstrel who warbled whatever he thought would make a tolerable sound and keep an audience in place. A Hegel could ask for no more. Such deference! Pierrot bespeaks a set of academic tweeds and practices the steps of basic ontology.

And yet he is still Pierrot, the motley shows under the tweeds, and a fiddle faddles his basic ontology. How serious in fact is literature? On one side, I note that a little poem about a girl and a sparrow, a "nothing" poem, survives all the murders of time for two thousand years to be read, reread, retranslated, and reanthologized without end in sight. But on the other, I see *War and Peace*, I see *The Metamorphosis*, I see *The Magic Mountain*, I predict two thousand years for them as well, give or take a few centuries. Even in my own poems—perhaps in the poem you read a quarter of an hour ago—there may peep now and then an "instructive" thought—a "position," heaven bless me, I need not be extravagantly modest about. So then, it appears that now we minstrels have positions, and now we don't. The conclusion must be that significant thought (expressed or implied, old or original) is but one of many "musical lines" available to the ambitious minstrel. It is a powerfully helpful line, but not an essential one. Minstrels can achieve immortality with or without it. Professional thinkers only with it.

What no one can take away from us minstrels, however, is the enviable part we play in the *dissemination* of significant thought, especially in the department of dissemination charged with inseminating the young. Of course, a highly valued work of art which happens to perform significant thoughts is both conveyor and article conveyed. It disseminates and is disseminated. But here I confine my interest to the first of these two roles. Minstrels make the transfer of culture pleasurable. Few youngsters will ever work their way through treatises of theology, history, psychology, and the like, but almost all of them will have well-seated ideas on these and a mass of other subjects, ideas for which minstrels will have been in good part responsible. Though poetry in the narrow, strict sense plays a minor role in this process today, surely novels are extremely influential, and motion pictures and television's fictions almost frighteningly so. The young person matures, continues to be educated in part by minstrels—though less so than in his early life—and finds it easy at last to credit, in Sidneyan fashion, the artists who so excitingly fleshed out ideas instead of the less accessible thinkers who truly invented them.

Here then is a two-tiered theory of literature, according to which the young or inexperienced *learn* thoughts from literature, while the mature *enjoy* them. This sentence compresses any number of complexities, but stands up, I believe, to sharp examination. Another way of putting it is that for the mature reader, significant thought in the body of a text has been absorbed and digested into the aesthetic experience.

No one need blush for having tasted of ideas at the hands of Dante, Milton, Thackeray, Tolstoy, Proust, Mann, Kafka, or the hundreds of contemporaries he is more likely to read; nor for having learned "volumes" from all his Saturday nights at the movies. But as far as *truth* is concerned, the movies suggest an obvious warning concerning Pierrot which you may find harder to accept when it is directed at Dante. Taste from Dante (I say nonetheless) as prudently as you should from a film. For Pierrot lours in the sleeve even of the artist who most solemnly dons the robe of philosopher or prophet. The artist has finally no obligation to be "scientific"—to verify his propositions through assiduous research or icy logic, or to curb his peculiar passions. One never knows when the artist-in-the-artist will drub the philosopher-in-the-artist off the stage. For the professionals of theoretical thought, it is unseemly to call on "special effects." But special effects are practically the artist's whole business. Rebellious as he may be to the notion, what is expected of him is the administration of a shock of pleasure. Even Céline, even Beckett must comply, *have* complied, willy-nilly. The artist's obligation is to the Muse, and in deference to that mischievous lady he may well lead you astray the moment a better rhyme or a more awesome image occurs to him. Plato was right and Aristotle was wrong. History is more philosophical than Poetry, and Philosophy is more philosophical than Poetry.

Drink, my gullibles,
drink the decanter dry
where truth ferments
to savory lie.

Christ barked his orders,
the gospel sings.
Let us pretend
we have wings.

Another consideration to be placed in the balance on the side of modesty is that a bad work of art—and I simply mean a work of art whose reputation with the elite has stabilized itself at a low watermark—may bear within itself ideas quite as significant and positions quite as remarkable as our most applauded classics. The reason is simple. A sociologist or psychologist who publishes what is destined to be called an important contribution cannot mar it so long as the contribution—the significant position—is intelligible. But of Pierrot the public makes other demands. With him, the position must be performed—Kafka must produce the unforgettable cockroach—and a dull performance can easily (ah, how easily!) lead a commendable theme to the dustbin.

By the same token, though supreme works of art may be excellent disseminators of culture, so are, and far more efficiently, the lowliest yarns screened in drive-in movie houses. Again and again, you see, the realities thrust the artist back to the stronghold of pleasure that is truly his, and remind him that all his other effects are excursions, sallies into a surrounding countryside controlled by his friends, I might say his suppliers.

It is even conceivable that a strikingly innovative concept may do an artist more harm than good. A strong innovative concept is, as such, aesthetically profitable, that is to say, it is excellently pleasing in itself. An artist who "owns" such a concept may therefore be tempted (unconsciously, of course) to let it do the aesthetic work nearly all by itself and allow his imagination to rest. If the concept is as strong and new as he thinks it is, his work may win a considerable crowd of admirers. But concepts cannot be new for long. As his innovative position becomes the next generation's commonplace, the poverty of his performance of it becomes apparent, and his once successful work slides into obscurity. Instead, ideas that are well-worn to begin with solicit the imagination to begin with. They seem to say, "You had better do something amazing *with* us, friend; for upon our bare backs you shall never ride to glory."

Not that this hypothetical scenario should discourage innovative thinking. It comes seldom enough, so if it does come, welcome it by all means, but without relaxing your aesthetic impulse. In my opinion, incidentally, the minstrel's best chance of "saying something new" comes when he haunts the interstices of philosophy or captures the thousand and one variants of the large principles which the nonaesthetic disciplines seek to cover. The minute explorations of Nathalie Sarraute come to mind. Beckett, it seems to me, composes parables whose ground is well trodden, but Sarraute has perhaps dug out unexplored recesses of "out there" (or rather "in here") reality. Such happy discoveries must still be performed, but they will possess an intrinsic power that is far from negligible. And they may even—the thing has happened—set in motion and direct toward significant abstractions the thoughts of those who make thinking their profession.

If all or much of what I have said so far is true, what lesson emerges for the discipline of criticism? If I am not mistaken—and I had bettter confess that the shorter my time on eath becomes, the less I am disposed to read droning books about lively books— most of the critical activity today concerns itself with *meaning*. "Signifiers" fill the air. The questions posed address themselves to individual texts, to single authors, to groups of authors, to movements and epochs, to literature *in toto*, or even to all the arts, and, as I have said before, extremely meaningful works have been written denying the possibility of meaning altogether; but these distinctions are not the issue here. I am questioning wholesale this passionate inquiry into the cognitive element—positive or negative—of the minstrel's products. The brief quotation I exhibited, concerning "logical geography," is typical and represents the main thrust of critical thought. Under this head hostile factions unwittingly maneuver on the same ground: Marxist and psychoanalytic critics, for instance. For critics are men and women of learning. Almost without exception, they work out of colleges and universities, where learning is enthroned. The objects of their studies stand or fall according to the delight they give, but their own studies stand or fall according to the instruction or conviction they bring about. By an easy *glissando* of the mind, they transfer their own function to the artists they study and to art as such, and soft step by soft step they lose sight of the defining mission of art—so much so, it seems to me, that the proverbial visitor from Mars might spend a year at their feet and hardly get to suspect that giving pleasure is so much as a tail-end mission of literature: comic pleasure, tragic pleasure; erotic, macabre, delicate, sadistic, sentimental, and scores of other species of pleasure—not always redounding to the intelligence or the moral elevation of mankind; pleasure for the simple, pleasure for the specialists, pleasure for all manner of human groups.

Consider another paragraph from a typical critic:

> "The Rhetoric of Temporality" is Professor de Man's most openly metaphysical essay. His position emerges clearly in his debates with the chief American interpreters of romanticism, Wimsatt, Abrams, and Wasserman, who claim for major romantic poets a "working monism," a "radical idealism" in which the priority of the subject is asserted over that of objective nature. De Man thinks that the assertion of the subject's priority is a confusion of the critics, generated by periodic confusions of the romantics themselves; it is a view, in any case, not compatible with the overall poetic practice of the romantic poets whom he finds giving a "great deal of importance to the presence of nature" and to an "analogical imagination that is founded on the priority of natural substances over the consciousness of the self."

More and more debates of this sort have taken to spinning loose and failing to connect—cog meshing into cog—with the driving aesthetic wheel. For fifty writers who investigate the question whether, for the Romantic poets, the self creates nature or nature creates the self, barely one (if we are lucky) will try to understand why we read Wordsworth but throw Southey away. For fifty writers who inform me about the workings of Keats's "analogical imagination," one, at best, will show me how he energized his imagination into a high art forever locked away from Rogers. How is it, one wonders, that Keats and Stevens have not made their way into our textbooks of philosophy? Might it be because philosophers know better than literary critics?

I have before me now an impressive essay by Thomas LeClair entitled "Avant-Garde Mastery." Its author praises a recent direction taken by certain novelists on the interesting ground that they are searching for "orders and patterns" in the cosmos, whereas the *old* avant-garde (how these avant-gardes do jostle one another!) gave in to entropy-ridden notions of disintegration, fragmentation, deconstruction, and disorder. The good new avant-garde accepts "relativity, fragmentation, and the artifices of knowledge as givens" (whatever that means) but goes on to make "new intellectual maps." It offers "homologies and hierarchies that give . . . information new contexts for understanding." *Therefore* it is superior. As he draws toward the end of his essay, the critic acknowledges that readers may be bored by these wonderful novels, but this is nothing to the fact that "instructive and original wholes are being created." The key words are "understanding" and "instructive," and the key concept (implicit) is that if work of art A is superior to work of art B in the quality of its instruction, it is *ipso facto* superior to work B as art. We might call this the *academic fallacy*. It is a dangerous one for artists to fall into. For the fact is that tediousness, not simplicity of mind or erroneous philosophy, is the one crime we *never* forgive a work of art. What the writer of this essay failed to do—what, I will guess, it never occurred to him to do—was to show that concepts of order have somehow a better chance of begetting good art than concepts of disorder. The exegetical gear never engaged the aesthetic gear.

My unease is the same with respect to intellectual inquiry within the single text. Enjoyment is more quickly exhausted than understanding. The understanding—as modern criticism has generously proved—can keep going almost forever. So the Tower of Babel ran endlessly up and disappeared into the clouds. But the critic who ascends from meaning to higher meaning forgets what he should have come for if he fails to pause at each step in order to ask *whether, how, how well*, and *for whom* a discovered or proffered meaning contributes to the quality of the text, that is to say, to the probable, the predictable thrust of pleasure it can deliver. Once more I suggest that above a certain and of course variable level, a law of recession sets in, and further exegesis begins to spin without meshing. It threatens to become an exercise in the all too prodigal possibilities of language as such, or else to subserve disciplines of naked fact like biography and history instead of addressing the moving, beautiful, powerful text.

Taking up a hint I dropped before, I concede that minstrels (seduced, I think, by the critics) do not always accept the limits to our philosophical destiny or importance which I perceive, nor my contention that our primary, essential, indispensable allegiance is to the Muse that governs the fiddle. Remember the drumroll with which I began this meditation. Our so-called commercial artists, like the lowly jugglers of the Middle Ages, do not object to being called entertainers. But in the upper reaches of entertaining, where that word itself becomes obnoxious— among the princely trouvères—another view often prevails. Serious artists often see themselves as above all metaphysicians, patriots, servants of God, explorers of social or psychological realities, emancipators of slaves, political revolutionaries, agitators for women's rights, and so on almost ad infinitum, and but secondarily as minstrels. They are mistaken. But the Lord moves in mysterious ways. It is a beneficent paradox that the mistake such artists make about their place in the universal scheme may be the necessary source of their best minstrelsy, for a moral or intellectual passion will usually energize a writer (inspire him, in romantic English) to better purpose than vacant ambition or an exclusive devotion to literature. The judgment passed upon a literary work will always be aesthetic; but the impulse to write it is free to come from anywhere the spirit blows.

— 3 —

I have now moved from the instructive mission of literature to its moral or persuasive mission. These missions—or powers—are not easy to separate, for they are often bound together in a single image, personage, or episode. Nevertheless, they are distinct enough to permit a separate little chapter for each. A Romantic nature-poem, for instance, may provide us with a number of "hard facts" concerning a landscape or a season, which, if we so please, we can mentally separate from the moral approval that emanates from such a poem. Let it, however, be understood at once that when I say "moral," that is to say, addressed to the good or bad, the loved or hated, the admired or despised, I include "political," and make no generic distinction between an effort, say in a novel, to promote the chastity of nubile girls and another to give power to the underdogs.

With so many Marxist and other "committed" critics writing nowadays, the political sector of this redemptive mission is amply recognized. Too amply, perhaps. These critics are so respectful of minstrelsy's power that they see it at work even in our omissions, our silences. If we sing of sparrows and pretty girls while, in Willy Loman's famous words, "the woods are burning," we are dubbed agents of reaction and repression. We are so powerful, in other words, that we move even when we say nothing. All the greater the respect we command when we do take open sides, although it is sometimes forgotten that a poet is likely to become a serious political force only *after* acquiring fame for his texts, and not *through* these texts, even when the latter speak to political issues.

Deserved or partly deserved, this estimate of our political influence is nowhere more flattering to us than in the minds of tyrants—Hebrew, Christian, Moslem rulers, absolute monarchs everywhere, and gangster–dictators of the right and left in the twentieth century. So respectful of Art are the gross masters of the Soviet Union, for example, that they are prepared to exile, starve, and kill a man for daubing a square and a circle on a piece of canvas: this, it appears, is violently antiredemptive. Naturally, even more zeal has been applied to the slaughter of immoral artists whose medium is language. The odd conclusion is that serious artists in the Soviet Union and other rigid countries long, or ought to long, for a more skeptical opinion of their political importance—something of the protective blank that stagnates between American bards and their presidents. Soviet artists are oppressed because they are believed to matter: enviable wretchedness!

But—I repeat—the political is merely a subsection of the moral, and it is to the larger picture that I now turn. Considering how passionately moral (or immoral) most works of art are, it is a wonder of our intellectual culture that critics show only the faintest interest in this feature of the textual landscape. Perhaps they avoid it because a stale odor of Victorianism lingers over the subject whenever it is not politically oriented. In the meantime, fortunately, artists continue to preach and denounce, to love and to hate, and to do it so emphatically that he who runs may read, and he who reads will understand. One encourages the life of the gut over the life of the brain, another makes homosexuality reputable, a third sings in praise of cowardice, a fourth rouses women to rebellion against male tyranny, a fifth makes himself the advocate of drugs. Of course I am listing here on purpose a few "nonconformist" opinions. Most artists, whether they address the elite or the masses, partake of the moral attitudes we vaguely call liberal. Few recommend, explicitly or implicitly (and now I mix again the political and nonpolitical sectors), torture of political prisoners, Negro slavery, ridding the world of inferior breeds, branding adulterous women, gouging hillsides for minerals, keeping the poor in their places, the beauty of avarice, or giving fathers absolute power over the family. If they did, critics would quickly drop their "deconstructions" and other playthings and make great moral clamors again—like the Victorians.

These are, I realize, drearily bald lists of moral positions. The advantage of baldness is in the clarity provided by a lucid dome; but I hope I am not blind to the power of things which manifest themselves without clear surfaces and hard edges. Moral pressure is often inchoate and subtle, an unformulated seepage into the mind proceeding from what might be called, metaphorically, a glow rising out of a text rather than a specific light bulb—Chekhov, perhaps, as against the later Tolstoy. I am not, in short, dealing here simply with propaganda art, though propaganda art can be superb and is very much a part of my discourse.

These moral "gravitational waves" reach both the subconscious and the alert mind, and form our ideals and our feelings, and sometimes even dictate our actions, as certainly as does clear pleading or attack. The younger we are, the more we are affected in the unlit areas of the mind. Moreover, these waves can be mutually contradictory—even within a single text—and thus we learn that "there are few simple answers in life." We also learn from listening to a multitude of minstrels that moral positions strange and even odious to us have been firmly held by others, and are so held today. Some works, besides, raise moral questions they do not answer. Others oscillate, they are ambiguous. Then again, if they do exert a distinct pressure, and obtain a definable effect, are these necessarily what the minstrel intended? Of course not. But then, how unerring is the fire even of professional preachers? Nothing of this diminishes the sheer moral power of the minstrel—which, you have gathered, is such that now the

humility that transpired from my introital verses seems to have
vanished, and I show you Pierrot in the plenitude of his wordly-
worldly powers, no more the "entertainer"—fie!—but a grand
force for mankind in its clambering up the ethical slope—a force
hardly lesser than that of parents, teachers, and friends—and
quite possibly greater than that of priest, mullah, and rabbi. If
you are skeptical of the clambering, and believe that Stone Age
man had morals as good as ours, still—minstrels have at least
kept the ideals before our eyes, and kept us from falling back.

A question that arises in my mind is whether a literary work is
ever completely devoid of moral tendency. I am sure—and I will
be returning to this point—that a minstrel can "choose" to mute
this instrument, just as he can play down significant thought.
But I am not sure that, once he achieves intelligibility with
respect to a given audience, this audience is ever moved sheer out
of the moral realm. Shall we not rather prolong the parallel with
the instructive weight of all texts, and affirm that, just as all
intelligible texts bear by definition a minimum of "thought," so
all intelligible texts exert a minimum of moral pressure? This
would derive from the fact that the artist will always be arousing
our emotions, and our emotions are in a sense lived valuations,
they necessarily carry a plus or minus sign, a verdict.

Be that as it may, here we have Pierrot impressively mantled,
singing his loves and his aversions, and inseminating his listeners with responsive feelings and judgments. And yet we must
not allow him to parade oblivious to his true nature. Let him
not forget his motley, nor his fiddle. Several considerations I have
urged in connection with his role as philosopher will apply
again; and again, to begin with, I feel that a sound theory of art
must be split into two theories, one for the young, the unformed,
the immature, and the other for all their opposites. As usual,
reality declines to be cut up so neatly; but we override her objections, content to stuff the body of her into slots and to let the
spillovers take care of themselves. Do we not know there is a
substantial difference between a child's appreciation of *Gulli-
ver's Travels* and yours?

Making a division between—in brief—the young and the mature enables us to reimpose a degree of modesty on our poets. For
they are evidently far stronger with respect to the first group than
the second, so much so that we must study their operations

among the mature before we fully grasp that moral power is but a variable secondary power, while the minstrel's primary power remains, inflexibly, aesthetic.

For the young, the aesthetic and moral powers of a work of art are virtually undifferentiated. I note three phenomena. First and most interesting: a work they experience as beautiful, gripping, powerful (and so forth) will influence their moral thinking and sometimes their manifest behavior; and will so influence them whether it practices open propaganda or whether its effect is of the subtler kind I have spoken of already. I leave aside again the problem of unintended effects, of misunderstandings, for my topic is simply any substantial effect at all.

Second, when young or unformed readers take in a work of art whose detectable moral position echoes their own (for even the young, and certainly the unformed, have moral positions) they will tend to "love" such a work, failing again to differentiate between the moral and the aesthetic.

And third, what we call the aesthetic power of a work of art may cause them to *change* their moral position from one side to another.

Pierrot the moralist is thus a fine cock of the walk at the level of low sophistication.

At the upper level, he loses much of his power and returns to his fated place in the world. For again and again, the mature reader separates in his mind the aesthetic pleasure he has received and the moral positions openly or covertly advertised by the delightful or powerful work. The three effects I have discussed do not by any means vanish. But the mature are immensely less likely to be formed or changed by a work of minstrelsy. For them, moral position, like significant thought, has become absorbed into the aesthetic experience. They "appreciate" poems, novels, plays, motion pictures, and paintings whose moral positions they would, if questioned, qualify as "acceptably" different from, or even contrary to, their own. "How moving!" they will cry, but they will in no way be moved from their real moral, political, and metaphysical positions. I myself, for instance, can be "impressed" by Hemingway's work without suffering the slightest alteration in my moral feelings. For the young and the unformed, this separation of effects is hard to accomplish. But at a certain level of experience, it is made automatically. Only at the aesthetic and ethical poles can these faculties collapse into each other again. Extreme aesthetic delight and extreme aesthetic revulsion may just possibly cause a moral shift even in the best-read readers, and extreme moral approval or disapproval will certainly affect aesthetic reception. No one can prize a work that expresses "idiotic" or "infamous" values. To be quite honest, our aesthetic appreciation will often be swayed a little by even moderate moral approval and disapproval: we cannot help giving a slight preference to works on *our* side of a question over those which espouse a cause distasteful to us. But in the large space between extremes where most of our experiences take place, the artist's ethical passions do not graft themselves on his sophisticated public, which perceives them as an ingredient in the aesthetic mix. This audience knows, too, that mere moral passion—even a moral passion it admires—cannot in itself make a great work of art, just as the absence of moral intensity cannot prevent greatness. Much less will such an audience ever suppose that the attested, historical moral/political influence of a work of art is an index to its quality.

By an interesting paradox, our two-tiered theory of art confirms Pierrot in his supreme role of minstrel precisely for the educated audience which has so consistently pressed a supposedly higher dignity on him. I venture to say that a kind of bad faith distinguishes this audience from the more candid masses. It rewards Pierrot for his artistry, yet except for a half-hearted subordinate clause, the citation mentions only political or metaphysical "vision."

The two-tiered theory also shows that tyrants have a point when they take the arts seriously. They may grasp, in a recess of their small minds, that loyal intellectuals will not "break" if exposed to dissident art, and that dissidents will not be converted by a program of loyalist films and novels. But excellent results will be obtained if the huge population of the young and their unsophisticated elders is fed thrilling conformist art and at the same time kept away from thrilling dissident art. And incidentally—or, for the artists, not so incidentally—cunning dictators will not discriminate between "high art" and "junk" on the false theory that the elite enjoys the one and the masses batten on the other. The slovenliness of human affairs is such that the masses may love, and therefore be influenced, by either. This discrimination between high and low is made by the elite and does not govern the tastes of the unsophisticated.

These tyrants pick up our story where the priests left off. Both groups—along with a host of moralizing critics in ages past who routinely treated the arts as teachers of virtue—took or take the redemptive view of the arts. And for the artists themselves, a paradox we have met with before appears once more: it may be good for them, good for their art, to believe that they work for a redemptive cause, religious or secular. By all means, says the Machiavellian voice, by all means let them believe that a poem is, or can be, "the trumpet of a prophecy."

The valedictory question I ask of "I cannot build the house where I'm alive" is why it stopped where it did without allowing me, in a second part, to rise a little from the satirical shambles. Why was it in a prose, in this Elaboration, that I went on to qualify, investigate, and complete? The prose, being philosophical, took on the responsibility of seeking the truth, a truth, some sort of truth, an area of cultural consent—call it what you like—and agreed to stand or fall on its ability to generate acquiescence. The poem, instead, came to a halt in compliance with the "rules and regulations" of minstrelsy, and blithely violated those of sound thinking. For, in not going farther, it fell mendaciously short. But Pierrot was apparently content. He had, he thought, a leading "position" that an audience might cheer as interesting. That was the foundation of his performance. What he did thereafter, and how long he was busy in his workshop under sun and moon, pertains to his mystery. But it can be stated that, after the concept, after a choir of subconcepts, and after the moral stand, the big perspiration was still to come.

— 4 —

A pleasant feeling of virtue takes possession of me as I look back now at my effort to call Pierrot out from the wings into which "l'esprit de sérieux" keeps pushing him, in order to set him up once again center-stage, in the role he was made for. Service to truth is always virtuous, of course, but I am thinking more of a pair of oddities—the first being that I am myself a member in good standing of the academic world, and the second, that my own verse is brazenly "intellectual"—unless I am brazenly mistaken. Does not this, for instance, merit the name?

Empty House

In the middle of a house
a clock strikes one
(strikes one?)
to no one.

Vibrations lunge
(who knows)
at chairs and sleeping
bibelots.

Why does the world
bother to be
without me?

At two,
a shift of dust
proves a vibration
was and must.

Or did it shift
to rendez-vous
with my two eyes
at two?

Why does the world
bother to be
without me?

Stars fiddling
ten billion years,
and not even
a pair of ears?

My virtue, then, consists in a willingness to resist the temptation my own work dangles before me of embracing the academic fallacy, and thereby helping my little poems cut a figure among the professionals who count.

At the same time, I gladly recognize that critical jousting is a pleasure in itself. The brain likes to play tennis too. A good battle between two concepts stirs my blood. I grant that the concept on whose behalf I am hoisting my lance is no maiden seen for the first time upon the dais, but among dowagers one of the hoariest. Alas, as hoary dowagers know, age does not always bring about the veneration it merits. See how serious-minded thinkers are always belittling my dear, venerable concept. "Mere pleasure!" they sneer. For them, to say "pleasure" is to place *Finnegans Wake* on the same shelf as some gushing best-seller beckoning from the supermarket rack. So then, old as the concept is, it needs to be defended in the lists again and again.

But finally, this urge to reproclaim the centrality of pleasure has a higher purpose I have kept in hiding till now. This purpose rests upon a very particular postulate, to wit, that the "serious" arts of our century—*all* the arts—are remarkable for undigested tedium, nastiness, and gloom—separately or in combination. Let me be excused from entering all the qualifications and explanations which a "mouthful" of this sort requires before it can be legitimated. Instead, I shall take up this space for a gloss upon the term "undigested." I mean that serious twentieth-century artists have all too often—have characteristically—made their works tedious, nasty, or dispiriting without attempting to press these recalcitrant effects into the service of pleasure, or without offsetting them through compensatory joy-giving effects. These two strategies—making a sort of chemical alteration in tedious, nasty, and dispiriting materials, or else placing them in the vicinity of contrasting, consoling materials—I call "digesting." Thus the difference between present and past is not that we alone have opened the doors of serious art to elements of tedium, nastiness, and gloom (though we have undeniably thrown them open wider than our predecessors dared), but that typically we have allowed the visitors to monopolize the place.

This much postulated, I argue next that, together or separately, the academic and redemptive fallacies have *empowered* these three invasive elements. In effect, critics have taught serious artists that giving pleasure is not their business, any more than it was the business of John Calvin. They are not to expend their best creative talents on *that* low line of work. Giving pleasure is the business of a separate class of persons, usually rejoicing in fat bank accounts, and known to one and all as "commercial entertainers." A serious artist, even when he is writing a comedy (a *dark* comedy, of course) has nobler goals: expressing his innermost secrets, declaring his "vision" of the universe, or putting an end to iniquity. A favorite motto is "uncompromising honesty." It places advocates of pleasure in the awkward position of objecting to an ideal more sacred to intellectuals than motherhood. Serving under this motto, and animated by a cause more honorable than providing an hour of pleasure, artists have become free to "torture" their public. And that is how we descend from the tragic beauty of *King Lear* and *Macbeth* to Edward Bond's nasty *Lear* and Ionesco's nasty *Macbett*. Typically, the good and evil of old dissolve into a common repulsiveness. How illuminating, by the way, is the fact that the eighteenth century sentimentalized Shakespeare, while we brutalize him. Or we descend from the sprightliness of meaningful literature to the extinguishing tedium of a literature which, in the name of an attack on, or a critique of, bourgeois positivism, and stimulated by the aggressive, intimidating rhetoric of theorists (bristling verbiage serves intellectuals as the horn helps the rhinoceros and talons provide for vultures), has been fragmenting, collaging, scrambling, decomposing, mauling, and randomizing meanings for over a century. Demeaning meaning has proceeded as an enterprise within the arena of meaning, in high contempt, more often than not, of the aesthetic imperative of art. Fortunately, in the arts, poetic justice is always done, and it is the torturers who die. The select public of connoisseurs and special experts endures the torture for a while for reasons to be unearthed by social psychology, and then discreetly files out.

This same public (preceded by the more naive elements) will also forsake and therefore condemn to oblivion a very special sort of tedious literature which academic criticism has blessed, encouraged, and I believe created: that worst kind of literature whose occupation is to explore the tools and features of literature itself. Then again, critics must take the responsibility for easing on their way the innumerable experiments in poetry undertaken by "alienated" poets—not one of which ever had pleasure as an even remote object. Poetry is the most vulnerable of the arts. That is why, when giving pleasure evaporated as a purpose, it succumbed more swiftly and more completely than the other arts. "Everybody" once read the Victorian poets. "Nobody" reads poetry today. One can very nearly dispense with the inverted commas.

Have critics then so much power to influence artists? They have. Not always, and not over every artist: see how Shakespeare and Lope de Vega bearded *their* pompous lords of criticism. But whole generations have been intimidated and misled by the reigning Cornutus and Clauserus types, and yes by the Sidneys too. No one, I regret to say, has as yet written the history of their corrosive power, perhaps because academicians are loath to flog their own profession. I take heart only because on rare occasions critics have also done a mite of good in the world. So fortified, I indulge myself in a fantasy of seeding a new, amiable critical program, to be promoted by men and women in influential positions in the critical world, and intent on persuading serious artists in all media that such matters as intellectual vision, social justice, private inner necessity, formal experiments, and explorations of the medium itself must be digested, must be performed, must be effective, must delight the chosen audience—or must *go*. Such is Pierrot's Law. Already, I am serenely sure, history is marking for deletion all the artists who, their unquestionable genius notwithstanding, have failed to tremble before that law.

WHO'S DIPHILUS?

Who's Diphilus? His works are lost.
He was a poet, won
some prizes, dented time
in Greece among the better men,

And got thrown out one time because
he wrote a stupid comedy.
Ten scholars now remember him;
that too is immortality.

Immortality, we sometimes forget, comes in different sizes. It is such a grand word that it resists a little when it is called upon to humble itself and recognize that beside a Sophocles immortality, a Diphilus immortality is also to be reckoned with. After all, our encyclopedias and textbooks are crammed with Diphiluses, each "forever alive in human memory," even when only ten living souls happen to remember. Diphilus, therefore, reminds those of us who are low-minded enough to work, in part, because we hunger for that immortality—low-minded enough to hunger and high-minded enough to confess it—that the boon we ask for may be granted without stirring much dust about our names. Like some heedless wish in *The Arabian Nights*, this one might disappoint in coming true. And yet, and yet. A name known to ten snickering scholars or a snide entry in a compilation; I hardly know why, but even this seems better than utter erasure.

What folly! And how noisy ambition is! How mean! And how admirable are the quiet people who merely live, but live in the purest way, loving, caring, and doing their duty without making speeches. The only real saint is he (but usually she) who does not become one. The others have already made too much noise.

First published in *The American Scholar*, Spring 1982, and reprinted in *The Key Reporter* (Phi Beta Kappa), Winter 1982–83

You see how I tack about from one view to another. For on the Diphilus side, it must be granted that without his likes, mankind would never move forward at all. Even those who but reach to the knees of genius are summoned. They are Nature's sergeants. Sergeants and generals—Diphilus and Sophocles—all are conscripted so that the wheel may be invented, and all the rest. They constitute the species militant. Of course, it is easy to tack about once more and ask what all that militancy is for. Why not stay home and cull the easy banana from its tree? In a quiet hour Diphilus understands that doubt. But it does not stop him. He carries it in his sack on the march.

Nature, then, has implanted this egomania in certain persons in order to "get things done" and prevent the baboons from inheriting the earth. Another trick of hers, useful for keeping ambition hot, is to prevent our imaginations from representing ourselves as genuinely dead. When I think of myself defunct, the self that is thinking merges subtly with the reclining cadaver and animates it. The cheating cadaver stealthily raises itself on its elbow to look around and watch the reading public that makes immortalities both large and small. In short, by a Heisenbergian twist, zero cannot be imagined without becoming something. If it is zero, it cannot be imagined. If it is imagined, it cannot be zero. Thus the dream of immortality—neither the first nor the last infirmity of minds both noble and ignoble—continues to beckon to inventors who no longer believe in the immortal soul.

This Diphilus, besides so luckily surviving for ten or twenty scholars as a name supporting a couple of anecdotes, was certainly a personage of some visibility in Athens while he lived. His mediocrity did not obscure him. It was (I shall guess) generally acknowledged; but being generally acknowledged, it made him a general figure. I picture him rising at dawn for his stroll to the bathhouse and the barbershop, and getting his mediocre dignity saluted by everyone who was anyone. The Scythian policeman raised his hand to his cap and the stonecutter looked up to say "Good morning, Mr. Diphilus; regaling us with another comedy this season?" (With a private tee-hee.) Athens was a small city; Attica a small province; Greece a small state. Mediocrities writing plays were pretty rare; only a little less so then geniuses. Nearly everybody read or heard nearly everything scratched on clay or papyrus.

In our century, instead, poor Diphilus is lost in the crowd of his peers. We flood one another. No one recognizes him as he loads his basket in the supermarket. What grievous fits of melancholy have I not suffered in one of our larger urban bookstores, gazing at the hundreds, thousands, tens of thousands of books on shelves and tables. And what are they to the hundreds of thousands, the millions that dawdle in our research libraries? More books than Noah saw raindrops. How many readers will read a given one of them—mine, yours—in their lifetimes? And how will it be in the distant future? Incomprehensible masses of books, Pelion upon Ossa, hordes of books, each piteously calling for attention, respect, love, in competition with the vast disgorgements of the past and with one another in the present. Neither is it at all helpful that books can even now be reduced to the size of a postage stamp. Avanti! Place the Bible on a pinhead! Crowding more books into small spaces does not cram more books into our heads.

Here I come to the sticking point that unnerves the modern Diphilus. The number of books a person can read in a given time is, roughly speaking, a historical constant. It does not change significantly even when the number of books available for reading does. Constants are pitted against variables to confound both writer and reader.

Having launched "constant" and "variable," I propose to amuse you with a few fanciful numbers whose only object will be to give "a local habitation and a name" to my melancholy. One constant, I repeat, will be the number of books read, or partly read, or (in Athens) heard declaimed in the course of an average year. By books I shall mean long poems, sets of poems, and plays, as well as novels, philosophical treatises, scholarly works, anything we habitually call serious without being purely technical or administrative. My second constant will be the ratio of writers to readers—writers, let us agree, who aspire to making what is generally called a permanent contribution, whether in belles lettres, in philosophy, or in scholarship. This particular constant is undoubtedly less constant in its constancy than the first, but no philosophical harm will come to us in the game we are playing if we keep it fairly steady.

Three variables now enter the graphs. First: an enormous increase in the absolute number of serious readers. Second (as a consequence of our second constant): an enormous increase in the absolute number of writers, hence in the number of serious written works. And third: the steady growth of the stock of books and authors surviving from the past, that is to say, endowed with some or much of the permanence these authors desired.

The next step is to invent illustrative figures, one set referring to Diphilus then and the other to Diphilus now. In the first set we assign ten thousand persons who regularly read or hear works of the aspiring sort I have mentioned before. These persons constitute the cultural elite. If most of them are acquainted with one or more of the works of Diphilus, it is fair to claim, albeit a mite loosely, that "everybody" knows him.

Each of these reader-hearers absorbs on the average twenty serious works per year. We will make our speculations a little easier by postulating that these twenty serious works are written by as many writers.

Diphilus is lucky in that, in the year 300 B.C., the treasures of the past are as yet comparatively scarce, so that most of these twenty works are by authors still alive. Let us say arbitrarily that seventeen of them are current works.

How many rivals for attention does Diphilus contend with in a given year? Let us use the figure of one serious writer for each one hundred of our serious readers, so as to picture one hundred serious living writers in our "aware" population of ten thousand.

Next I eliminate such pressures as genius, the finger on the public pulse, good publicity, and happenstance ("Have you heard that Diphilus has been keeping three wives? I'm dying to hear his latest comedy!"). In my simplified world of imaginary numbers, every writer enjoys the same chance of being known as his comrades-in-quill.

Since I have posited a single work to be ascribed to each writer, we can visualize each of our ten thousand as scanning, over a period of a year, the field of one hundred highbrow works in order to read or hear seventeen of them by living writers. Each writer has therefore a 17 percent chance of being chosen. In a period of two years his chances fail to double, because some of the ten thousand who knew him have died, and their young replacements begin from naught. Therefore we limit the increase of his chances to 30 percent. In five years, however, his chances of having been read or heard by nearly all the ten thousand have become excellent, even if we keep allowing new readers to come in and old ones to die out, and (more important) even if we reintroduce some of the pressures I eliminated at first. For, of course, there will be the best-sellers—deserving or lucky—that will skew the figures. Nevertheless, we can rest assured that, aspiring if mediocre, Diphilus will indeed be recognized by "those who matter" (and therefore many others) as he leaves the barbershop smooth-cheeked and smelling sweet.

Our second set of imaginary yet revelatory figures transfers Diphilus to the United States after World War II. There we shall create a serious audience of one million readers. We appeal to our constant ratio of one serious writer to one hundred serious readers and obtain ten thousand persons producing books in the domains of belles lettres, essays, and general scholarship. Though imaginary, this is not a fairy-tale figure. I see in the *American Book Publishing Record* that some thirty-seven thousand new titles appeared in the United States in 1980. It is at least a plausible proposition that ten thousand of these should be serious, and that as many serious writers should be producing them.

Our neo-Diphilus must, however, square off against a legion of dead writers whose works rival his for the public's attention. And that attention, worse luck, is limited by the one constant that proves fatal. The reader today can absorb no more in a year's time than his ancestor did in Athens. Microfiche, retrieval systems, all the electronic gear you care to think of—nothing helps. To each one of our million aware readers we continue to assign twenty serious works per year, each again, for the sake of simplicity, written by a different author; but now, only fifteen of these authors are alive. If we continue to let each author produce one work per year, then each one of our million readers will be scanning a field of seventy-five hundred works by living writers in order to read fifteen of them. As a result, the chance of being chosen, which had been 17 percent in our invented Athens, is now reduced to 0.15 percent for our hapless modern Diphilus. And here it may be observed how unimportant is the accuracy of any of my illustrative figures; for change them as you will, as long as they have any intention of capturing the realities of our time and place, they will reduce our Diphilus to a pitiable cipher.

His chances of being recognized by anybody as he emerges from the hairstylist's are nearly nil. Each of our ten thousand Diphiluses has, in fact, his separate, minute fraction of the massive audience. An implacable constant creates for us, in the flesh, the fragmented society we hear so much about.

The only help comes from forcing the curve to skew in someone's favor. One writer has a genius that compels the attention of so many of our million that it can be fairly said of him that "everybody" has read or at least browsed him. Another benefits from outstanding publicity. A third is particularly well attuned to some ephemeral taste or need or curiosity. And a fourth owes his success to an extraneous circumstance—like the scandal instanced before. Each time, of course, that the curve does skew in someone's behalf, the chances of being a "well-known author" diminish from the already diminutive 0.15 percent for our honest, interesting, worthwhile, but less than towering Diphilus. On the other hand, were it not for these celebrities—some of them rewarded for nothing else than genuine merit—poetry, philosophy, and scholarship might well die out altogether. Fortunately the heroes exist, and their existence encourages every newcomer in the field to wrestle with that curve and to try to flex it in his own favor.

If the curve resists, Diphilus, worthy of something better than nullity, repines. It is a wonder to him sometimes that he can lift his fingers to the keyboard of his typewriter at all. You will undoubtedly interject, and scornfully too, that a true poet, philosopher, or scholar writes from pure inner compulsion.

> I do but sing because I must,
> And pipe but as the linnets sing.

And you are repelled by this harping of mine—so Greek and so unchristian—on fame, glory, immortality. Nature, you say, favors curious, inventive, creative human beings, but she does not ask them to be motivated by a lust for what Thomas Huxley called "pudding and praise." Let me then offer a softer picture of creative man, and to show its universality, I yield the floor to a sixteenth-century Chinese, Li Chih, who was surely not touched by the Faustian West. "Their hearts," he says, speaking of literary geniuses, "were filled with such terrible anguish, their throats knotted in such pain, that they wanted to—yet dared not—spit everything out. They had so many things to say on the tip of their tongues without having anyone to whom they could say them that at last it grew too much, nothing could any longer dam up that accumulated force." And so they committed their passion to paper.

The admirable point of this passage is its implicit wedding of two overpowering needs: to express oneself, yes, but to express oneself *to someone.* The Chinese were too level-headed, I trust, ever to conceive of the artist as content to express himself *to* himself. But as soon as we cry or print our message to others, we become ambitious—ambitious to convert, to instruct, to delight—in sum, ambitious to be known.

A fine parable of this double condition can be found in Coleridge's *The Rime of the Ancient Mariner.* The Mariner, like one of Li Chih's artists, has had an overwhelmingly important experience. He is driven to utter it—that is to say, he is inspired. But he utters it only in the presence of a listener—a stranger-listener, it is worth adding, not his own admiring mammy.

The truth, sad or otherwise, is that poets, philosophers, and scholars are finally taken in by their own propaganda, and they forget that they are members of the tribe, even when they are found pouting by the outermost paling. They perform in the same vulgar psychological arena as athletes, politicians, and businessmen. The inspiration that animates them is the same that swells your football player, tycoon, and senator as they engage in their own battles. They too love the thing in itself. Everyone who practices any art whatsoever, from embroidery to conquering the world, has been seized by a powerful compulsion. This compulsion fuses at once with a latent ambition. To be the "leader of the pack," and I stress the animal image, each person has as a matter of course chosen the discipline he loves. Alexander has chosen soldiering, Shakespeare versifying. And the moral is: if Diphilus is melancholy, leave him alone and save your scorn. Plucking the harp before his mirror would make him inhuman, a romantic monster, but a monster.

Another grim thought for writers today, to wit, that the cinema is inexorably "marginalizing" them, is also well founded. But why is this happening? Is it because the picture is replacing the printed word in our deteriorating culture? Not so. The picture is doing no such thing, and our culture is not deteriorating especially: its deteriorations are merely better publicized than they were in the past. Then is it because movies can be seen by our elite million all at once? They can, but books can be read by a million readers simultaneously too. Is it because each person can or does take in vastly more films per year than books? Not so either. True, a person who likes both watching films and reading books is apt to consume more of the first than of the second, but not so many more as to make a difference in the character of our civilization.

The true cultural advantage of films over books is, prosaically but paradoxically, that films are very expensive to make. As they require huge investments of capital ($8.5 million for the average feature production in 1980), relatively few get made in a given time. Against the thirty-seven thousand new book titles mentioned before, the record shows about two hundred new motion pictures in America in the same year. This means that one of our crucial constants—the ratio of serious authors to serious readers—is exploded, as if to adapt itself to the exploding population. We had postulated a reasonable single serious writer per hundred serious readers. Let us now assume that out of two hundred (or three hundred) films produced, one hundred fifty are of a sort that our million members of the elite might deign to see. Pretending again that each of these is made by a different creative spirit, we discover that only one serious filmmaker appears for every 6,666 of our million. Let us now suppose that each serious viewer consumes—between the moviehouse and his television screen—not twenty but thirty pictures a year. This leads us to a 20 percent chance for each serious film to be seen in a year's time by each member of our elite. In short, these figures confirm what, philosophically speaking, we knew all along: the cinema has restored us to the happy Athenian condition. A given film stands an excellent chance of making itself known to "everybody." Even a mediocre film. Even a Diphilus film. And this is what verifiably occurs. During a normal meeting of family, friends, lovers, colleagues, or strangers, the conversation soon turns to the movies. The ritual exordium, "Have you seen *Shell Shock*?" (or the like) is advanced with a sanguine anticipation of assent. If, however, the answer is negative, two remedies are available. "Be sure to catch it, it's one of the best pictures I've seen in months"—advice which has a high probability of being heeded and is therefore by no means an empty formula; or, "What about *Clandestine Kisses?*"—for it will not be long before the response is a vigorous "I saw it last week!" Whereupon the picture in question will be discussed with the same enthusiastic vigor that got Diphilus thrown out ages ago and some fellow playwright awarded a tripod.

Again, notwithstanding the worldwide human billions (language barriers fall at the first subtitle or dub), motion pictures are relatively so few in number that, in a rough manner of speaking, the entire output can be grasped by the entire public. That is why the cinema is as much the central art of our times as the theater was that of Athens, Elizabethan London, or the Sun King's Paris. Indeed, the very word *theater* has been humiliated in the United States, where it has come to signify the place where motion pictures are shown: a superb example of the son killing the father.

We leave this new theater and return to the bookstore. There stands a friend of Diphilus among the masses of hopeful hopeless tomes. He looks almost as melancholy as our poet and, at moments, as his eyes wander from shelf to shelf, more so. He is the serious reader, depressed by the consideration that in his entire lifetime, though he should live to be a Circassian one hundred twenty, he will be able to devour no more than a small fraction of the books standing and lying around him here; a smaller fraction yet of the books in his language currently in print that the bookstore has not seen fit to carry; a minute fraction of all worthwhile books that have survived since the beginning of bookmaking; and nothing whatsoever of all the serious, worthwhile, important untranslated volumes written in languages he does not read. Depressed, he pours himself another dram of anguish by anticipating the melancholy of some reader like himself a thousand—why not ten thousand—years hence, whose powers of absorption will be the same misery of books per year as his own, unless a lucky mutation intervenes, or some electronic technique for packing, say, the complete Proust into the human brain in an hour, with all its qualities intact.

Thoughts like these were not so much as born in Athens when Diphilus, emerging from the daily trim of his beard, quickly ducked home to his wife and mother-in-law, and got to work on his next entry at the festival, confident of restoring his crumbled reputation.

Lucky, but also unlucky Diphilus! For the anonymity which the new numbers enforce on us standard serious mediocrities does have its compensation. Long ago, an over-brave drama of mine concerning Francesca da Rimini went into production. Opening night came to a satisfying conclusion. Admiring crowds, or crowds feigning admiration, shook my hand in the lobby. The actors and I embraced in the dressing rooms. The talk afterward over coffee turned coffee to champagne. A couple of days later, a newspaper compared me not unfavorably with, inevitably, the Bard himself. As my evil star would have it, this was a paper read only by the unlettered masses. The second newspaper, the one "everybody" was in the habit of consulting, reported that my play was no better than police-blotter trivia done up in fancy costume. I was annihilated. The actors sulked to my face. I dared not leave the house or answer the telephone. Surely the whole city must be laughing at me. But it turned out that only four or five of my friends, relations, and acquaintances had so much as glanced at the fatal review. The tens of thousands who constitute the "everybody" in town had read only the film columns. A few, interested in drama, had failed to retain my unknown name and had quickly confused this particular review with a dozen others read that week. Thank God and alas, it was safe for me to go in and out of my barbershop all day long. There was a knife in my back, but no one to notice it.